The Control of Imports and Foreign Capital in Japan

Robert S. Ozaki

The Praeger Special Studies program—utilizing the most modern and efficient book production techniques and a selective worldwide distribution network—makes available to the academic, government, and business communities significant, timely research in U.S. and international economic, social, and political development.

The Control of Imports and Foreign Capital in Japan

PRAEGER SPECIAL STUDIES IN INTERNATIONAL ECONOMICS AND DEVELOPMENT

Praeger Publishers   New York   Washington   London

PRAEGER PUBLISHERS
111 Fourth Avenue, New York, N.Y. 10003, U.S.A.
5, Cromwell Place, London S.W.7, England

Published in the United States of America in 1972
by Praeger Publishers, Inc.

Library of Congress Catalog Card Number: 79-181697

Printed in the United States of America

To My Parents

It is a curious fact in Japanese economic studies in the West that, while the protectionist policy pursued by the Japanese government has often been noted as an outstanding aspect of foreign economic policy in postwar Japan, no book has thus far been written in the English language that specifically deals with Japan's control of imports and foreign capital since World War II. I am grateful to the American Council of Learned Societies for responding favorably to my interest in filling this research gap by awarding me a fellowship that largely financed the research underlying this study and enabled me to travel to Japan and work there in 1968 and 1969 collecting data and interviewing Japanese economists and government officials.

During my stay in Japan I accumulated large debts to many individuals who helped me with bibliographical information, hints and useful ideas, research facilities, discussions that corrected some of my preconceptions, and in numerous other ways. While I am thankful to all of them, I cannot refrain from acknowledging my particular sense of appreciation to the following individuals for their assistance: Yoshinobu Namiki (Ministry of International Trade and Industry); Shuntaro Shishido (Economic Planning Agency); Hisao Kanamori (Japan Economic Research Center); Ichiro Takeuchi (Bank of Tokyo); Keiichiro Nakagawa (University of Tokyo); Kazuo Noda (Rikkyo University); Yoshio Okamoto (JETRO); Yushiro Eto (Kyowa Bank); Fukutaro Watanabe (Gakushuin University); Tsuneo Nakauchi (International Christian University); and Teruaki Fukumoto (Aoyama Gakuin University).

I should also like to express my gratitude to the following librarians at the East Asiatic Library of the University of California, Berkeley, for their help in bibliographical information: Eiji Yutani; Yukiko Monji; Hide Nagata; and Kiyoko Yamada. Last, but not least, my thanks are due to Cecilia E. Levine for her superb editing and secretarial assistance. Needless to say, all the above-mentioned individuals are not responsible for the contents of this book.

There is an enormous amount of institutional data on the import and foreign capital controls in postwar Japan. The intent of this study is merely to present an outline of the hitherto neglected subject. The author's wish will be largely fulfilled if this study closes the existing research gap in a modest way and helps stimulate further research in this area.

Spring, 1971

LIST OF ABBREVIATIONS

AA	Automatic Approval
ADR	American Depositary Receipt
BNT	Brussels Tariff Nomenclature
EDR	European Depositary Receipt
ESB	Economic Stabilization Board
FEFTCL	Foreign Exchange and Foreign Trade Control Law
JETRO	Japan External Trade Research Association
MITI	Ministry of International Trade and Industry
MOF	Ministry of Finance
OECD	Organization for Economic Development and Cooperation
OEEC	Organization for European Economic Cooperation
PRS	Price Ratio System
SCAP	Supreme Commander for the Allied Powers

This is a study of the control of imports and foreign investments in postwar Japan. The subject constitutes a striking feature of foreign economic policy as well as an inseparable component of the overall growth strategy in postwar Japan. The performance of the Japanese economy is well known. Rising from the ashes of World War II, her economy has managed to grow at an annual average rate of some 10 percent in real terms. In terms of gross national product the Japanese economy became the third largest in the world in 1968, surpassed only by the United States and the U.S.S.R. The Japanese GNP reached $200 billion in 1970 and is expected to rise to $400 billion by 1975. Her exports approached the $20 billion mark in 1970; consequently, the weight of her exports in total world trade increased to about 6 percent in the same year whereas the similar weights were 3.2 percent in 1960 and 1.3 percent in 1950.

Japan's postwar economic growth presents many interesting problems in economic policy and theory. A high degree of competition seems to have persisted within the domestic economy, but the economy itself has been carefully protected from foreign competition. The country has been operating under a system of private enterprise, but the system is a "sponsored capitalism," highly manipulated by the government. The policy mix has managed to generate sufficient aggregate demand in order to accelerate growth. What is striking is that somehow aggregate supply has caught up with the demand as rapidly as it did.

The logic of Japan's growth strategy has been a simple one. The central concern was to maximize the output capacity of the national economy, and this was to be achieved by accelerating capital accumulation and concentrating resources on the building of important industries. The static interpretation of the Ricardian comparative-cost doctrine was summarily rejected because the doctrine would have led to the policy choice of encouraging the development of light and labor-intensive industries. Instead, the dynamic (long-run) inter-pretation of the comparative advantages of Japanese industries was emphasized. For this objective, protection of those industries which were considered strategically important by the government was taken for granted. Anything else—such as consumer welfare and social overhead—was not so much ignored as deemed to be of secondary importance in view of the primary task of promoting Japan's industrialization. Japan's postwar growth may be characterized as a gigantic experiment in the "young-economy" argument for protection; but, in terms of the policy suggestions based upon the existing economic literature on trade and development, Japanese protectionism has been remarkably thorough and extensive. A policy question—whether or not Japan's protectionist policy has truly been worth its costs—remains to be answered.

If the promotion of exports represents the offensive side of foreign economic policy, the control of imports and foreign capital refers to the defensive side. This study is primarily a survey of the defensive mechanism, i.e., the legal and administrative network of control over imports and foreign capital transactions, together with discussions of related problems.

Part I deals with the import restrictions, and Part II with the control of foreign capital. The two Parts are symmetrically arranged; each begins with a discussion of the legal and extralegal framework of control, then focuses on the liberalization of regulations as it took place at different points of time during the postwar period, and ends with a survey of Japanese views on the subject. While frequent remarks in the nature of appraisals are made, our main interest is to bring out empirical and institutional information on the system of control and to reveal the Japanese mentality concerning the virtue of their particular strategy. A quantitative, cost-benefit analysis of protection is not attempted inasmuch as the institutional complexity of the subject makes it exceedingly difficult to expect a fruitful result from such analysis.

Part III, entitled "Source Materials," is mainly a collection of documents concerning the control of imports and foreign capital in postwar Japan that supplement the contents of Parts I and II. These documents, most of which were translated into English from Japanese, constitute important chronicles of a phase of Japan's postwar economic history, previously inaccessible to Western readers.

Part III includes the Foreign Exchange and Foreign Trade Control Law and the Foreign Investment Law, the two legal foundations for Japan's protectionism with respect to imports and foreign investments. Also included in this Part are official statements of historical significance in connection with the stages of trade and capital liberalization, statements by various business organizations and a labor group—all of which illustrate "Japanese views" on the subject.

The bibliography is, to my knowledge, the most extensive—though by no means exhaustive—collection of Japanese sources on the particular subject of this book that has thus far been prepared in the West. It is hoped that it will be useful to those who wish to conduct further research in the area.

THE CONTROL
OF IMPORTS

**THE
TRADE
AND EXCHANGE
CONTROLS**

PREWAR SYSTEM

The practice of direct and extensive control over foreign trade and exchange transactions by a national government is, by and large, a fairly recent phenomenon that typically arises in response to compelling circumstances, such as a major war or a severe depression. In the case of prewar Japan the period prior to 1930 was one of relatively free trade; whatever conscious measures the Japanese government had adopted then were mainly directed toward promotion of exports rather than toward direct control of external trade and exchange.*

It is an interesting, historical question to ask if, in the absence of the large sums of war indemnity claimed by Japan from China as a result of the Sino-Japanese War (1895) and of the windfall profits to Japan through the export boom during World War I, Japan would have been confronted with balance-of-payments difficulties of such severity as to induce her to abandon substantially the principles of free trade before 1930. The picture began to change after World War I and with the coming of the Great Depression. Chronic stagnation spread throughout the world economy. An increasing number of

---

*For example, the Regulatory Rules concerning Habutae Exports (1905); the Raw Silk Exports Inspection Law (1926); the Silk Fabric Exports Regulations Law (1927); the Exporters' Associations Law (1925); and the Important Exporters-Manufacturers' Associations Law (1925).

countries were faced with the problem of rising import surpluses.
One by one, major nations went off the gold standard and chose to
pursue the path of narrowly conceived national interest, in lieu of enhancing their own welfare through closer international economic relations with the rest of the world. Japan was no exception. The method
of yen depreciation was invoked in order to cope with her external
deficits. The Yen Bloc was formed, encompassing Manchuria, the
Kwantung province, and China. After the Manchurian Incident, Japan's
move toward a war economy, including stringent control of foreign
trade, became definitive.

The core of the prewar system of trade and exchange control
was established within the decade preceding the outbreak of the Pacific
War. The Capital Outflow Prevention Law was promulgated in 1932.
This law was incorporated into the Foreign Exchange Control Law of
1933. The control became more thorough and comprehensive with the
passing of the Law concerning the Reform of the Foreign Exchange
Control Law in 1941. Other related laws were promulgated during
the same period: the Law concerning Adjustment of Trade and Pro-
tection of Commerce in 1934; the Law concerning Adjustments of
Foreign Trade and Related Industries in 1937; the Law concerning
Extraordinary Measures for Exports and Imports in 1941; and the
National Mobilization Act of 1941 which included provisions for the
Foreign Trade Control Decree.[1]

There are some basic differences between the prewar and postwar systems of trade and exchange control. The prewar version
technically consisted of two separate legal systems, one controlling
movement of commodities and another regulating exchange transactions. In contrast, under the postwar system, control over goods and
exchange is unified. The prewar version was an integral part of the
overall war-oriented economy, involving far-reaching vertical control of production, distribution, and foreign trade. Under the postwar
system, on the other hand, control of foreign trade and exchange as
a rule has been isolated from that of production.

Despite these differences it is ironic to note that the postwar
system, which was a product of radical political-economic reforms
carried out under the directives of the Occupation authorities after
the war in order to liberate Japan from the maze of control and
regulations, came to resemble the prewar system in its coverage and
effectiveness. The Foreign Exchange and Foreign Trade Control Law
that emerged after the war has its origin in the prewar Foreign Exchange Control Law. Many other postwar laws pertaining to regulation of foreign trade find their prototypes among the laws promulgated

for similar objectives during the decade of 1930's. The basic reason
for the similarities between the prewar and postwar systems was that
Japan faced a common set of problems before and after the war. In
both periods Japan was in acute need of accelerating industrialization.
The paucity of domestic supply of industrial raw materials meant a
rapidly rising level of imports, whereas there was no automatic assurance that Japan's exports would be expanding as fast as imports.
The rationale for control was that the Japanese economy was struc-
turally so vulnerable that without control and regulation Japan was
unable to maintain her balance-of-payments equilibrium. Not only
imports but also exports as well had to be regulated because overpopulation and low wages allegedly were prone to cause excessive
competition among Japanese producers and traders, which would lead
to harmful disruptions of overseas markets.

POSTWAR TRADE CONTROL[2]

The Pacific War came to a close with Japan's acceptance of
unconditional surrender to the Allied Forces in August, 1945. All the
external economic transactions of the country were placed under the
jurisdiction of the Supreme Commander for the Allied Powers (SCAP).
The previous legal means of economic control such as the National
Mobilization Law, the War-Time Emergency Measures Law and the
Export-Import Extraordinary Measures Law were nullified by the
end of 1945.

The basic principles of trade control were stated in Article 11
of the Potsdam Declaration and in Section 6 (International Trade and
Financial Relations) of Part 4 of the occupation policy directives
issued on September 22, 1945. The directives stipulated that SCAP
would exercise complete control over all exports and imports of goods
and services, as well as all foreign exchange and financial transactions,
in order to ensure that Japan's external transactions would not violate
the objectives of the occupation. Furthermore, Japan's acquisition of
foreign currencies to purchase foreign goods was permitted only to
fulfill minimal needs of the country. Direction and execution of all
of Japan's external trade and finance became subject to SCAP's
approval and supervision under the provisions set forth in Item 7
(Imports and Exports) of SCAP's Memorandum No. 3 dated September
22, 1945, and Memorandum concerning Imports of Important Commodities dated October 9, 1945.

The Trade Bureau of the Ministry of Greater East Asian Affairs
was dissolved in August, 1945. The administrative task of this Bureau

was taken over, on an interim basis, by the Trade Section in the Bureau of Commerce of the Ministry of Commerce and Industry.

In early 1946 the Foreign Trade Agency was created under the jurisdiction of the Ministry of Commerce and Industry. Under the directions and supervision of SCAP the Agency was charged with the responsibility for carrying out export and import transactions via the newly established Foreign Trade Funds Special Account. Since it was impossible for the Agency to handle all the transactions, some seventy exporters' and importers' associations were organized as subagencies, each in charge of a certain commodity category. Under each association were dealers and traders directly engaged in foreign commerce. Meanwhile, the Japanese government prohibited unauthorized transfer of all then existing, exportable goods within the country.

The Foreign Trade Extraordinary Measures Decree, issued on June 20, 1946, spelled out much of the legal basis for the export procedures as prescribed by SCAP. This Decree continued to be the basic legal foundation of trade control prior to the Foreign Exchange and Foreign Trade Control Law of 1949. The critical nature of the times is reflected by its contents. The Decree mainly prescribed that: 1. No person other than the government as represented by the Foreign Trade Agency may engage in export or import activities; and 2. in order to make available sufficient quantities of goods for export, the government may issue orders requiring mandatory transfer of goods as deemed necessary.

In 1947 four trade corporations were established under the Foreign Trade Corporations Law. They were public corporations, fully financed by the government and charged with the task of carrying out export-import transactions as intermediaries between the government and domestic traders. Each corporation covered one of the four major commodity categories: mineral products; textiles; food; and raw materials.

With reference to exports, the Foreign Trade Agency, acting in accordance with SCAP's directives and supervision, placed orders via the Foreign Trade Corporations with domestic dealers for goods to be exported. Goods were purchased at domestic official prices which had little to do with concurrent international prices. Funds to purchase those goods from domestic export firms came from the Foreign Trade Funds Special Account. Foreign exchange earned through exports was deposited in the special dollar account held and controlled by SCAP.

With respect to imports, funds for imports were provided out of SCAP's special dollar account. Imported goods were first held by SCAP, then released to the Foreign Trade Agency. The Agency in turn delivered them through appropriate Foreign Trade Corporations to domestic dealers at prices which, as in the case of export prices, had little to do with international purchase prices. Yen receipts to the Corporations were deposited in the Foreign Trade Funds Special Account.

In short, Japanese foreign trade was still a case of strict state trading, controlled by the Occupation authorities. There was no official rate of exchange between the yen and other currencies. There was as yet no settlement of trade involving the normal, foreign exchange transactions.

In 1947 Japan's industrial production and volume of trade began to expand noticeably. This was also the time when U. S. policy toward Japan was being radically revised. The initial policy to discourage Japan's industrial recovery in the name of destroying all the seeds of its war potential and keeping Japan as a land of agriculture and insignificant commerce proved too costly to the U. S. Treasury (and hence to American taxpayers). Furthermore, given the intensification of the Cold War, the new occupation policy shifted its focus to emphasize the importance of accelerating Japan's economic recovery. As a means of achieving that end, expansion of trade was now deemed essential.

On June 10, 1947, SCAP issued a special directive, indicating August 15, 1947, as the date for the partial reopening of private trade. Under the new policy spelled out by the directive the basic framework of trade control was to be retained. In specified conditions, however, entry into Japan of representatives of foreign trading firms and direct communication between foreign and Japanese traders would be permitted, and the results of their negotiations could be put into effect with the approval of SCAP and the Japanese government.

In August, 1947, SCAP established the Foreign Trade Revolving Fund as a financial basis for promoting Japanese trade with an initial endowment of $137 million. A year later (August, 1948), a new contract system was introduced whereby: 1. Japanese private exporters were allowed to represent Japan in negotiating contracts with foreign importers; 2. trade transactions could now be financed by city banks under specified conditions; 3. private dealers were now held responsible for the quality of exports as well as for the settlement of claims;

and 4. exports were to be priced in accordance with the floor-price system as determined by the Japanese government.

These were the highlights of steps taken in preparation for full resumption of private trade. In actuality, however, the Foreign Trade Extraordinary Measures Decree was still in effect. All exports were technically still subject to examination and approval by SCAP. Strict regulations continued concerning the use of foreign exchange, the manner of pricing exports and imports, and the allocation of important raw materials. In February, 1949, the Foreign Trade Agency became the sole authority whose validation was necessary for exports. At this date, however, complete state trading with respect to imports remained in effect.

Turning to the foreign exchange aspects of trade control in early postwar years, the Ministry of Finance Ordinance No. 88 (October, 1945) formally laid out the legal basis for prohibiting free foreign exchange transactions. This ordinance contained only ten articles, of which three dealt with foreign exchange control. The essence of these three articles was that exports and imports of precious metals, transfer of means of external payments, use of valuable papers in connection with trade finance, all foreign exchange dealings, business contracts involving aliens—all of these had to be approved by the Ministry of Finance. Since little was ever approved during the early postwar years, this ordinance meant de facto a total ban on all private foreign exchange transactions. In contrast to the prewar Foreign Exchange Control Law which listed numerous, specific items to be restricted (thus providing a loophole for those items which escaped mention in the list), the Ordinance No. 88 deliberately employed abstract expressions such as "foreign exchange transactions" in order to make the control general and complete. Literally interpreted, it was an extremely powerful ordinance. It would be more apt, however, to view it as an emergency restraining order compelled by the extraordinary situation right after the war. The fact of the matter was that at the time the ordinance was issued there existed no formal application procedures. The Economic Bureau of SCAP handled the use of all foreign-currency funds, and Japanese private dealers and banks were allowed to use only the yen currency. In effect, there were no "foreign exchange transactions" in the true sense of the term as far as Japanese nationals were concerned.

In October, 1948, an interim measure to establish a system of exchange rates was taken. Known as PRS (Price Ratio System), the system divided all exports and imports into commodity groups, and the exchange rates between yen and foreign currencies were set with

respect to those groups. It was a case of a multiple rates system.
For exports the yen price of a dollar ranged from 200 to 600 yen, and
for imports the rates varied between 67 and 350 yen. On April 7, 1949,
the rate of exchange for imports was unified at $1 to 330 yen. On April
23, 1949, the Ministry of Finance Notice No. 237 officially announced
the single and universal rate of exchange, $1 to 360 yen, which has
remained unchanged throughout the postwar period in contrast to the
experiences of such major countries as Great Britain, France, and
Western Germany. This date marked a turning point in Japan's postwar economic history; the yen was for the first time after the war
linked with other currencies in the world through a single, official
rate of exchange.[3]

On May 25, 1949, the Ministry of International Trade and Industry
(MITI) was established. The Foreign Trade Agency was absorbed into
this newly created Ministry. On March 13, 1949, the Foreign Exchange
Control Committee was organized. Attached to the Prime Minister's
office, it began its activity four days later. The major functions of
this committee were: 1. to administer control of government funds
for trade and exchange transactions that were located within Japan as
well as abroad; 2. to determine the criteria for approving methods
and procedures concerning settlement and execution of foreign trade
and exchange dealings; 3. to make recommendations to the government
for formulation of foreign exchange policy; and 4. to examine extents
and ways of participation by Japanese and foreign banks and the customs
office in the administration of exchange control. The committee received transfer of dollars and pounds from SCAP, and deposited them
at foreign banks under its name (the Foreign Exchange Control Committee Account) as representative of SCAP. The committee was dissolved in July, 1952. Most of its work was then taken over by the
Ministry of Finance, and the funds hitherto administered by the committee were transferred to the MOF (Ministry of Finance) Account.

Slow but steady steps of normalization were being taken even
before the Peace Treaty. In November, 1948, permission for Japanese
to travel abroad at the invitation of foreigners or foreign institutions
was granted. In July, 1949, the Cabinet Order concerning Priority in
Use of Foreign Currency Funds for Export Promotion approved the
use of foreign-currency funds earned through exports for overseas
travels directly related to promoting exports and inporting specified
raw materials. In October, 1949, the floor price system for exports
was abolished. The Cabinet Order concerning Extraordinary Measures
for Foreign Exchange Banks (October 25, 1949) approved dealings in
foreign exchange by foreign exchange banks, other authorized banks,
and certified private exchange dealers.

THE FOREIGN EXCHANGE AND FOREIGN
TRADE CONTROL LAW[4]

Before 1949 there had existed no single, unified law concerning the control of foreign trade and exchange. What had existed were numerous memoranda and directives of SCAP combined with scattered ad hoc orders, ordinances, and notices of the Japanese government. They were so diverse, confusing and complicated that even the experts could hardly grasp all the rules and regulations. In order to develop legal systems of control that would be intelligible and coherent, the Ministry of International Trade and Industry and the Ministry of Finance worked on the Foreign Trade Control Bill and the Foreign Exchange Control Bill, respectively. At the same time, the Economic Stabilization Board (ESB) directed its effort toward drafting the Foreign Capital Induction Promotion Bill.

By August, 1949, a general agreement had been reached among MITI, MOF, ESB, and the Foreign Exchange Control Committee that it was undesirable to treat trade control and exchange regulations separately as had been done previously and that there should be a unified legal system which would cover all the external transactions involving foreign trade and exchange. The result was the External Transactions Regulations Bill which was jointly drafted by a group of representatives of various Ministries. This Bill was submitted to SCAP which gave a negative reply to the Japanese government through the Memorandum concerning Private Exports (October 20, 1949) and the Memorandum concerning Private Imports (October 21, 1949), suggesting that exports and imports be treated separately under the control system. In response, the Japanese government hurriedly drafted Export Trade Extraordinary Measures Bill (which became the predecessor to the later Export Trade Control Decree) and the Import Trade Extraordinary Measures Bill (which became predecessor to the subsequent Import Trade Control Decree). There was a further policy reversal on the part of SCAP as it advised the Japanese government on November 15, 1949, to scrap the above two Bills and instead prepare a general and comprehensive trade and exchange bill for submission to the Sixth Extraordinary Session of the Diet. Already bewildered by the preceding turn of events, the Japanese government frantically began to work on the bill, and managed to bring it to the Diet on November 24, 1949, the scheduled closing date for the 6th Diet Session, while extension of the Session was obtained at the last minute. After five days of deliberations both the House of Councilors and the House of Representatives passed the Bill in its original form. This was the manner in which the Foreign Exchange and Foreign Trade

Control Law (FEFTCL) was born. It was promulgated on December 1, 1949, with a provision that it become effective by a Cabinet Order no later than June 30, 1950.

The Foreign Exchange Trade Control Law was initially an integral part of the overall scheme of direct and stringent economic control practiced by the Japanese government during the early postwar period. Given the urgent task of recovery from the war, SCAP and the Japanese government felt that it was essential to regulate the flow and distribution of exports, imports, and foreign exchange. The supply of every major resource was critically scarce, and the free market mechanism could hardly be relied upon as the means of achieving optimal allocation of resources for accelerating economic reconstruction of the country. The character and content of the Law have been changing through time. However, it is generally agreed that the Law has been one of the most significant legal factors in molding the pattern of Japan's postwar economic history.

The Law itself is rather brief, and written in such a manner that it is enforced through those Cabinet Orders, Decrees, Ministerial Ordinances, Notices, and the like which are issued in accordance with the provisions of the Law. In other words, it was designed in such a way that substantive changes in government control of foreign trade and exchange could be made not by rewriting the law each time the need for revision arose but rather through issuing new orders, ordinances, etc., which could be executed more expeditiously.

The Law applies to practically all external commercial transactions involving foreign trade and exchange. It provides a legal basis for invoking the state's authority to intervene with activities of private business firms and individuals in pursuit of private gains if and when those activities are believed to be in conflict with the public interest. The vast coverage of the Law has somewhat unavoidably made its language and objectives conspicuously abstract. The alleged objectives of the Law are the sound expansion of Japanese foreign trade, maintenance of the balance-of-payments equilibrium, and the effective use of foreign exchange funds. The actual implementation of the Law has been far more flexible than those formal objectives tend to suggest. For example, the Law has been instrumental in mitigating excessive competition in the home market and strengthening protection of domestic industries.

Foreign trade and exchange transactions do not take place in a vacuum. They are conditioned and restrained by the complex of international treaties, business practices, private rules of trade and exchange, the commercial and civil codes, and the like. FEFTCL does not try to replace the existing network of laws, rules, and conventions. Instead, it uses this network as a foundation upon which certain regulations over private commercial activities are to be enforced. As an illustration, if a Japanese importer attempts to do what is perfectly legal under the Japanese Commercial Code, his action may still be blocked by FEFTCL. If he fails to withdraw his action, he will be subjected to a sanction under the provisions of FEFTCL, while nothing thus far has invalidated the existing Commercial Code. FEFTCL is allegedly a temporary measure for steering the badly damaged ship of Japan through rough seas after the war. The Law itself states that as the self-supporting capacity of the Japanese economy increases, the rules and regulations under the Law will be reduced and totally removed eventually.

RELATED LAWS[5]

FEFTCL is surrounded by a large number of other laws, and there are many areas where the two overlap to varying degrees. This section mentions only a few of the relatively more important and closely related ones.

The Foreign Investment Law

This Law attempts to encourage (at least in theory) and regulate the inflow of foreign investments into Japan. Most of the in-coming foreign technology and capital has been subject to examination and validation by the Japanese government. The competent Minister's authorization has typically been required before a foreign investor puts into effect a contract of technical assistance which involves transfer of foreign currencies. A similar authorization has been required of the foreign investor in Japan who wishes to acquire certain, specified shares of stock, beneficiary certificates, loan rights, etc. Government approval means that outward transfer of foreign currencies by foreign investors including their earned interest, dividends, royalties, and the like in accordance with the terms of the contracts will assuredly be free and open.

Those parts of FEFTCL which pertain to the inflow of foreign investments are the objects of the Foreign Investment Law, and those cases which have been approved by the Foreign Investment Law are automatically to receive protection and preferential treatment by the Japanese government. In this sense this Law may be viewed as a special law based upon FEFTCL.

There is much overlapping between those sections of FEFTCL which deal with foreign exchange and similar rules under the Foreign Investment Law. To avoid confusion on account of this overlapping, the interpretation has been that those cases which come under the Foreign Investment Law are exempted from FEFTCL, and those which have been approved under the former are not subject to further approval under the latter. In actual practice, the matter has not been quite as simple and clear-cut as this formal interpretation seems to indicate. There have been numerous complications whereby one is required to apply for validations under both Laws as, for example, a Japanese firm tries to acquire a technical license from a Western firm which involves importing goods and equipment.

The Export-Import Transactions Law

Japan's postwar Anti-Monopoly Law prohibits, in general, all cartels. Under the Export-Import Transactions Law, exporters and importers under certain conditions are allowed to form cartels with reference to price, quantity, quality, and design of goods concerned. If approved, those cartels are exempted from the Anti-Monopoly Law. The assumption of the Law is that some cartels are necessary and desirable to avoid overt disorder and instability of the market. The approach in implementing this Law, however, is a passive one. In contrast to cases of direct control whereby the government explicitly prohibits specified transactions and deeds of dealers, under this Law the government merely approves or disapproves those cartels which the exporters and importers have initially and autonomously proposed. The traders may on their own initiative dissolve previously approved cartels even if such dissolution is not to the liking of the government.

Difficulties arose in connection with "outsiders," i.e., those exporters and importers who did not join the cartels and thus disrupted the market. To cope with this problem, the 1953 reform of the Law allows the Ministry of International Trade and Industry to issue, if and where necessary, "Outsiders Regulation Orders" which makes it mandatory for the outsiders to comply with the rules of the existing cartels.

The Staple Food Management Law

During the postwar period the Japanese government has practiced stringent control over the distribution of rice, wheat, and barley. The legal basis for the control has been the Staple Food Management Law which requires approval of all exports and imports of staple foods.

After promulgation of FEFTCL in December, 1949, there arose many complications due to extensive overlapping between FEFTCL and the export-import provisions of the Staple Food Management Law. This problem has been resolved through the inter-Ministerial executive agreement between the Ministry of Agriculture and Forestry and MITI which provides that no separate license is necessary under FEFTCL when one imports staple foods as commissioned by the government under the Staple Food Management Law and when one exports staple foods which have been sold by the government. The agreement further provides that when the Minister of International Trade and Industry authorizes export of staple foods under the provisions of FEFTCL and when the same Minister allocates foreign exchange funds for import of staple foods, he may beforehand consult with, and obtain an agreement from, the Minister of Agriculture and Forestry.

The Specified Commodity Imports
Extraordinary Measures Law

Direct control of imports means that the supply of certain commodities is artificially restricted within the domestic economy because such restriction is presumably necessary and essential for allocating greater resources toward more strategic areas in accordance with the economic policy of the government. Depending upon the intensity of internal demand for those commodities whose imports are controlled, however, their prices in the domestic market may reach astronomical heights. Other things being equal, this means that those firms which manage to obtain import licenses are entitled to exorbitant profits. There develops then a serious question of equity.

The Specified Commodity Imports Extraordinary Measures Law, which is said to be a curious by-product of FEFTCL, purports to eliminate excess profits resulting from the quantitative control of imports by selectively taxing those firms which acquire import quotas for the scarce commodities in question. The rates of the special import duties are set in terms of quota size, commodity categories, and availability of foreign exchange funds. The tariff revenue thus collected is credited to the Industrial Investment Special Account of the Ministry of Finance.

Other Laws

The list of those laws which are interconnected with FEFTCL and which fall within the purview of the criminal code includes: the

Vegetables Disinfection Law; the Livestock Epidemics Prevention
Law; the Narcotics Control Law; the Poisons and Powerful Drugs Control Law; the Gunpowder Control Law; and the High-Pressure Gas
Control Law. The Tariff Law similarly contains provisions for restricting imports of those pictures, sculptures, publications, etc., which
may have adverse effects on public safety and morality.

The Cultural Assets Protection Law as a rule prohibits exporta-
tion of "important cultural assets" as designated by the Japanese
government. The Export Approval System which operates under the
Export Trade Control Decree which in turn is based upon FEFTCL
similarly extends its jurisdiction over "national treasures" and "important cultural assets."

The Cabinet Order concerning Acquisition of Properties by
Aliens mainly pertains to the disposition of real estate involving
aliens. There is much overlapping between this Order and the provisions of FEFTCL. The general rule of reconciliation has been that
those cases which have been covered by this Order are not subject to
FEFTCL, and vice versa. The essence of this Order is that the state
preserves the right to overrule private contracts, i.e., acquisition of
properties in Japan by aliens may be null and void without approval
by the competent Minister. As in the case of many other government
rules and regulations, this Order has undergone numerous revisions.
As of 1967 the Order applies only to citizens of those Communist
countries with which Japan maintains no diplomatic relations.

EXCHANGE CONTROL[6]

Residents

Under FEFTCL every person is either a "resident" or a "nonresident." Simply defined, a resident is one who maintains a domicile
in Japan; a nonresident is a person who is not a resident. Minute
details of the legal definition of a resident have been changing over
time. However, the following definition which was operative as of
1962 gives the general idea.

In the case of natural persons who are Japanese citizens, nonresidents refer to: 1. those who live abroad with an intent to stay
overseas for more than two years; 2. those who live abroad and are
employed by foreign institutions; 3. those who have lived abroad for
more than two years regardless of their intents; and 4. those in

1, 2, and 3 above who temporarily return to Japan for less than six months. Those who are not nonresidents are classified as residents. Those who go overseas to work at Japanese government offices abroad are classified as residents.

In the case of natural persons who are aliens, residents refer to: 1. those whose places of work are located in Japan; and 2. those who have lived in Japan for more than six months. Those aliens who are not residents are nonresidents. Diplomats, consulate officers, and associated employees, as well as those aliens who work for foreign governments and international organizations in Japan are classified as nonresidents.

As a rule, the residency status of dependents (family members) is the same as that of the person who pays their living expenses, providing that the dependents concerned live with that person.

In the case of juridical persons (and others) the following classification applies. Foreign branches of Japanese juridical persons are nonresidents. Branches in Japan of foreign juridical persons are residents. Embassies and consulates, located abroad, of the Japanese government are residents. Embassies and consulates of foreign governments as well as international organizations that are located in Japan are nonresidents.

With respect to the U. S. and United Nations armed forces stationed in Japan, their members, members' families, civilian employees who are aliens, as well as those directly affiliated organizations, are nonresidents.

Framework of Control

The yen transactions between residents are not subject to regulations under FEFTCL. However, when yen is used as a means of external payment (or receipt) of any sort, it becomes "yen exchange" which is under the jurisdiction of FEFTCL. When a resident makes payment in yen to a nonresident, typically the yen is deposited in the nonresident yen account at a foreign exchange bank. As a rule, yen in this account cannot be converted into a foreign currency without government authorization. Under the Foreign Investment Law (Article 9-2), there is another nonresident account called the foreign investors deposit account. Yen in this account is usually given conditional convertibility in that it may be converted into another currency after a specified period of time. Given the restrictions on its marketability and convertibility, it is dubious whether the yen in these accounts can properly be described as "yen exchange."

There are two kinds of convertible yen: 1. the yen that can be converted only by nonresidents; and 2. the yen with universal convertibility for all. By the end of 1958 restoration of convertibility with respect to nonresident accounts in most countries in Western Europe had been completed. The case was hardly the same with Japan.

A currency refers to bank notes and coins denominated by the common unit of account. The Japanese currency is the currency whose unit of account is yen. That currency which is not the Japanese currency is a foreign currency. One aspect of the mechanism of exchange control in postwar Japan is known as the Designated Currencies System. The idea behind this system is that the use of "bad" currencies should be prohibited for those transactions which affect Japan's balance of payments. A "bad" currency is one that is not convertible, is of unstable value, and is not able to circulate internationally. It is assumed desirable for the government, which ultimately must absorb all the exchange risks under the existing control system, to prevent Japanese foreign exchange banks and traders from acquiring these "bad" moneys. Article 8 of FEFTCL stipulates that the currencies whose use may be approved under the Law are those currencies which have been "designated" by the Ministry of Finance. Changes in the list of designated currencies are implemented by the Ministry's ordinances. The number of designated currencies continued to increase along with restoration of convertibility of yen as well as other currencies and with the abolition of bilateral trade agreements between Japan and other countries. In early 1963 there were no restrictions left on the currencies to be used for external payments, while the designated currencies (including yen) for receipt purposes numbered fifteen. FEFTCL makes provisions so that nondesignated currencies, with an appropriate authorization, may be used under some exceptional circumstances.

From the standpoint of FEFTCL there are four main categories of foreign exchange: 1. external means of payment; 2. securities; 3. claimable assets; and 4. precious metals. External means of payment include bank notes, government notes, small-value paper money, coins, checks, bills, postal checks, certified notes, etc., provided that they are denominated in foreign currencies and can circulate abroad. Yen is regarded as an external means of payment if it circulates abroad through "legitimate" channels. Because of this legitimacy test, the Hong Kong yen which circulates in black markets outside Japan, may be a de facto external means of payment, but is not so classified under FEFTCL. Domestic means of payments are those which are not external means of payment. Securities refer to those public-corporation bonds, corporation bonds, stock shares, investment certificates, national bonds, mortgages, profit certificates, etc., which may be redeemed abroad and/or are denominated in foreign currencies. Claimable assets chiefly refer to time and demand deposits and insurance certificates. Precious metals mostly consist of monetary gold. In postwar Japan all precious (monetary) metals have been held and managed by the government through the Precious Metals Special Account. However, they have seldom been actively used by the government as a means of its foreign exchange market operations.

Other than authorized foreign exchange banks, there are four main categories of participants in foreign exchange transactions: 1. the general public; 2. shippers and insurance dealers; 3. trading companies; and 4. exchange brokers. With reference to the general public, any person may himself engage in foreign exchange transactions for commercial purposes, travel, transfer of money to families abroad, or for any other reason. Whether he is a resident or a non-resident makes much difference as to what he may or may not be allowed to do under FEFTCL. Shippers in general and international insurance dealers are legally part of the general public. In practice, however, they receive different treatment. Shipping companies, airlines, insurance companies, etc. are given much more freedom in exchange dealings than the general public in connection with external payments for transportation costs, fuel costs, insurance premiums, and so on. Trading companies are those firms which carry out export-import business or which act as agents for other firms' export-import transactions. They not only influence the supply and demand conditions of the exchange market but also often actively engage in speculative transactions, acting and reacting sensitively to market changes. While FEFTCL gives no special status to trading companies as a category distinct from other business firms, they have received some preferential treatment. For example, the Inter-Branch Mutual Accounts System provides for a comprehensive approval of external payments to be made by those trading companies which maintain overseas branches, and the leading trading companies have been given a special right to hold foreign currencies under the Trading Companies Foreign Currencies Holding System. Foreign exchange brokers played an active role in prewar Japan. However, the postwar system of exchange control has made little room for their activities. Consequently, there has been no significant development of exchange brokerage as a well-defined business.

Foreign Exchange Banks

Foreign exchange banks assume important tasks and responsibilities, and are exempted from many standard regulations. Authorized foreign exchange banks refer to those authorized under Article 10 of FEFTCL (including the Japan Export-Import Bank, Japan Development Bank, and Long-Term Credit Bank) and those authorized under the separate Foreign Exchange Banking Law. The latter are known as Foreign Exchange Specializing Banks. Each foreign exchange bank is either Class A or Class B. A Class A bank is permitted to engage in all phases of foreign exchange business, while a Class B bank is subject to some restrictions. The latter may not open correspondent relationships with foreign banks, may not create credit, and may not hold certain designated currencies. Foreign banks which have been authorized as foreign exchange banks receive the Class A status.

The main business of foreign exchange banks is to sell, purchase, and insure external means of payment, and to act as agents for others concerning payments and receipts of foreign exchange induced by trade (and other) activities between Japan and foreign countries. FEFTCL commissions foreign exchange banks to carry out much of the actual administration of exchange control in behalf of the government. This semi-official role of the banks was designed presumably to minimize red-tape and to implement control efficiently and effectively. From the standpoint of the banks, this has meant a thankless task of absorbing the tremendous burden of administrative chores. Specifically, there are four kinds of interrelated obligations imposed upon the banks: 1. to confirm whether or not clients fit categories that are within the jurisdiction of FEFTCL and related laws (Article 12, FEFTCL); 2. to sanction against those who violate the existing rules and regulations by canceling permits, refusing access to the banks' service facilities, etc. (Article 13, FEFTCL); 3. to administer the system of exchange control; and 4. to report to competent Ministers on their operations.

Operating side by side with foreign exchange banks, money changers and the Post Office receive special treatment under FEFTCL insofar as they deal with foreign exchange. Money changers mainly refer to travel companies and hotels. For convenience of foreign travelers, they are authorized to sell or buy foreign exchange and handle foreign travelers' checks (Article 14, FEFTCL). However, they are not permitted to accumulate foreign currencies, and are obliged to sell them,

except for the specified amounts, to foreign exchange banks. The
Post Office has the legal monopoly in dealing with postal checks,
postal money orders, drafts, etc. Those who acquire foreign currencies
via postal service are obliged to sell them to the Post Office which in
turn muct sell them to foreign exchange banks.

Exchange Concentration

During World War II many national governments in the world
adopted the method of concentrating all foreign exchange available in
their hands as part of wartime economic control. In 1941 the Japanese
government took possession of all foreign currencies and monetary
gold as a wartime emergency measure. After the war the exchange
control in Japan was taken over by SCAP, and from 1949 until the
Peace Treaty the control rights were reverted to the Japanese government. In 1952 the Foreign Exchange Funds Special Account was established at the Ministry of Finance. This Account has been used as a
main instrument of exchange control and of financing foreign exchange
transactions of the government. Funds from this Account may be used
to supplement inter-bank transactions and to stabilize the foreign exchange market. Funds may be deposited as secondary reserves for
the government (known as MOF deposits) at, or loaned (for interest
income) to, Japanese foreign exchange banks as well as foreign banks.

The system of exchange concentration purports to achieve the
optimal use of available foreign exchange by distributing it in accordance with policy and planning rather than leaving the problem of its
allocation to the market. During the early postwar years the rule of
concentration was severe and thorough. No one other than the government was allowed to hold foreign exchange of any sort. Subsequently,
the rule was gradually relaxed, and the direct allocation of foreign
exchange by the government became increasingly something of an
exception. Foreign exchange banks were allowed to hold increasing
amounts of exchange in their own accounts.

The system of exchange concentration bears two implications:
1. All foreign exchange in the country is to be controlled by the
government; and 2. all exchange risks are to be borne ultimately by
the government, and any person may call upon the government for
supply of exchange. The system assumes, however, that private
holding of exchange is justified only for the convenience of carrying
out international economic transactions and only if there exists no
danger of capital flight. The system further assumes that the government may, if necessary, force transfer of exchange from nongovern-
mental holders to itself. Specific application of the rule of concentration depends to a large extent upon one's residency status and whether

or not an institution concerned is a foreign exchange bank. The question of who is allowed to hold how much foreign exchange is answered mainly by Cabinet Orders and Ministerial Ordinances. Article 8 of the Foreign Exchange Control Order states that the Ministry of Finance may order foreign exchange banks to sell their external means of payment to the Foreign Exchange Funds Special Account and, under extraordinary circumstances, may order residents to sell their external means of payment that are registered at the Bank of Japan to the same Account.

NOTES

1. Among the works that deal with trade control before and during the war are the following: Yoshio Ishimaki, Gaikoku Kawase Kanri Ho Seigi [The Foreign Exchange Control Law] (Tokyo: Bunga Do, 1939); Mitsuo Midorigawa, Shihon Tohi Boshi Ho no Kaishaku to Unyo [Interpretation and Application of the Capital Flight Prevention Law] (Tokyo: Daido Shoin, 1932); Uichi Noda, Kaisei Gaikoku Kawase Kanri Horei Kaisetsu [Explanation of the Revised Foreign Exchange Control Order] (Tokyo:Okura Zaimu Kyokai, 1941); Isamu Hishinuma, Senji Keizai to Boeki Kokusaku [The Wartime Economy and the National Policy on Foreign Trade] (Tokyo: Sangyo Keizai Gakkai, 1941); and Nishizo Uesaka, Senji Boeki Jitsumu no Chishiki [Knowledge of Wartime Trading Business] (Tokyo: Tokyo Hobun Sha, 1941 .

2. The list of standard works that cover the subject of trade control during the early postwar period include: Ministry of International Trade and Industry, Nihon Boeki no Tenkai [Expansion of Japanese Foreign Trade] (Tokyo: Shoko Shuppan, 1956); Economic Planning Agency, Sengo Keizai Shi [Postwar Economic History] (Tokyo: Okura Sho Insatsu Kyoku, 1957); and MITI, Sengo Keizai Jyunen Shi [Postwar Ten-Year Economic History] (Tokyo: Shokokaikan Shuppan Bu, 1954).

3. A collection of articles discussing the implications of the exchange rate policy for Japan's postwar economic growth appears in Keizai Hyoron, (October, 1964).

4. The English translation of this Law is given in the Source Materials, beginning on page 143. A single volume that discusses this Law most extensively in Boeki Jitsumu Koza Kanko Kai, ed., Boeki Kawase Kanri Ho [The Trade and Exchange Control Law] (Tokyo: Yuhikaku, 1967).

5. For legal backgrounds concerning FEFTCL and related laws, see Boeki Jitsumu Koza Kanko Kai, ed., Boeki to Horitsu [Foreign Trade and the Law] (Tokyo: Yuhikaku, 1966); Yoshio Kanazawa, Keizai Ho [Economic Laws] (Tokyo: Yuhikaku, 1968); and Yoshio · Kanazawa, ed., Boeki Kankei Ho [Laws concerning Foreign Trade] (Tokyo: Nihon Hyoron Shinsha, 1956).

6. Among numerous works pertaining to exchange control during the early postwar years, Makoto Watanabe's Kawase Kanri Kaiso [Recollections on Exchange Control] (Tokyo: Gaikoku Kawase Boeki Kenkyu Kai, 1963) stands out as unique as it gives the personal re-collections of the author who was a high-ranking official deeply in-volved in the administration of exchange control. The publications available in English include: Bank of Japan, Manual of Foreign Ex-change and Foreign Trade Systems in Japan (Tokyo: January, 1956); Ministry of Finance, Report on the Japanese Exchange System and Related Matters (Tokyo: June, 1956); U. S. Tariff Commission, Post-war Developments in Japan's Foreign Trade (Washington, D.C : U S. Government Printing Office, 1958), pp. 18-22. For background materi-als, see MITI and Ministry of Foreign Affairs, eds., Sengo Nihon no Boeki Kinyu Kyotei [Trade and Financial Arrangements between Occupied Japan and Other Countries] (Tokyo: Jitsugyo no Nippon Sha, 1949); and Seeichi Kase, "Yen Kawase Ron" [On the Yen Exchange], Tsusho Sangyo Kenkyu, (December, 1958), pp. 2-16.

OBJECTIVES

The system of import control in postwar Japan has been based upon FEFTCL in that the technical details and actual operations of the system were worked out and implemented by those numerous Cabinet Orders, Ministerial Ordinances, special rules and regulations enforced by various branches of the government, etc., which were issued in accordance with the provisions of FEFTCL. The ultimate goal of the system is the same as that of FEFTCL. Namely, recovery and expansion of the national economy, balance-of-payments equilibrium, stability of the Japanese currency, optimal use of foreign exchange reserves, and other objectives of FEFTCL are at the same time the concerns of the import control system. The basic assumption of the system has been that the critical nature of Japan's postwar economic condition dictated the use of direct control in the sphere of external trade and that "managed" trade rather than free trade was a better alternative under the prevailing circumstances. Emphasis on particular objectives has shifted with time. At first, economic recovery from the war was the main concern. After the recovery was completed, more emphasis was placed upon growth and stability of the national economy.[1]

If one is to judge the relative importance of a given objective in terms of how frequently it is quoted in official statements, the most important one has been the balance-of-payments equilibrium. Japan's heavy dependence upon foreign trade for sheer economic survival renders the goal of maintaining external balance an exceedingly significant one. The official position has been that, while the general efficacy and usefulness of fiscal and monetary policies are recognized,

23

these more orthodox policy tools are not always too reliable as a means of achieving balance-of-payments equilibrium because of the time lags involved in applying these policies and because of the danger that the goals of rapid economic growth and full employment might be seriously jeopardized when fiscal and monetary policies are invoked to such an extent as to achieve the country's external balance. Postwar Japan is said to have been beset by persistent excess demand for imports which induce major outflows of foreign exchange. In order to avoid critical deterioration of the balance of payments, direct trade control was thought to be the logical alternative to take.

Protection of domestic industry has been another important objective of the import control system. The Japanese government does, however, recognize the virtues of free trade. The economic welfare of the nation would be enhanced through freedom of imports. On the part of consumers, removal of barriers against the inflow of goods made by foreign firms would lower prices and improve qualitative standards of goods available to the consumers. A greater variety of goods entering the home market would enable consumers to diversify their tastes. Over the long run, domestic producers would also benefit from free trade. Keener competition coming from foreign producers would motivate domestic firms to strive harder to raise the efficiency and productivity of their operations. The pace of absorption of the more advanced foreign technology would be faster under free trade. The freedom to import industrial raw materials would enable domestic firms to achieve the optimal allocation of resources.

It has been the interpretation of the Japanese government, however, that these virtuous effects of free trade are realizable provided that a certain ideal condition prevails, namely, the country is already sufficiently developed and devoid of elements of vulnerability and weakness on the domestic front. In the context of postwar Japan as viewed by the government, this ideal condition definitely did not exist. The Japanese economy as a whole was seriously weakened by the war. Modern industries had to be developed fast to catch up with the West. Overpopulation and surplus labor made competition in the domestic market excessive—in many areas to the point of being wasteful of resources. Small businesses have been notably backward in technology and vulnerable to competition from abroad. As a matter of national policy, agricultural production had to be protected. It was the belief of the government that, given all these conditions, the tariff, a more conventional method and the least disrespectable form of protection, was hardly sufficient.

Price stabilization has been another objective of the import control system as a supplement to fiscal and monetary policies.

Reasonable price stability is desirable in order to achieve stable growth of the economy. However, the mix of fiscal and monetary policies alone may fail to mitigate excessive business fluctuations. If so, the method of direct import control is to be invoked as a means of assuring sufficient imported supplies of goods and materials, of reducing excess demand for imports at the time of overheating of the economy, of preventing speculative imports, and of making other necessary adjustments in conjunction with internal business fluctuations.

Import finance is an important part of total finance in the nation. In a trade-dependent country such as Japan, one cannot speak of an effective implementation of monetary policy divorced from import finance policy. While finance in general is a matter of concern for monetary policy, practically all phases of import finance—including Japanese imports financed by aliens, import credit from foreign banks, from foreign exporters, etc.—have been subject to the import control system under various provisions of FEFTCL. In this sense, the import control system may be said to be a branch of monetary policy.

Articles 1 and 52 of FEFTCL stipulate that the government shall exercise control over imports so that goods will be imported most advantageously and effectively. What this means is that the import control system operating under the provisions of FEFTCL, regards the optimal use of (scarce) foreign currencies funds as one of its prime objectives. However, what is most advantageous and effective is a matter of debate. Under the free trade approach foreign currencies funds available in the country will be allocated in accordance with the dicta of the market as consumers and producers freely decide what they want to purchase from abroad. Maximum use of available foreign exchange under the principles of free competition will lead to those imports which maximize the economic welfare of the nation. The contention of the Japanese government has been, however, that this happy result may occur in the very short run, but whether such an approach would truly be advantageous to the country over the long run is highly dubious. Most of the foreign currencies funds are used to finance imports. Therefore, what goods shall be imported becomes an important question—too important to be left to the market alone—from the standpoint of accelerating the rate of capital accumulation in the country. The free trade approach may result in too much import of consumer goods (including "nonessentials") and too little import of investment goods and industrial raw materials. The free import system may cause deterioration of the Japanese terms of trade as domestic producers, pressed by excess demand, bid up import prices. The official statements and discussions in general have

remained silent on the question as to whether the alleged excessive
competition among producers in search of foreign exchange funds was
due to the "wrong" rate of exchange adopted by the government. At
any rate, at the existing rate of exchange, strong excess demand for
foreign exchange was generated, and this provided a setting for an
easier and more effective implementation of the import control system.
Thus, the government has been able to control, to varying degrees in
shifting contexts, not only categories of imports and individual items
in each category but also who should be allowed to import—with
emphasis on the importation of those items which are believed to be
of strategic importance from the viewpoint of the government's growth
objective.

   During the early postwar years bilateralism as a form of international trading was popular among many countries, including Japan,
as a result of the then acute dollar shortage. In the case of Japan,
bilateral trade was carried out through the "open accounts" which
Japan maintained with other individual countries, each account specify-
ing the amount of export and import as well as the credit limit for a
given year as set by the bi-national trade agreement. FEFTCL came
into being when bilateral trade was still extensively practiced by Japan.
Consequently, one of the implied intents of the import control system
was to regulate the contents and the direction of imports so that
Japanese exports to those countries with which Japan held bilateral
trade agreements could be promoted at a planned pace and in a manner
consistent with the open account requirements. As world trade recovered from the shock of the war, the number of open accounts continued to diminish. But this did not mean that export promotion and
adjustment as a goal of the import control system lost its relevance.
While convertibility of West European currencies was largely restored
toward the end of 1958, most of the countries in Western Europe retained
waivers and reservations that were discriminatory against Japan.
Consequently, the Japanese government had to continue to cope with
the problem of balancing trade with those countries. At the same
time, even after the open accounts were removed, many of the underdeveloped countries suffered from chronic and critical balance-of-payments disequilibrium. Therefore, sufficient imports from them
frequently became a precondition for expanding Japanese exports to
those countries.

FOREIGN EXCHANGE BUDGET

   Prior to April, 1964, the Foreign Exchange Budget System had
played a central role as an instrument of import control. The budget

was to be determined by the Cabinet Council. The Minister of International Trade and Industry made announcements, after the budget was finalized, concerning those imports which were subject to approval. The same Minister might make no such announcements if the Cabinet Council so decided. The importer of those goods which were classified as quota items had to apply to MITI for a foreign exchange allotment. After MITI validated his application, the importer then was to apply to a foreign exchange bank for its approval. As part of the application for import approval, the importer was required to deposit at the foreign exchange bank an import collateral as set by MITI.

The government imports, imports by the U. S. and UN armed forces stationed in Japan (and others classified as free import items) might require no approval. But branches of the Japanese government other than MITI had to consult with the Minister of International Trade and Industry when they planned to purchase goods from abroad. External settlements of intermediary trade were to be executed only with MITI's permit, i.e., intermediary trade was generally outside the jurisdiction of orders and ordinances that applied to regular imports.

The Cabinet Council was chaired by the Prime Minister and had six other members: Ministers of Foreign Affairs, of Finance, of Agriculture and Forestry, of International Trade and Industry, of Transportation, and the General Secretary of the Economic Planning Agency. Decisions of the Council were to be unanimous. The president of the Bank of Japan participated in deliberations of the Council as an advisory member.

While public announcement of the import limit was made in accordance with the decision of the Council, the import collateral ratio was set by the Minister of International Trade and Industry with the concurrence of the Council. The Bureau of Foreign Exchange of the Ministry of Finance acted as secretariat of the Council.

Administrative agencies for the import control were the Ministry of International Trade and Industry, and the Ministry of Finance. MITI was mainly responsible for trade control, regulated related nontrade transactions, and prepared a foreign exchange budget for those items which came under its jurisdiction. The Ministry of Finance determined the standard settlement method, cross-examined and consolidated various foreign exchange budget plans gathered from different branches of the government, and submitted its own plan to the Council. It expressed its views to MITI concerning the nonstandard settlement method, yen imports, intermediary trade, etc.

The Bank of Japan under the provisions of FEFTCL assumed administrative tasks of import control as commisssioned by the competent Ministers. The Bank was charged with examination of the foreign exchange budget, post-import checks, collection of reports from importers, and part of the administration of the Foreign Currencies Special Allotment System.

Democratic control was said to be one of the central characteristics of the import control system in postwar Japan. The role of administrative agencies of the government was confined to one of determining basic policy directions. Actual control and regulations were to be carried out uniformly and routinely within the broad framework, i.e., no arbitrary execution of the rules by the administrative agencies was permitted, and all the procedures and other technical details of the control system were open and announced to the general public.

While FEFTCL let Cabinet Orders and Ministerial Ordinances work out technical details of trade control, the same law originally contained many explicit statements concerning the Foreign Exchange Budget which was not a temporary ad hoc matter but was meant to be a declaration, in a unified manner, of the common interest of the various branches of the government concerning the import control. In the beginning the first-come-first-served principle was widely employed. If the importers' demand for foreign exchange exceeded its supply, lottery was used as a means of allocating the limited exchange funds. Later, a more deliberate allotment system came to be heavily relied upon.

The competent Ministers were not allowed to approve the use of foreign currencies in the amounts exceeding those specified in the Foreign Exchange Budget. Thus the budget set a limit on how much foreign exchange could be spent in each fiscal year. The budget figures, however, were not directly related to actual amounts of foreign exchange used during the same period on account of time lags between appropriation and actual spending.

During the early period the currency-wise budgeting was important, as much consideration was given to the convertibility of the foreign currencies involved. Later on there was a shift of emphasis to the global budget which did not distinguish between currencies in terms of projected imports. The shift became notable after 1958 as restoration of convertibility of European currencies rendered such currency distinctions insignificant in the budgeting process. The budget routinely included the exchange reserve for contingencies.

The budget was formulated on the basis of careful prediction of availability of foreign exchange in connection with import as well as nontrade demand for exchange, and external and internal economic conditions affecting Japan's balance of payments. Sufficient reserves
were provided so that the probability of default involving Japanese
importers was minimized. Budget changes were permitted only under
extraordinary circumstances. The budget in its final form took effect
at the same time as the government made a public announcement of
the imports list.

The two allotment criteria were used. One is known as the
"pure trading firms allotment" criterion. Primarily meant for importation of consumption goods, this method relied upon past records
of the importing firms. From the standpoint of optimizing the use of
limited foreign exchange, the past records were used as evidence to
show that the firms were capable of effectively utilizing the exchange
funds. The data on import prices, volumes, and kinds of transactions
of the applicant firms were examined. However, even the government
has acknowledged the built-in bias of this system, namely, the older,
established firms are allowed complacency whereas the new entrants
tend to be discriminated against.

Another method was called the "domestic demand" criterion.
Applicants for exchange allotment were importers responding to internal demand in excess of internal supply. This method tried to
examine what goods were to be imported, whether or not such imports
were good for the national economy, who the importers would be,
whether the importers had good past records, and whether such imports would cause problems of import substitution in conjunction with
the government's economic plans. This second method was employed
mainly with respect to importation of investment goods. The "domestic demand" criterion was at times supplemented by the "order limit
notification" method, an example of administrative guidance, whereby
the government instructed the firms to limit their import orders
within bounds specified on the basis of the firms' productive capacities
and export records. The method was invoked typically with respect to
those domestic producers who required large volumes of imported
industrial raw materials. Despite the allegedly democratic procedures
and the fairness principle, these allotment methods involved an inherent trap of encouraging favoritism and discrimination.

The Special Allotment System applied to special categories of
imports such as raw materials for processing deal, compensatory
trading items, materials for tourist hotels in Japan, imports for the
U. S. troops stationed in Japan, and "specified goods." The last

category refers to those consumer goods for which excess demand
in the home market is notably high on account of the trade control,
e.g., bananas, canned pineapples, salmon eggs, etc. Importers of
these "specified goods" have been subject to excess-profit taxes.

An allotment certificate issued by MITI remained valid in general for four months within which time the importer was required to
obtain import approval from a foreign exchange bank. In principle,
every prospective importer applied for the quota under his own name.
However, he might commission, or might be commissioned by, another
person. For instance, the manufacturing firms which imported raw
materials typically commissioned their representative associations
to apply for approval of their imports.

THE APPROVAL SYSTEM

Determination of the Foreign Exchange Budget meant that the
basic framework of import control for a given fiscal period was laid
out. While administration of the control was conditioned by the budget,
actual information useful to the importers came from the Imports
Announcement. This Announcement was made in accordance with
Article 3 of the Import Trade Control Order by MITI on the basis of
the Cabinet Council's decision and contents of the budget. It cited
approved import items in terms of commodity categories, currencies
to be used for settlement, and other related matters. The Announcement was published in the government journals (Kampo and Tsusan
Sho Koho). The meaning of Imports Announcement has been varying
considerably depending upon the weights of the Automatic Approval
System as against the Foreign Currencies Funds Allotment System.
Under the former system foreign exchange banks immediately began
approving the supply of foreign exchange once the Announcement was
made, whereas under the latter system the importer was obliged to
apply for an allotment of foreign currencies to MITI. In April, 1962,
the format of the Imports Announcement was switched to the so-called
"negative list" that cited only those import items which did not come
under the Automatic Approval System.

When the import control was in full force during the early postwar period, some foreign exporters on occasion took advantage of the
open system of Imports Announcement by deliberately raising their
prices of those goods for which Japanese import demand was intense
as judged by the contents of the Announcement. This abuse led to the
adoption of the selective nondisclosure rule applicable to key import
items under the Foreign Currencies Funds Allotment System. The

significance of the Imports Announcement diminished as trade liberalization progressed in later years.

Authorized foreign exchange banks approved (or disapproved)
applications for imports, if and where such approval was required.
The banks' task was primarily to check applications to see if they
were consistent with the contents of the Imports Announcement and
constraints of the Foreign Exchange Budget. In some exceptional
cases (e.g., imports involving the nonstandard method of settlement
and imports of unspecified origins), MITI's separate pre-import permit was required. In these cases the banks were responsible for con-
firming that the pre-import permits had been duly granted. Where
relevant, the banks were also responsible for checking to see if the
import-collateral requirements had been met. The banks' import
approval remained valid as a rule for a period of six months. The
idea behind this time limit was that too long a time lag between the
import committment and the actual payment for imports was believed
to tend to create difficulties on the part of the government's balance-
of-payments policy and that the absence of a time limit was presumed
to encourage speculative (and other "unsound") imports. The time
limit might be shortened or prolonged by MITI. Once approved, the
contents of the approved imports might not be changed. If a change
was necessary, that would call forth a separate approval.

Under the Authomatic Approval System imports were approved
automatically as applications were submitted to the foreign banks as
long as the balance of exchange in the budget remained positive. The
banks merely checked with the Bank of Japan (acting in behalf of MITI)
to see if enough exchange funds were left. The Cabinet Council set
aside a lump sum for the Automatic Approval System without specify-
ing how much exchange was allocated for which import items, the sum
being sufficiently large so that unexpectedly sharp increases in import demand for particular items would not cause a complete drain
of the total reserve. The working rule was that applications for imports covered by the System were never to be refused or sorted by
some rationing device (such as a lottery), and, in the event of an
abnormal increase in import demand of a speculative nature, the con-
tingency reserve would be activated rather than invoking an administrative intervention with the process of automatic approval.

In April, 1964, the Foreign Exchange Budget System, the Cabinet
Council responsible for the budget, and the associated Foreign Currencies Fund Allotment System were terminated as part of the preparation for compliance with Article 8 of the International Monetary
Fund (IMF) Charter.

STANDARD SETTLEMENT

Standard settlement refers to a method of import control whereby the government sets certain "standards" concerning external payments. If these standards are met, foreign exchange banks approve
imports routinely (subject to other restrictions that may apply). If
the standards are not met, this means that the importer is employing
the nonstandard settlement method, and is therefore obliged to apply
for a special permit from MITI.

The rationale for government intervention here is that if what a
private importer regards as a good, reliable, and advantageous method
of external payment is not considered likewise by the state, that method
should be classified as nonstandard and be subject to restrictions. The
general criteria for nonstandards are as follows: 1. The method in
question may be effective and advantageous in particular cases but, if
generalized, is believed to be disadvantageous to the national economy
as a whole; 2. the method may be good as far as individual importers
are concerned but may generate adverse effects from the standpoint
of the government's monetary and financial policies; and 3. the method
will violate, or is believed to violate, the existing trade and payment
agreements with other countries.

Distinction between standards and nonstandards is made in terms
of period of settlement, currencies used for settlement, origins of
imports, import prices, etc. Technical details of the standard settlement method are determined by the Ministry of Finance. Restrictions
are imposed concerning four aspects of external payments: prepayments, post-import payments, import prices, and settlement currencies.

With reference to restrictions on prepayments, it is standard
to make a payment after receipt of cargo or of documents duly certifying loading of cargo at foreign ports. All "others" are nonstandard.
Prepayments are discouraged mainly to prevent deterioration of
terms of settlement. Granted that prepayments may provide advantages
such as greater assurance of receiving cargo, saving on interest and
price reductions, it was feared (especially during the early postwar
period) that foreign exporters would exploit the "weaker" position of
Japanese importers by imposing terms more advantageous to foreign
suppliers than to Japanese importers. Similarly, it was feared that
freedom of prepayment would encourage speculative imports, causing
excessive depletion of the nation's limited exchange reserves.

As to restrictions on post-import payments, the importer must
as a rule pay for imports within four months after customs clearance
of said imports. If payment is made later than four months, it is
classified as nonstandard. Delayed payment may be desirable as it
reduces outflow of foreign exchange and enables Japanese importers
to have greater access to trade finance in foreign money markets.
In the government's view, however, too much delay in payments will
cause problems such as technical difficulties in connection with administration of the nonexchange imports, with implementation of the foreign exchange budget policy, and with execution of internal stabilization policy due to inflow of much credit from foreign sources.

Concerning restrictions on import prices, it is standard to pay
the whole import price as specified by the Ministry of Finance (usually,
the contractually agreed import price plus related service charges).
Payment of a part of the import price is deemed nonstandard mainly
as a means of discouraging illegal transfer of foreign exchange and
illegal (or extralegal) opening of yen deposits in Japan owned by nonresidents.

Restrictions on exporting countries and settlement currencies—
designed to economize the use of hard currencies and to cope with
the existing treaty obligations—lost much of their meaning after restoration of convertibility of European currencies in 1958. Before then,
the world was divided into three currency areas: the dollar area, the
sterling area, and the open account area. Standard currencies to be
used for imports from the dollar area were U. S. dollars, Canadian
dollars, and Swiss francs. Currencies acceptable for imports from
the sterling area were British pounds, West German marks, and
French francs. Payments for imports from the open account area
were settled in compliance with whatever bilateral trade agreements
existed between Japan and other countries in the open account area.
After restoration of convertibility of European currencies, the world
was redivided into the open account area and the "other" area. The
weight of the open account area steadily diminshed as Japan continued
to withdraw from bilateral trade agreements with other countries.

OTHER ASPECTS OF CONTROL

Import Collateral

Under the import collateral system, the import collateral is a
condition for approval of proposed imports. The system purports to

discourage unsound or speculative imports and to assure the actual
carrying out of imports. Approval of imports technically does not
oblige the importer to purchase foreign goods. But if he does not
import, this would be unfair to others who applied and failed to obtain
approval. The argument here is that those imports which have been
approved should be carried out so as to optimize the use of limited
exchange reserves. If no imports take place, the collateral, as a rule,
will not be refunded. On the other hand, the collateral may be used to
pay part of the import price.

The system has at times been invoked as a means of suppressing
import demand (somewhat in the manner of margin requirement) in
conjunction with the government's tight money policy. For example,
in 1957, the year of severe balance-of-payments difficulties, the
collateral ratio was raised up to the maximum of 35 percent. Whether
this measure was truly effective as an instrument of deflationary
policy remains uncertain. The system has been criticized as discriminatory against small importing firms which can be gravely affected by
change in the collateral ratio in contrast to large trading companies
which are known to be insensitive to the ratio changes. Employment
of the import collateral ratio policy may be viewed as a manifestation
of inadequacy and underdevelopment of the framework of monetary
policy which usually consists of discount rate policy, required reserves
policy, and open market operations.

The Minister of International Trade and Industry determines
collateral ratios applicable to various categories of imports (Article
13, Import Trade Control Order). Collaterals may be in cash,
national bonds, national railways bonds, telephone-telegraph bonds,
or time deposit certificates. The Minister of International Trade and
Industry may impose restrictions upon the kinds of collateral that are
acceptable. The collateral in the right amount and of the right kind
is to be submitted to the foreign exchange bank as part of the application for import approval.

The collateral may be refunded by foreign exchange banks or
only with the approval of the said Minister. The collateral may be
returned by the bank where it was deposited in the following manner:

1. If the proposed import is not approved, all collateral will be
   returned;

2. If the bank gives a partial approval of the import, that portion
   of the collateral which refers to the unapproved part of the
   import will be returned;

3. If the importer returns the import approval to the bank, all collateral will be refunded; and

4. If, within the effective import period, goods are imported in a value exceeding "certified import value" which equals the value of the approved import times the ratio set by MITI (usually 0.8), all collateral will be refunded.

If there are no imports, or if the value of actual imports falls below the "certified import value" within the effective import period, there will, as a rule, be no refund of the collateral. When the importer has legitimate reason for failing to import the proposed amount, he may petition the said Minister within ten days after the end of the effective import period. The reasons that are acceptable to the government for refunding the collaterals are: 1. unexpected export bans or restrictions imposed by foreign governments; 2. wars or revolutions in foreign countries; 3. bankruptcies of foreign export firms; 4. cancellation of export permits by foreign governments; 5. destruction of cargo-carrying ships by fire, storm, etc.; and 6. other reasons that are deemed legitimate by MITI. The foreign exchange banks will transfer those collaterals which have not been refunded to the government account one month after the end of the effective import period.

Customs Clearance

Customs procedures are prescribed by the tariff law, and represent a legal system separate from FEFTCL. However, activities of the customs are linked with the framework of import control. The main objective of customs inspection is to check to see if the actual imports are the same as those described on paper in connection with the provisions of FEFTCL. All the pre-import controls are formal and implemented through documents. At customs one can really observe whether or not the control mechanism is working properly and effectively.

When the customs office discovers major discrepancies between actual imports and those described in the approval documents, clearance may be refused. In the cases whereby discrepancies are believed to be deliberate, importers are subject to penal sanctions. In practice, minor differences are waived at the discretion of customs inspectors. If the discrepancies are due to the importers' misunderstanding or ignorance about laws, customs, and conventions of exporting countries, the cargo may be shipped to designated factories for minor alterations and adjustments so as to make the imported goods fit sufficiently the

descriptions in the approval documents, or the matter may be referred
to MITI and/or the Ministry of Finance for their advice and instruction.
Those imported goods which fail to be cleared are either shipped back
to the import origins or auctioned off in accordance with the provisions
of the tariff law.

Nonexchange Imports

Nonexchange imports in general refer to those imports which
may be paid for in yen, or those imports which do not require the use
of foreign exchange with respect to total or partial payments of their
prices. In a way, it is peculiar that even imports of this category
have been subject to control inasmuch as they do not involve foreign
exchange, the scarcity of which has been one of the central concerns
of the government. The control of nonexchange imports has been
justified: 1. because it was deemed necessary to maintain the overall effectiveness of the entire control system; 2. because one of the
main objectives of the control system has been protection of domestic
industries that are affected by any imports aside from whether they
require the use of foreign exchange; and 3. because it was feared that
leaving this category free would tempt importers to abuse the system
by importing as much as possible under the category of "nonexchange"
imports and paying for them illegally or extralegally.

The structure of control over nonexchange imports is simpler
than that for regular imports. Nonexchange imports have been free
of constraints and rules pertaining to Imports Announcement, the
Foreign Exchange Budget, the standard settlement method, and the
import collateral. The Minister of International Trade and Industry
approves nonexchange imports and validates prolongation of their
effective period. The definition of nonexchange imports technically
includes gifts, foreign goods that physically enter Japan for repairs
only, those imports which are settled in foreign currencies other than
those designated by the government, those imports which are paid for
in foreign currencies borrowed outside Japan, and those imports
which are paid for through cancellation of notes receivable from nonresidents.

Intermediary Trade

Intermediary trade refers to the movement of goods between
two countries that involves a dealer (or an agent) in the third country.
Under FEFTCL it is defined to be trade between two countries other

than Japan in which residents of Japan are involved concerning trade contracts, a typical example being a Japanese firm's purchase of a machine in the United States to be shipped to Burma where the same firm is building a new factory. The cases whereby 1. residents of Japan collect service charges but are not involved in actual sales contracts, and 2. residents of Japan are involved but goods move only within one foreign country are not classified as intermediary trade under FEFTCL.

It is said that intermediary trade helps the growth of Japanese trading companies. What initially began as a casual, insignificant deal may later lead to more substantive trade relations with foreign firms. Intermediary trade may act as an effective publicity medium for know-how, technical competence, and reliability of Japanese firms. On the other hand, it may turn out to be harmful to Japanese exports as every intermediary export means a loss of potential export of output produced in Japan. Sometimes the importing countries maintain the import quota system which classifies "intermediary" imports technically as those from Japan even though they physically came from elsewhere. The control of intermediary trade was intended to cope with these negative aspects. However, the weight of intermediary trade in Japan's total external trade has been negligibly small throughout the postwar period. Intermediary trade is subject to approval by the Minister of International Trade and Industry with consensus of the Minister of Finance.

Others

Notes Receivable. If the importer obtains a note receivable in connection with his imports, he is obliged to collect it, as a rule, within three months after it becomes due. Notes receivable of this sort are drawn typically for settlement of overpayments, discounts, service charges of agents, compensation for loss and damage and the like, that occur in connection with transportation, ship chartering, insurance, storage, inspection, and post services.

Post-Import Inspection. The Bank of Japan, as commissioned by MITI, routinely examines all import documents to see if foreign exchange banks and importers are complying with the existing rules and regulations of FEFTCL. Separate from the Bank of Japan's inspection, MITI also periodically audits foreign exchange banks mainly to see if import collaterals are being duly deposited or transferred to the government account.

Free Imports. No approval is required of the following imports: 1. personal belongings of residents; 2. materials to be used in building public facilities; 3. belongings of nonresidents entering Japan; and 4. commercial samples that meet certain conditions. All free imports, however, are subject to customs inspection.

Government Imports. The Import Trade Control Order does not apply to government imports. Instead, internal rules within the administrative branches of the government are to be complied with. Before April, 1964, what might be imported by the government fell within the confines of the Cabinet Council's decisions and was subject to the approval of the Minister of International Trade and Industry. Foreign exchange required for government imports then was included in the regular Foreign Exchange Budget.

Military Imports. FEFTCL generally does not apply to imports by and for the U.S. and UN armed forces stationed in Japan. Article 3 of the U.S.-Japan Mutual Security Pact (originally signed in April, 1952) gives exemption to the following cases: 1. goods imported by the U.S. armed forces for official purposes; 2. goods imported by the U.S. sales agencies (e.g., PX) that serve military personnel and their families; and 3. goods imported by the U.S. military post office and banks. These military or military-related imports into Japan are subject to approval by the U.S. government. At the time of the Korean War similar provisions prevailed with respect to the UN troops in Japan.

NOTE

1. The system of import control in postwar Japan has been vast and extremely complicated. The detailed description of the system that includes a chronological survey of changes and reforms would easily fill several volumes. This chapter intends to give merely an outline of the control mechanism. Sources that should be consulted by those interested in greater details of the subject include: the Bureau of Foreign Trade and the Bureau of Trade Promotion of the Ministry of International Trade and Industry, ed., Saishin Boeki no Jitsumu [A Complete Guide to the Up-to-Date Business Practice in Foreign Trade] (Tokyo: JETRO, 1968; MITI, ed., Tsusho Sangyo Roppo [Laws Concerning Foreign Trade and Industry] (Tokyo: Foreign Trade and Industry Research Association, 1968; and the Foreign Exchange Research Association, ed., Gaikoku Kawase Sho Roppo [The Laws Concerning Foreign Exchange] (Tokyo: 1968). Sections on trade policy in MITI's annual Tsusho Hakusho [Foreign Trade White Paper] mention changes and reforms of the import control system that may have taken place in a given year.

3

**LIBERALIZATION
OF
IMPORTS**

BEFORE 1960

During the period prior to 1959-1960 no substantive liberalization of of imports (namely, removal of quantitative control of trade in the forms of import quotas and associated exchange restrictions) had been undertaken by the Japanese government. There was a mild trend toward trade liberalization, but the trend was mixed with short-run setbacks and policy reversals as the country continued to experience periodic balance-of-payments crises and a perennial shortage of foreign exchange relative to the rising import demand. Until April, 1952, the Cabinet Council responsible for formulation of the Foreign Exchange Budget remained under the supervision of SCAP. The elaborate mechanism of FEFTCL exerted its regulating force to all phases of Japanese foreign trade. The mood for freer trade was fermenting in business and industrial circles, but the general attitude was one of caution and "wait and see." The government had not yet developed a central, unified plan for major liberalization. If we express the extent of liberalization as a ratio of the amount of foreign exchange budgeted for those imports which come under the AA (Automatic Approval) system to the total foreign exchange budget for commodity imports minus normal reserves, the ratio was as small as 15.8 percent at the end of 1955. Similarly, the ratio was 22.9 percent in 1956, 21.0 percent in 1957, 25.7 percent in 1958, and 31.5 percent in 1959. It is somewhat misleading to interpret these ratios as an index of liberalization because it was only after restoration of convertibility of West European currencies toward the end of 1958 that most Japanese imports became "global," i.e., prior to that time even many AA items were subject to secondary regional restrictions in terms of the currency areas of the world from which goods were to be imported.

Since its promulgation (1949) there have been numerous moves to change the character of FEFTCL. Before 1954, however, they were faint voices of discontent and opinions barely audible amidst the nation's preoccupation with problems of postwar chaos and reconstruction. Once the occupation was over, there arose a sentiment within the Japanese government favoring revising FEFTCL, a product of the occupation era, as a way of manifesting its newly gained political autonomy and independence. Such sentiment was reflected in the Master Plan for Reforms of Laws and Regulations, drafted and announced on March 9, 1954, by the Special Committee on Administrative Reforms of the then governing Liberal Party. While the Plan was concerned with the entirety of the postwar legal system in Japan, it contained many suggestions pertaining to FEFTCL. Inter alia, the Plan recommended that: the Cabinet Council be retained but its functions be reexamined; the definition of precious metals include only gold; the method of certifying import payments be simplified; the exchange fund allocation system be reexamined; the import collateral and post-import check systems be simplified; and a special committee be established to study and improve the administration of trade and exchange transactions. While the reform movement as suggested by the above Plan was a reaction of the Japanese government to the occupation policy, namely, an attempt to revise the administrative structure that was established during the occupation period, the political and economic climate was hardly ripe for actual implementation of the Plan. The major changes in FEFTCL did not occur until years later   The only minor revisions that took place in 1954 were the new definition of precious metals that included only gold and the new rule by which an importer became able to establish the legitimacy of his complaint without bringing a formal suit to the court (Law No. 138, 1954).

In early 1956 the Federation of Economic Organizations conducted an extensive survey concerning improvements of the existing foreign trade and exchange control system. It covered practically all major firms in trading, production, banking, insurance, and transportation. While the survey was then criticized as too comprehensive and disorganized, the Federation submitted to the government the survey results which generally indicated a rising desire of the business community for reduction of trade control in light of the changing economic circumstances. In March, 1956, the Japan Foreign Trade Association, another powerful business organization, issued a policy statement entitled, The Re-examination of the Trade and Exchange Control System, which recommended the relaxation of the Foreign Exchange Concentration System, introduction of the yen exchange, greater liberalization of imports by way of expanding the global AA list, and the abolishment or simplification of the existing Foreign Exchange Control Orders. These recommendations of the Federation of Economic Organizations and the Japan Foreign Trade Association were motivated by the sustained economic growth and prosperity at home, the expansion of Japan's foreign exchange reserves and the steady trend of trade liberalization in Western Europe. At the same time they helped strengthen a climate of opinion that the time had come for Japan to start preparing for the inevitable liberalization of her imports. In November, 1956, there took place a series of reforms of the Export and Import Control Orders. In May, 1957, another note of rising consciousness concerning trade liberalization was registered as the Tokyo Chamber of Commerce and Industry issued the Recommendations for Establishing a Committee on Reforms of the Foreign Trade and Exchange Control Laws and Regulations.

In December, 1957, sixteen experts (mostly from private backgrounds) held the Conference on the Trade and Exchange Control Systems from the Standpoint of Promoting Exports under the auspicies of the Ministry of Finance and MITI. The conference was initially meant mainly to explore ways and means of encouraging exports through adjustive changes in the control system as Japan experienced a drastic fall of exports and severe balance-of-payments difficulties in 1957. Discussions at the conference, however, ranged over all aspects of FEFTCL. After its promulgation in 1949, the central principle had been to regulate all trade and exchange transactions. Numerous laws, regulations, orders, ordinances, rules, notices, etc. had been written to implement FEFTCL. The result was a maze-like apparatus of control, so huge and complex that few people could possibly understand it. The experts at the conference expressed their view that the time was ripe for a fundamental change of FEFTCL. Specifically, they recommended drastic restructuring and simplification of the control apparatus, total trade liberalization as a new principle with adequate provisions for partial restrictions if and where necessary, and instituting a committee of experts on the fundamental reform of FEFTCL as adjunct to the Ministry of Finance and MITI. Such a committee was organized a year later in December, 1958.

In late 1957 the Federation of Economic Organizations once again surveyed the views of its member organizations, and circulated the survey results as Recommendations Concerning the Reform of FEFTCL. The contents of these recommendations closely paralleled those of the above experts' conference. They included, inter alia, immediate liberalization of foreign exchange transactions, drawing a specific time table for trade liberlization, and accelerating industrial reorganization as a means of enhancing internal readiness for the liberalization through revision of the Anti-Monopoly Law and adoption of appropriate fiscal and monetary measures.

On November 19, 1959, the Foreign Trade Constitution of Japan (Nihon Boeki Kensho), unique and somewhat unusual as constitutions go, was promulgated at the second All Japan Trade Promotion Conference (at Hotel Teito in Tokyo) held under the auspicies of the Japan Chamber of Commerce and Industry, the Japan Foreign Trade Association and JETRO (Japan External Trade Research Organization). Its high-sounding rhetoric aside, the Constitution is reproduced in full below as it illustrates the rising consciousness at that time of the business community in Japan concerning the approach of trade liberalization.

The Foreign Trade Constitution of Japan

Recognizing that foreign trade is an effective means of promoting prosperity and peace for all countries through international division of labor and efficient use of resources in the world and that foreign trade is indispensable for raising standards of living and cultural enrichment of the Japanese people, we hereby promulgate this Foreign Trade Constitution of Japan as a way of expressing our belief in the following principles which should guide the direction of Japanese foreign trade. This Constitution shall be defended through constant efforts of every Japanese citizen.

Article 1 (Expansion of Foreign Trade)

Foreign trade shall be expanded in the atmosphere of freedom and mutual harmony, and the international market shall be maintained as the common ground for promoting economic prosperity in the world.

Article 2 (Respect for Mutual Benefits)

Foreign trade shall be guided by the principle of respect for mutual benefits and shall be contributory to economic development and rising standards of living in the countries of all trading partners.

Article 3 (Fair Trade)

Foreign trade shall be fair and in accord with the principles of international trust and economic order.

Article 4 (Foreign Trade as a Matter of National Policy)

The expansion of foreign trade shall be a fundamental objective of national policy and all other policies
of the Japanese government shall be consistent with that
objective.

Article 5 (Principles of Imports)

Imports shall be understood as an effective tool of
enhancing not only growth of the Japanese economy but
also expansion of exports and development of resources
on the part of those countries from which Japan imports.

Article 6 (Principles of Exports)

We shall constantly strive to improve the quality,
design, and after-service of our exports, and shall be
sensitive to the market conditions, wants and needs of
the importing countries.

Article 7 (Promotion of Science and Technology)

We shall endeavor to improve our science and
technology in order to develop and innovate new and more
advanced products for export.

Article 8 (Research and Advertising)

We shall make every effort to increase our knowledge and understanding of the overseas markets and to
publicize to the rest of the world our culture, industry
and economic capabilities.

Article 9 (Cooperation of Related Firms and Agencies)

All firms, organizations, and government agencies,
directly or indirectly involved in foreign trade, shall
cooperate closely with one another for promotion of
Japan's external trade.

Article 10 (National Principle)

Realizing that the nation's economic life is critically
dependent upon foreign trade, every Japanese citizen shall
make positive efforts on the job and in daily life toward
achieving the national goal of promoting external trade.

THE MASTER PLAN

The Japanese government announced the Master Plan for Liberalization of Foreign Trade and Exchange on June 26, 1960, thus making explicit its policy position concerning removal of trade and exchange restrictions. Prior to 1958 there was little serious concern on the part of the government with the problem of trade liberalization. Given the strong, conservative mood in business and industry as well as within the government that lingered on even in early 1960, the pronouncement of the Master Plan was something of an epoch-making event that signified the commencement of a new era in Japan's postwar economic history. In 1956-1957 the government was compelled to tighten its import control amidst the balance-of-payments crises; unthinkable then was the question of trade liberalization. The psychological mood of the nation was basically the same in 1958. The restoration of the convertibility of currencies in Western Europe in December, 1958, made the Japanese realize that sooner or later Japan would have to start liberalizing her trade; but as a matter of concrete policy action rather than of abstract thought, few policy-makers in Japan were as yet seriously concerned.

From the second half of 1959 on, some significant changes began to take place. The legal limit on the amount of foreign exchange that could be held by trading companies was raised. Some restrictions on transfer of funds from the nonresident yen accounts were lifted. Regulations of overseas travel were partially eased. In December, 1959, the Plan for Liberalization of Textile Raw Materials was announced. As of March, 1960, the AA (Automatic Approval) list included 1,067 items accounting for about 40 percent of total private commodity imports.[1]

In the fall of 1959 the annual meeting of IMF was held in Washington, D.C. The Japanese delegation brought to the meeting proposals to liberalize nine remaining AA items whose imports from the United States were still restricted, and to relax the peg on yen by allowing 0.5 percent fluctuations below and above the official parity. The U.S. government reacted with coolness to this offer as being far less than expected, and reminded Japan that the pace of her trade liberalization was unjustifiably slow in light of her growth records and balance-of-payments position. In the winter of 1959, the 15th annual meeting of the General Agreement on Tariffs and Trade (GATT) was held in Tokyo. Japan registered her complaints to those Western countries which still invoked Article 35 for discriminating against Japanese goods as a violation of the spirit of GATT. In return, Japan was criticized by the Western delegations for the persistence of extensive trade control in Japan, and was reminded that Article 35 was still used lest their markets be flooded by "cheap" Japanese goods. These experiences compelled the Japanese government to realize that as an international bargaining tool, if nothing else, the early liberalization of her trade became a matter of necessity.

In the spring of 1960 the Japanese government established the Coordinating Council for Promotion of Trade Liberalization. Specific plans were studied and drafted mainly within the Economic Planning Agency before they culminated in the Master Plan of June 26. The Master Plan was based upon eight broad policy objectives: 1. rapid economic growth with reasonable stability; 2. expansion of domestic employment and increase in labor mobility; 3. promotion of exports and economic cooperation with other countries; 4. greater advancement and modernization of Japanese industry through freer trade; 5. modernization of agriculture, forestry, fishery, and small businesses; 6. improvement of social overheads to increase efficiency of business firms; 7. establishment of orderly markets; and 8. reform of the tariff system. According to the Master Plan, products of the advanced industries would be liberalized immediately or soon. The less internationally competitive goods would be liberalized later. Backward industries would remain under protection till they become sufficiently strong vis-à-vis foreign competitors. In all cases, for those items to be liberalized there would be corresponding, adjustive changes in tariff rates. In essence, the guidelines for liberalization of imports were formulated in accordance with the infant-industry argument for protection.

The liberalization of imports meant an augmentation of the AA system, i.e., an increase in the weight of those imports which were to be automatically approved in Japan's total private commodity imports. In calculating the liberalization ratio as an index of the extent to which Japanese imports are free of restrictions, fiscal 1959 (April 1959 - March 1960) was chosen for weights to make the statistics comparable to those used by the Organization for European Economic Cooperation (OEEC) countries. The ratio refers to that of those imports under the AA system to total commodity imports less government imports in fiscal 1959 weights. Government imports which primarily consist of rice and wheat are excluded because they are normally not subject to liberalization as an obligation of membership in GATT. Calculated in this manner, the ratio was approximately 40 percent as of April, 1960. According to the government plan the ratio was to increase up to 80 percent in three years (or to 90 percent if coal and petroleum would be liberalized).

The above liberalization ratio requires some interpretation. Suppose oil import weighs 10 percent in fiscal 1959 and 15 percent in 1964. If oil import is liberalized in 1964, it is counted as 10 percent liberalization, not 15 percent. The smaller the weight of a given item in the base year, the greater is the extent to which the ratio underestimates actual liberalization. Similarly, if the weight decreases from the base year to a later year, the ratio tends to exaggerate the real extent of liberalization. As Warren Hunsberger puts it: "Items that were important [in 1959], like raw cotton or crude petroleum, carry heavy weight in measuring liberalization. . . . And items not imported at all in 1959 do not affect the liberalization calculation, no matter how much or little of them is later permitted entry, or on what terms."[2] While the Japanese government contended that the calculation method was patterned after what was used by the OEEC countries, the London Economist reported:

> When your correspondent was in Tokyo in the summer of 1962, Japan was preparing, with a fanfare of trumpets, to march forward in the following autumn into what it hoped it would be able to call 90 percent liberalisation of imports. It had better be said straight away that this most certainly does not mean that it envisaged that 90 percent of all that might be imported into Japan would be free of restrictions. In the first place, the figure refers only to 90 percent by value of Japan's spending on imports in 1959; if imports of anything were nought in 1959 (and imports of very many things were) 90 percent of nought is still nought. Again, imports were still to be authorised only within the limitations set by an overall foreign exchange budget; it was pretty clear that liberalization was being steered into fields where the government hoped that domestic producers would be least hardly hit; and some tariffs had already gone up to counter the effect of the quota restrictions coming down.[3]

The Master Plan classified all imports into four categories in terms of Japan's competitive position in the world market: 1. those which could be liberalized immediately; 2. those which would be liberalized within three years; 3. those for which no specific time limits were set but which should be liberalized as soon as possible; and 4. those whose liberalization was deemed difficult for a long period of time. The first and second categories refer to those goods which were to be liberalized so that the liberalization ratio would be 80 percent within three years according to the Master Plan. Those included in the third category were of two kinds: products of those industries which were still considered "infant" in 1960 but were classified by the government as those which would play strategic roles in the future course of Japan's economic development; and products which would require protection for some time, given Japan's particular factor endowments. The former subcategory referred to automobiles, heavy electrical machinery, chemical equipment, industrial electronic equipment, manufacturing machinery, and the like, whereas the latter subcategory included walnuts, chestnuts, mushrooms, black tea, paper pulp, paper and paper products, copper, lead, nickel products, petro-leum, and coal. Among the most sensitive items was coal as there was a virtual certainty that the sudden liberalization of petroleum would give a hard blow to the coal industry which had long been beset by rising production costs and unemployment. The fourth category (for those which were not expected to be liberalized for a long time) included sulphur, manganese, various fruits, confections, and products of the coastal fishing industry.

AFTER 1960

The OEEC countries began to liberalize regional trade among themselves in November, 1949. The overall ratio of their regional trade liberalization reached 90 percent at the end of 1958. The pace of liberalizing their imports from the dollar area was slower, but in 1960 their trade with the dollar area became about as free as among the OEEC members. On the other hand, they continued to discriminate, even after 1960, against Japanese goods such as textiles, synthetic fibers, binoculars, leather goods, toys, cameras, sewing machines, and ceramics. As late as 1969 France discriminated against 65 items from Japan; Italy, 64; Austria, 116; Benelux, 28; Norway, 59; Sweden, 47; West Germany, 19; and Denmark, 25.

Japan had practiced regional discrimination before restoration of convertibility of West European currencies at the end of 1958, but after that most trade restrictions in terms of currency areas were abolished. Particularly after 1960 Japan's trade liberalization has been of a global kind. Japan began to liberalize later than European countries. Allowing for the time lag, however, the speed of Japan's liberalization was faster than that of some European countries. The trade liberalization in Europe was mixed with short-run setbacks and temporary policy reversals; in the case of Japan there have been no policy reversals since the Master Plan of 1960. A sequel to the Master Plan which laid out a broad framework of liberalization, the Trade and Exchange Liberalization Promotion Plan which the govern-ment announced in September, 1961, provided a more specific time table. The new target according to this Promotion Plan was to raise the liberalization ratio up to 90 percent by October, 1962.

At the end of 1961 the liberalization was already 70 percent. In April, 1962, the ratio was up to 73 percent. On April 1, 1962, the Japanese government switched from the "positive list" to the "negative list" method, namely, the previous practice of announcing the AA items was replaced by the new method of citing only the restricted BTN (Brussels Tariff Nomenclature) 4-digit items.

In October, 1962, there was a major liberalization: as many as 230 items were liberalized, including crude oil, vitamins, nylon tire chord, soap, auto tire tubes, papers, nylon stockings, automatic vending machines, ballpoint pens, slide fasteners, etc. As a result, the number of items on the negative list sharply decreased down to 262. The liberalization ratio became 88 percent—slightly below the target ratio of 90 percent only because liberalization of heavy oil was postponed for the sake of the coal industry.[4] The October liberalization was significant in several respects. Previously the liberalization typically meant removing restrictions on raw materials. Now a new principle was adopted so that only those items whose liberalization was believed to cause undue difficulties with virtual certainty were exempted, and many items which were merely potentially problematical were added to the AA list. At the same time the Japanese government assisted domestic firms by providing advance information, closely coordinating with the producers' associations and making precautionary adjustive changes in the tariff rates. Furthermore, the government employed for the first time a tactic of deliberately postponing liberalization of some items for bargaining purposes via-à-vis the European countries which continued to discriminate against Japanese goods. In November, 1962, Great Britain gave sizable concessions to Japan in exchange for Japan's liberalizing eight items including woolen yarn, synthetic fabrics, and razor blades. Japan made similar bargains with Italy and France in 1963.

Those items which remained restricted in 1963 were roughly of four kinds: 1. those exempted from GATT obligation such as weapons and narcotics, and the government imports of rice, wheat, tobacco, salt, etc.; 2. those which required protection in view of Japan's particular factor endowments, e.g., many dairy products, coal, sugar fruits, soyabean oil, and certain nonferrous metals; 3. "strategic infant" items such as electronic computers, heavy electric generators, large heavy machinery, and automobiles; and 4. those which were reserved for bargaining vis-à-vis the Western countries which continued to discriminate against Japanese products.

As an increasing number of items were liberalized from the mid-1960's on, there prevailed in Japan a widespread fear that Japanese markets would be flooded by foreign products. Given the elaborate mechanism of trade control and the umbrella of protection under which domestic firms had been operating during the previous years, this fear was understandable. In retrospect, however, their anxiety turned out to be unfounded. In an overall picture there is no evidence that Japan's balance of payments has been adversely affected by the liberalization of imports. This observation comes as no surprise inasmuch as even during the heyday of trade control prior to the Master Plan of 1960 the government as a rule permitted imports of industrial raw materials in quantities that would sufficiently satiate internal demand, and after the Master Plan the government has generally followed the path of gradualism in avoiding high-risk cases with respect to imports of finished and semifinished products. Japan's total imports show a high degree of covariance with cyclical swings of domestic industrial production. Individual import items show different behavioral patterns subject to secular trends as well as cyclical, seasonal and stochastic variations. It is therefore not easy to identify the cause-effect relationships between the import behavior and the timing of liberalization. Concerning the impact of liberalization on Japanese imports, a MITI survey of 1963 made the following observations:

1. Some import items showed little change after the liberalization: e.g., radio receivers, knives, forks, spoons.

2. Imports of some items rose sharply after the liberalization, and soon afterward returned to the previous levels: e.g., buttons, brushes, laundry soap, internal combustion engines.

3. Imports of some items rose to and remained at higher levels than before the liberalization: e.g., coffee beans, cocoa beans, household electric appliances, typewriter ribbons, sporting goods.

4. Imports of some items showed a rising trend after the liberalization: e.g., instant coffee, sewing machines, record players, leather goods, movie films.[5]

In April, 1963, various mineral products, honey, and bananas were liberalized; as a result the liberalization ratio became 89 percent. In August, 1963, the ratio reached 92 percent after liberalization of safety glass, certain cosmetics, air-conditioners, tape-recorders, batteries, etc. In 1964 the liberalization took place in January, February, April, May, and October; after the October liberalization, the ratio became approximately 93 percent.

In April, 1964, following the recommendation of IMF, the Japanese government began to comply with Article 8 of the IMF Charter. This meant that Japan was no longer permitted to practice foreign exchange restrictions on current transactions for balance-of-payments considerations. Consequently, the Foreign Exchange Budget System (which had played a vital role as the foundation of import control before 1960, and which became increasingly an imports projection device rather than a tool of trade control after 1960) was abolished as of April, 1964, together with the dissolution of the Cabinet Council which was directly responsible for appropriation of the budget. The Foreign Currencies Fund Allotment System was similarly terminated. Extensive, technical revisions and adjustments were likewise made in the then existing orders and ordinances of MITI, the Ministry of Finance, and the Bank of Japan in order to comply with Article 8.

As of October 1, 1966, the number of "unliberalized" items was 167. Of these, those which Japan was not obliged to liberalize in terms of GATT requirements numbered 43. The difference of 124, which refers to the so-called "remaining restricted import items," consisted of the following commodity categories: 1. eight mining and related products including coal, sulphur, tungsten ores, heavy and light oil; 2. forty-eight industrial products including various manufacturing machines, thermo electric generators, computers, wool fabrics, lace, leather shoes, certain cosmetics, color films; and 3. sixty-eight products of agriculture, fishery, and forestry, including beef, pork, fruit juices, apples, cornstarch, various products of the coastal fishing industry, wines, whisky, and brandy.[6] As of April, 1968, the numbers of "unliberalized items" and of the "remaining restricted import items" were 165 and 122, respectively.

On December 17, 1968, the Cabinet Decision concerning Promotion of Liberalization of Imports announced that the government would: 1. examine all remaining restricted items as to their readiness for liberalization; 2. liberalize a significant number of items within the next three years; 3. help accelerate industrial reorganization in Japan in order to facilitate the liberalization of additional items; 4. make better preparation to cope with sudden, unexpected disruptions that might result from the further liberalization; and 5. continue to strive to persuade other countries to end discriminations against Japanese goods. In order to materialize the above Cabinet Decision, the Joint Ministers' Conference passed a resolution in July, 1969, to reduce the number of restricted import items down to 60 (4-digit BTN) or less by the end of 1971. On October 17, 1969, the Coordinating Council of the said Conference announced the names of 55 items (a little short of the target of the July resolution) to be totally liberalized, along with a list of 12 items for partial liberalization. The Coordinating Council also made a pledge to endeavor to liberalize as many of the remaining restricted items as possible by the end of 1971.

On September 1, 1970, the Japanese government liberalized eight items, and announced its plan to further liberalize ten items by the end of April, 1971, and an additional twenty by the end of September, 1971, so that by the end of that year the extent of Japan's trade liberalizalization would have become comparable to that of Western Germany.

RETROSPECT

From the standpoint of economic logic the liberalization of imports was an inevitable course of action Japan would have to take sooner or later. The maturation of the ideas that liberalization is something desirable and beneficial to Japan was a slow process relative to the developments in the outside world, and this created an impression in the minds of Western observers that Japan was a stubborn protectionist who failed to understand the virtues of free trade and who would remove trade barriers only as a result of pressure from without. Allowing for the per capita income differences between Japan and the Western countries, however, the fact that Japan began her major liberalization of imports in 1960, several years later than West European countries, was hardly a breach of international expectation. It should also be remembered that from 1960 on the speed of Japan's liberalization was roughly comparable to that of many West European countries.

Most of the initially anticipated problems did not materialize. There were isolated, short-run difficulties, to be sure. But no major disruptions of the domestic markets occurred. The balance-of-payments position remained sound. While it is difficult to measure the impact of liberalization on the performance of domestic firms, there is little doubt that the liberalization greatly enhanced the overall efficiency of Japanese firms and improved the competitive environment within the domestic economy. During the period of tight trade control the firms were assured of sizable profits by merely managing to acquire a quota for imports of raw materials. The trade control system tended to cause overinvestments in many sectors of the economy as the quota was often determined on the basis of output capacities of the firms. The system was also bound to discriminate against new entrants. Once trade barriers were removed, laxity, inefficiency, and easy dependence upon the government were no longer permitted. For their very survival and growth the firms were compelled to concentrate more on gains in productivity and incentives. For the overall success of trade liberalization the government should, to a great extent, be credited for its careful timing of liberalizing specific items. The prospects of economic growth were enhanced by the liberalization. At the same time the process of liberalization was sustained without undue internal frictions by the viability and resiliency of the Japanese economy.*

Trade liberalization usually means imports of goods at lower prices than those of domestically produced counterparts. The liberalization is therefore expected to work in the direction of curving down inflation. Japan has been experiencing inflation—particularly that of consumer goods prices since around 1959. The major liberalization began in the middle of 1960. Apparently, the liberalization has had little substantive effect on decreasing the rate of inflation. One does not find many instances where prices of those commodities whose imports were liberalized began to fall sizably following the timing of trade liberalization. One explanation of this is that the government has been cautious about the timing of liberalization in connection with the "readiness" of domestic industries to be affected; namely, the government typically waited sufficiently long so that the competitive strength of domestic industries vis-à-vis imports became strong

---

*One of the most difficult problems has been the import of food. Kiyoshi Kojima writes: "Restriction on food import . . . presents a difficult problem for Japan's trade policy and one which is not easy to solve politically, since abolition would be a hard blow for a large number of small-scale farmers. Personally, as an economist, I would say that Japan cannot catch up with the Western standard of per capita income unless she liberalizes imports of foodstuffs, increasing imports of sugar, dairy products, meat, fodder for domestic animals and fruit, and concentrates agricultural production on efficient land and farmers. This is badly needed but it will take some time. However, previous trade liberalization, with its beneficial effects on our economic rationalization, is stimulating change into right direction." (Kiyoshi Kojima, "Japan's Trade Policy," Economic Record (March, 1965), pp. 73-74.

enough through productivity gains and industrial reorganization.
Consequently, there was no drastic increase in the volume of imports,
nor were there significant price decreases. From the standpoint of
the anti-inflation objective, this policy has been criticized by some
observers in that the government was not willing enough to optimize
consumer welfare through avoidance of inflation by adopting a more
vigorous approach to the liberalization.[7] Other objectives such as
rapid economic growth and capital accumulation received greater
priorities. It may still be held, however, that the alternative to let
prices rise less fast than they would otherwise have deserves some
merit, i.e., without the liberalization, the pace of Japanese inflation
would have been faster.

NOTES

1. MITI, Tsusho Hakusho-Soron [Foreign Trade White Paper-
General Survey] (Tokyo: 1960), pp. 10-12. See also, Subcommittee on
Foreign Economic Policy of the Joint Economic Committee, Congress
of the United States, 87th Congress, 1st Session, Trade Restraints in
the Western Community (Washington, D.C.: U.S. Government Printing
Office, 1961), pp. 17-18, which reports on developments in Japan in
1960.

2. Warren Hunsberger, Japan and the United States in World
Trade (New York: Harper and Row, 1964), p. 136.

3. Correspondents of the Economist, Consider Japan (London:
Gerald Duckworth, 1963), p. 95.

4. MITI, Tsusho Hakusho-Kaku Ron [Foreign Trade White Paper-
Detailed Survey] (Tokyo: 1963), p. 611.

5. MITI, Tsusho Hakusho-Soron [Foreign Trade White Paper-
General Survey] 1963, pp. 151-155. See also: Shunji Arima, "Nihon
no Yunyu Kozo no Tembo" [Perspective of the Structure of Japanese
Imports], Keizai Hyoron (March, 1963), pp. 29-34; and Toshio Shishido,
Nihon Keizai no Seicho Ryoku [Growth Capacity of the Japanese
Economy] (Tokyo: Diamond Sha, 1965), pp. 139-140.

6. Japan Foreign Trade Research Association, ed., Sengo Nihon
no Boeki Niju-nen Shi [The Twenty-Year History of Japan's Postwar
Foreign Trade] (Tokyo: Tsusho Sangyo Chosa Kai, 1967), pp. 470-471.

7. E.g., see Saburo Kawanishi, "Yunyu no Katsuyo to Bukka no
Antei" [Uses of Imports and Price Stability], Boeki to Kanzei (May,
1968), pp. 38-39.

4

**JAPANESE VIEWS
ON
FREE TRADE**

THE WEB SOCIETY

Japan is a nation of some 100 million people, and among them there are bound to be more than one view on any given subject. It is therefore distorting rather than revealing to speak of the Japanese view on free trade. During the course of trade liberalization much discussion has flourished in Japan concerning the virtues of free trade versus protection, and the discussion has been characterized not by the unanimity of opinions but rather by the diversity of views among groups and subgroups of discussants. Even within what appears to be a tightly knit bureaucracy of the Japanese government, positions of the various administrative branches with respect to trade liberalization have by no means been uniform and homogeneous. The Ministry of Foreign Affairs and the Ministry of Finance have maintained a relatively more progressive and forward-looking posture toward liberalization, whereas the attitude of the Ministry of International Trade and Industry and the Ministry of Agriculture and Forestry has been more conservative and in favor of a cautious and gradual approach to the removal of import restrictions. Variations on the theme of trade liberalization have been heard among businesses, big and small. To those industries which could effectively compete in the world market the thankless obligation to comply with a thousand and one rules and regulations of trade control constituted enough nuisance to advocate early liberalization. On the other hand, those stagnant, low-productivity industries, which could survive only under the umbrella of protection understandably favored a prolongation of import restrictions. Similarly, opinions of Japanese economists have varied. On the subject of trade liberalization Japan has had her share of Milton Friedmans as well as those who would put more emphasis on the "reality" and "facts" of the Japanese economy.

The purpose of this chapter is not to indulge in the impossible task of surveying all the divergent views expressed by different groups of people in Japan concerning trade liberalization but rather to focus on those aspects of the discussions which seem to differentiate the Japanese economic mentality from that of the Western countries.

As regards the socio-economic character of the Japanese, Warren Hunsberger wrote:

> Crowded into narrow islands, the Japanese people have through the centuries evolved customs that rely on strict observance of detailed rules to make human contacts peaceable and effective. Duty and discipline are central features of life in a society so intricately interwoven as to be called 'the web society.' In Japanese eyes self-expression can easily tear the fabric, and social pressure is extreme for maintenance and reinforcement of the web. The harsh environment reduces the scope for individual action and enhances reliance on the group. And it is in groups, rather than individual activity that the Japanese people have been most outstanding. No other Asian people have been able to cooperate so effectively in large private firms or government, civil or military organizations. Japanese objection to what is called 'excessive' and 'destructive' competition seems to reflect discomfort at 'undisciplined' conduct as well as a feeling that the nation's interests are less well served by impersonal market forces than by conscious decisions on the part of leaders, accepted and followed by others.[1]

Is part of the Japanese objection to OFI due to a fear of the unpredictable?

If an Adam Smith would feel ill at ease in Japan, Japanese officialdom has never reacted in comfort to the philosophy of laissez-faire and free competition which has flourished in the Anglo-Saxon world. Even the officialdom's doctrine allows for all the virtues of free competition—from survival of the efficient, optimization of resource allocation, to encouragement of entrepreneurial creativity—to be realized under ideal circumstances. The argument goes that in Japan competition prevails as a "process" but the results of competition are far different from those assumed by the theoretical model. In Japan competition is visibly "excessive" and allegedly causes tremendous waste in resources and harmful instability of the market. On the question of facts versus theory of competition Yoshihiko Ryokaku, a MITI official, wrote:

Diff. anti-Smithian view of competition.

The benefit of perfect competition is essentially an abstract
notion. More realistically we should seek practical ways to
gain from imperfect competition. Namely, in the actual
world benefits of competition are derived from various
forms of oligopolistic or imperfect competition. Oligopolistic competition is a middle road that tries to avoid adverse consequences of both monopoly and excessive competition, and it is the best market structure for activities
of the firms.[2]

According to Yoshihiko Ryokaku, to expect the present-day national economy to operate on the basis of the laissez-faire doctrine
of the nineteenth century is no less unrealistic than to hope to revive
the massive network of direct economic control of the war period.
Instead, he advocates for Japan "the economic system of harmony
and cooperation" which preserves the framework of orderly freedom
rather than chaotic laissez-faire, promotes stable market activities
without resorting to direct controls, and pursues goals commonly
upheld by private business and the government without invoking to-
talitarian schemes. How can this system be brought into existence?
He holds that it will be established on the foundation of contracts between private business and the government as equal partners. It is
a third alternative to the struggle and waste under excessive liberalism
and the harmful coercion under a controlled economy. The two major
characteristics of the system are: first, it provides a common ground
where the government representing public interest and private business motivated by private interest come together to discuss their
common problems, to exchange information and to examine strategies
for the future; and second, the system will lay out mutually agreed
rules of conduct which will condition activities of private firms and
which will guide the government in formulating and implementing its
policies aimed at maximization of welfare from the standpoint of the
entire national economy.[3]

Yoshihiko Ryokaku is not alone in expressing a fundamental
skepticism about the Western conception of free competition. The
following summary of a discussion by Naohiro Amaya, another MITI
spokesman, illustrates the sort of vision that is prevalent among
many officials of the Japanese government.

He holds that it is a uniquely American view to interpret private
monopoly per se to be evil. There is, however, no such social consciousness on the part of the majority of Japanese. Capitalism means

free competition, and competition is presumed to maximize economic
welfare. But free competition can lead to two extreme ends, private
monopoly, and excessive competition, both of which can be equally
harmful. In the United States monopoly historically yielded numerous,
undesirable results; hence, there arose a social consciousness that
monopoly is bad a priori. At the same time, excessive competition
with all its negative effects on the economy has never been a "problem"
in the U.S. context. The thesis that monopoly is necessarily evil is
irrelevant to the Japanese context. Japan is in need of large growth
firms capable of effectively competing with Western corporations,
and this "need" is absent in the United States.

Naohiro Amaya concedes that monopoly may become harmful.
Against this danger, however, the government can legislate new laws
to oversee monopolistic firms from the standpoint of safeguarding
and promoting the public welfare. What is evident in Japan is not the
evil of monopoly but the harm of excessive competition causing waste
in the utilization of resources, disruption in the wage structure, over-
production and overinvestment, cutthroat competition, and scrambles
for large market shares irrespective of the means employed. He
opines that the anti-monopoly philosophy which treats free competition
as a sacred cow is not pertinent to the Japanese context. He suggests
that Japan reject the imported idea and instead cultivate her own.
Japan should develop a new economic constitution that clarifies: 1.
what the modern market is; 2. the means by which obstacles in the
way of realizing that modern market in Japan can be removed; and
3. rules which will ban anti-social behavior of the firms.

According to him, the excessive competition observed in Japan
is essentially a social struggle of the firms that reflects the lingering
irrationality of the Japanese social structure. Conduct of the firms is
conditioned not by market rules but by Machiavellian principles of
behavior. Each firm attempts to win not as a Schumpeterian inno-
vator but as a merchant of Venice. Naohiro Amaya concludes that
"competition in Japan rests upon 60 percent reason, 20 percent mad-
ness and 20 percent faith that in crisis the government will step in
to help."[4]

ECONOMIC NATIONALISM

On the social psychology of Japanese intellectuals Tsuneo Iida
wrote: "Within the country's intellectual tradition lies a belief that
the Japanese economy is always beset by crises, together with a
masochistic tendency to find delight in the approach of anything

resembling a crisis."[5] This may be a rhetorical excess, but there
is an observable inclination among many Japanese to mix their discussion of economic issues with nationalsitic sentiments and an air
of desperation. Japan is a rather small country in terms of geographic space (about 1/21 of that of the United States) which her four
main islands occupy, but she is not a small nation in terms of her
gross national product or population (about 1/2 of that of the United
States). There is a deep-rooted notion in Japan that Japan is critically
dependent upon foreign trade despite the fact that on the basis of the
ratio of imports to national income she is no more trade-dependent
than comparable Western countries such as Great Britain and Western
Germany. In the words of Warren Hunsberger:

> Although as dependent as any nation in the world on access
> to foreign markets and on the chance to compete freely,
> Japan shows marked reluctance to permit foreigners to
> compete in its own market. There is only limited domes-
> tic pressure to make the country a living example of the
> kind of commercial and financial policies that would most
> benefit Japan if followed by other nations. In this regard,
> Japanese psychology is that of a small country—pressing
> other countries for favorable treatment without demon-
> strating a sense of responsibility for the general charac-
> ter of international economic relations or the rules and
> practices involved. Japan conforms to the international
> rules that prevail but does very little to strengthen or
> improve them, even when that would benefit Japan di-
> rectly. The multilateral trade that contributes so much
> to Japan's unprecedented prosperity is accepted for what
> Japanese traders can gain. But much Japanese thinking
> has not yet caught up with the facts of Japan's trade
> position today, let alone pictured an improved world
> trading pattern that would benefit Japan.[6]

This Westerner's observation is shared by Hisao Kanamori
who remarked (in 1966):

> When we think of Japan's economic problems in the context
> of world economy, it seems that too many people in Japan
> hold a paranoic notion about the effects of trade laberali-
> zation. The notion that it would do Japan more harm than
> good was strong four or five years ago, and it still re-
> mains strong. Given the vigorous growth rates of Japa-
> nese exports as well as GNP, however, it is other coun-
> tries rather than Japan that have been threatened, i.e.,

the impact of global trade liberalization has been more of
a threat to other countries than to other countries than to
Japan.[7]

The desire for freer trade has been strong in the postwar world.
Despite setbacks there has been a steady trend toward realizing that
desire. The Japanese attitude has been in opposition to this global
movement. Depressed industries such as coal and agriculture and
those industries making excess profits under the system of import
control have either exerted strong pressure against trade liberalization or shown general disinterest in gains from free trade. There
has been little positive movement to promote trade liberalization from
within the country. Japan was even unaware of the incompatibility of
her attitude with the global trend until strong complaints were registered by the United States and other Western nations on the occasion
of the GATT meeting held in Tokyo in October, 1954.

To destroy the order built under the system of import control
involves both gains and losses to different interest groups. In the
past history of Western nations the realization of free trade was often
preceded by long, heated controversies between free traders and
protectionists. It is curious that in the case of Japan there was no
systematic advancement of the free trade philosophy until and unless
she was reminded by foreign governments of its importance. Even
after the policy to move ahead with the liberalization was adopted,
there persisted in the country a popular view that Japan was being
forced to swallow by foreign pressure something which was really
disadvantageous to the country. As Hisao Kanamori suggests: "The
power of protectionism in Japan may be said to be a result not only
of economic factors but also of the underdevelopment of social consciousness concerning the virtues of free competition in general."[8]

While many Western observers have expressed their puzzle-
ment over Japan's reluctance to liberalize her trade, the Japanese
counterparts have maintained that there is much hypocricy and self-
righteousness on the part of the United States and other Western
countries. There is a strong feeling among Japanese observers that
the professed gains from free trade are realizable only if two trading
partners are of equal strength and that, given Japan's economic underdevelopment relative to the West, the true motives of Western nations
as they insist upon Japan's swifter move toward a full and complete
liberalization as something beneficial to Japan are not so pure and
innocent as they might appear on the surface. The point is illustrated
by Tomomitsu Ohba as he wrote:

Historically, free trade has been advocated by those countries with a strong competitive power in the world economy. Great Britain in the 19th century and the United States after World War II are cases in point. It was from the position of strength that the United States supported the IMF and GATT in search of freer trade.[9]

Similarly, Sakae Akamatsu commented:

The United States seeks and strives for removal of quantitative restrictions on imports and exchange controls all around and for restoration of free convertibility of currencies. The pressure coming in the same direction from IMF and GATT may be viewed as a response to the U.S. demand. The United States has now assumed the industrial leadership position in the world economy. As was the case of Great Britain in the 19th century, this position makes the doctrine of free trade particularly advantageous to the U.S.[10]

Sometimes the Japanese argument becomes fused with a flare of emotionalism. The following editorial appeared in a semi-official journal concerned with Japan's trade policy.

The compulsory self-restraining rule . . . this is the form of export policy adopted by Japan. It may sound like a method of trade control which Japan has autonomously developed. The truth of the matter is that it is the method of export control which the United States has imposed upon us. 'Autonomous regulation of exports' may sound peculiar to foreign ears. The fact is, it is a substitute for import control on the part of the United States, the importing country. The importing country naturally prefers voluntary export restraint by an exporting country to the imposition of import control because the latter is controversial, full of difficulties and appears deplorable to the outside world. While preaching the virtue of free trade to the rest of the world, the U.S. is actually restricting trade with Japan through the voluntary export restraint rule which now involves some 50 items. Many other items are threatened to be subjected to the same rule. The U.S. indicates to us that, unless we 'voluntarily' restrict our exports, the U.S. will raise tariff rates and invoke import quotas against Japanese goods. Much the same is true with European countries. Trade among the

advanced countries in Western Europe has been liberalized; but quantitative control against Japanese products is
still practiced. Our request for removal of their quantitative control is often met by a counter request that Japan
take up the voluntary export restraint rule. Great Britain
has been urging Japan to exercise export restraint on 60
items. As some argue, it is true that the export restraint
is less bad an approach than direct import control, and is
relatively less disadvantageous even to Japan. The fact
remains, however, that it is naked discriminatory control
of foreign trade all the same.[11]

FREE TRADE AND PROTECTION

Completely free trade has never existed in the past, and no one
expects that literally free trade will ever prevail in the future. Each
nation state is interested in promoting growth of its economy and
maximizing its economic welfare through the most effective means
available. Foreign trade is not an end itself but a means of achieving
those national goals. When there emerge inconsistencies between
means and ends, it is unavoidable that some restrictions be placed
on the means.

There are two basic approaches to economic growth. One is
through a greater international specialization, namely, through expansion of foreign trade; the other is diversification of domestic production or furthering of internal industrialization. As suggested by
the Ricardian doctrine of comparative costs, a nation can raise productivity and efficiency in the use of its resources by concentrating
on production of those goods in which the nation's comparative cost
advantage lies. In the short run this will optimize the allocation of
resources with respect to the initially existing set of factor endowments. Over the long run, however, this approach may result in un-
derutilization or underdevelopment of resources that are potentially
available for other alternative industries. Furthermore, the fact that
a certain industry has comparative advantage implies that resources
for that industry are available in abundance at the starting point; but
as the industry expands along with trade, abundance disappears and
the law of diminishing returns may begin to set in. To the extent
that this happens, it is rational for the nation to enhance diversification of internal production. Product diversification is a way of
avoiding the diminishing returns as well as of widening the potential
horizon of resource utilization. It induces changes in the initially
given factor endowments themselves.

International specialization and product diversification are not necessarily incompatible with each other, and the two should not be viewed as mutually exclusive alternatives. To develop a new industry implies alteration of the hitherto existing pattern of international specialization. That new industry is bound to be confronted with competition and pressure from other (more advanced) countries. This raises the issue of the infant-industry argument for protection. In other circumstances the less developed countries may be catching up, and the nation being caught up with must cope with the problem of protecting those industries which used to be internationally competitive but are now becoming stagnant and depressed.

The contents of international trade keep shifting along with development and growth of different countries. For a national economy to survive and keep growing there is a constant need to change the structure of domestic industries and to adapt the mode of internal production to the shifting patterns of world import demand.

Capital accumulation is necessary for greater international specialization because, in order to expand exports, the country must employ more mechanized methods of producing export goods. At the same time, product diversification also calls forth capital accumulation inasmuch as it typically implies development of new, advanced industries wherein production is more capital-intensive than that in the already existing industries.

Most countries follow steps of economic development from agriculture to light industry, then to heavy industry and so on. What was once a leading industry must be replaced with another in the context of changing world trade. Over the long run a nation's economic growth and survival require a skillful blending of the principles of international specialization and partial protectionism to its own advantages.

INDUSTRIAL POLICY

In the original writings of Ricardo a nation's comparative advantages are largely determined by nature. This premise is tenable if we speak of a group of heavily agricultural countries, since climate, soil conditions, and the like play an important role in differentiating relative costs of producing different commodities. In the modern world characterized by the heavy weight of the secondary (manufacturing) industry, the comparative advantages associated with a given national economy are typically not nature-induced but rather man-

made. What is the most effective way of shifting the nation's comparative-cost position through time and of carrying out with minimum
friction the transition from one stage of development to another from
the standpoint of sustaining economic growth and survival in the world
economy? Japanese officialdom's answer to this question consists
of emphatic disbelief in the "invisible hand" and a strong preference
for the "visible hand" of the state. That the state has played important roles in the course of Japanese economic development since the
Meiji period is well known.[12] During the postwar period the pattern
of Japan's industrial growth has not insignificantly been molded by
government guidance through multitudes of policy measures, rules,
and regulations that are often collectively referred to as "industrial
policy" (sangyo seisaku) of which foreign trade policy has been an
integral part.

    What is "industrial policy"? A precise definition is not avail-
able. It is an indigenous Japanese term not to be found in the lexicon
of Western economic terminology. A reading through the literature
suggests a definition, however: It refers to a complex of those policies
concerning protection of domestic industries, development of strategic
industries, and adjustment of the economic structure in response to
or in anticipation of internal and external changes which are formulated and pursued by MITI in the cause of the national interest, as the
term "national interest" is understood by MITI officials.

    Industrial policy may be outlined in the following manner.[13]

                        Defensive Measures

Supply of Basic Commodities

    A stable supply of basic products and services is indispensable
to the national economy. In order for Japan to function effectively as
a nation-state such basic industries as electricity, utilities, steel,
and petroleum should be well developed internally. However, these
basic industries require large-scale plants and equipment. The increase in supply, therefore, tends to show discontinuities whereas
demand may rise smoothly. If left entirely to the rules of free competition, the market will chronically suffer from gaps between supply
and demand. Every excess capacity tends to cause an excessive
drop in price since the price elasticity of demand for outputs of these
basic industries is typically low. At the same time, some excess
capacity guards against inflation. The government should cultivate
the subtle art of "adjusting" production and investment so as to

minimize market disruptions and stabilize prices. Administrative guidance and other methods are to be employed to this end.

Protection of Infant Industries

It is deemed desirable for Japan to develop the following industries: synthetic textiles, petrochemicals, automobiles, airplanes, and electronics. These industries are therefore to be protected by the tariff wall, import controls, and internal measures such as tax preferences, special depreciation allowances, and credit from public investment funds. Active induction of the latest Western technology into these industries is to be encouraged.

Gradual Liberalization of Trade and Capital Transactions

The liberalization will proceed in gradual steps. We must distinguish between the ideal and the reality of the world economy today. Despite the propagated virtues of a free system we still live in a nationalistic world where each government does what it believes to be best for the country. Labor is not allowed to move freely between countries. The movement of technology is not entirely free. Tariff rates are set in accordance with each government's preferences. Consequently, we cannot advocate and practice an unconditionally free system with respect to foreign trade and capital transactions, irrespective of Japan's preparedness. A sudden entry of Western firms into Japanese markets may gravely disrupt the existing internal order.

Offensive Measures

Development of Strategic Industries

Development of strategic industries is vital in promoting economic growth and achieving export expansion. Steel and automobiles are examples of today's industries in Japan that require protection for their further growth.

Industrial Reorganization

Industrial reorganization is necessary in order to improve Japan's competitive position in the world economy. At present too many firms crowd important industries such as steel, automobiles, machinery, electronic computers, petrochemicals, oil refining and synthetic textiles. They should be merged to form fewer but larger and more efficient firms capable of competing with world enterprises.

These guidelines should not convey the impression that Japan's postwar industrial policy since the very beginning has followed an always consistent path set by well-defined policy directives. While much discussion has flourished concerning industrial policy, the nature of policy itself has tended to be ad hoc rather than rational and coherent. The relationship between industrial policy, on the one hand, and more precisely defined domains of economic policy such as monetary and fiscal policies, on the other, has never been clear. Similarly, the concept of "national interest" that underlies the theory of industrial policy has always remained vague.

To what extent the record of Japan's postwar economic growth is attributable to the effective implementation of industrial policy as against the hard work and diligence of Japanese workers and management is debatable. However, the writings of MITI officials often reveal an air of self-confidence and a nationalistic sentiment mixed with a flavor of paternalism. The following quotation illustrates the point. Shigeru Sahashi, former Vice Minister of MITI, wrote:

> The older generation would remember that there was nothing left in Japan right after the war—no foods, no clothes, no houses. Who could then imagine the present-day picture of Japan? I do not think it is too presumptuous of me to say that the industrial policy of MITI is largely responsible for bringing Japanese economy up to the present stage. Speaking of recent parent-child relationships, it has become fashionable for a grown-up child to forget the pains and efforts of his parents and think that he grew up all by himself. A wise parent would not complain about such an attitude because the fact that his child has grown into adulthood itself signifies that the parents' wish has been fulfilled. This is analogous to the relationship between MITI and industry. We have done our best and should not brag about it. Our industrial policy has not been entirely satisfactory and flawless. We merely comfort ourselves by the thought that we have not made any major errors. The present economic condition in Japan is the result of our policy.[14]

TRADE POLICY

Japanese officialdom is not necessarily against free trade. It duly acknowledges gains to the nation from a greater international specialization. Officialdom simply takes a "realistic" and "practical" position and points out that, as free trade is practiced in the real world rather than in a theoretical, abstract universe, there are merits as well as demerits associated with it, and the two must be carefully examined and equated before a particular policy is formulated. The following are those "problems" of free trade which many official spokesmen have mentioned as factors a responsible government cannot simply ignore, and which constitute justifications of the particular trade liberalization policy that has been pursued by the Japanese government.[15]

Unrealism of the Comparative Cost Doctrine

There are many presuppositions that ought to be fulfilled before free trade bears fruit for all trading parties. Perfect competition is supposed to prevail all around. Ideally, labor, capital, and technology are expected to move freely between nations. Populations and economic powers are assumed to be evenly distributed. In actuality, few of these presuppositions are met. While all nations of the world aspire to industrialize, there exist tremendous gaps in terms of overall productivity, standards of living, and the stage of capital accumulation between the advanced and underdeveloped countries. Free trade forces the labor-abundant, poor countries to specialize in labor-intensive goods; thus their relative economic backwardness tends to be perpetuated. To mention Great Britain as an example of those countries which managed to industrialize in the context of free trade as an argument in favor of universal free trade in the present-day world is an exercise in absurdity. From the standpoint of the less-developed countries aspiring to accelerate internal industrialization, some protection is to be taken for granted.

Excessive Dependence Upon Another Country

Free trade may lead a country to develop a critically high degree of dependence upon a foreign nation with respect to the supply of vital goods and resources (e.g., food and strategic industrial raw materials). This economic dependence may also lead to a political dependence, and this possibility cannot simply be ignored in the world of power politics.

Balance of Payments

The commonly heard argument in support of general and complete trade liberalization tacitly ignores the associated balance-of-payments difficulties or discounts the potential gravity of the problem. Trade liberalization tends to expand imports, but trade liberalization as such does not immediately and directly increase exports inasmuch as the level of exports is largely determined by extraneous events over which the exporting country has little, immediate control. Some argue that the emerging external deficit may be settled through adjusting the rate of exchange. The fact remains, however, that in the postwar world we operate under the pegged-rates system, and changes in the exchange rate involve complications and potentially damaging, international repercussions. If external imbalance is adjusted through depreciation of the national currency, this implies the deterioration of terms of trade as well as inflation of the cost of imports both of which are undesirable to the country concerned. Furthermore, if and when a severe, global recession strikes the world economy, the nations practicing free trade may greatly suffer from the synchronization of falling demand as thay are no longer equipped with self-protective devices to cope with the impact of recession coming from without.

Japan's Economic Isolation

Regional economic integration has been one of the most conspicuous developments in the postwar world. The Common Market and the Free Trading Area are cases in point. Typically, regional economic integration is a collective effort to build a stable and expanding market which provides greater opportunities for productivity gains and economic growth on the part of member countries than are possible if each nation acted independently of the others. The member countries first try to build their mutual economic strength, and then, on the basis of that strength, move to compete in the rest of the world economy. In the case of the United States, its domestic market alone constitutes an enormous market; in addition, the United States and Canada form a highly integrated, huge regional market.

In contrast, Japan has belonged to none of the postwar trading blocs. Japan is geographically and economically separated from Western Europe. She is hardly "integrated" with the North American market. The United States and other Western countries, while propagating the virtues of free trade and practicing a liberal trade policy internally, have readily applied discriminatory import control against Japanese goods. Southeast Asia and Japan have failed to find sufficient common grounds to achieve a regional integration.

From the standpoint of Japan, the domestic market has been the only stable and reliable market, and all other external markets have comprised elements of uncertainty in one way or another. Given this position of basic vulnerability, it is unwise for Japan to liberalize her trade too hastily without taking sufficient, precautionary steps.

Internal Problems

There are numerous, internal problems that reflect Japan's "semi-developed" status. Many firms even in the advanced sectors of the Japanese economy are still not capable, without protection, of effectively competing with Western firms in the world market. Many Japanese firms are too small to enjoy the economies of scale. Their financial position is often precarious, as indicated by the low ratio of owned capital. Research and development expenditures are less than adequate, and in many areas Japanese technology lags considerably behind the West.

At the same time the Japanese economy still comprises many backward sectors from agriculture to small businesses where a high proportion of the labor force continues to be employed. With respect to the increasing number of labor-intensive goods, many small businesses are no longer able to compete with products of underdeveloped countries where labor is cheaper than in Japan.

The only long-run solution of these internal problems of Japan is to sustain her rapid economic growth be developing new industries and discarding the old, and by transfering resources from the low-productivity to high-productivity sectors. These adjustive processes are necessarily time-consuming and require much care and planning. Trade liberalization, therefore, must proceed gradually and with caution in order to avoid internal frictions such as the sudden spread of unemployment of a politically intolerable magnitude.

NOTES

1. Warren Hunsberger, Japan and the United States in World Trade (New York: Harper and Row, 1964), p. 377.

2. Yoshihiko Ryokaku, "Sangyo Kyocho Taisei Ron" [Theory of Industrial Cooperation], Tsusho Sangyo Kenkyu, No. 100 (1962), pp. 39-40.

3. Ibid., pp. 44-45.

70   IMPORTS AND FOREIGN CAPITAL IN JAPAN

4. Naohiro Amaya, "Jidai wa Wareware ni Nani o Motomete Iruka" [What Does the Present Age Expect of Us?], Anarisuto (April, 1967), pp. 56-96. The quotation is from p. 64. See also Naohiro Amaya, "Sangyo Seisaku no Hansei to Tenkai no Tameni" [Industrial Policy: Reflections and Thoughts for its Future Expansion], Tsusan Journal, Vol. 2, No. 5 (1969), pp. 26-27.

5. Tsuneo Iida, "Keizai Seisaku ni okeru Minshushugi no Genkai" [Limits of Democracy in Formulation of Economic Policy], Chuo Koron (March, 1968), p. 93.

6. Warren Hunsberger, op. cit., p. 378.

7. Hisao Kanamori's remark in Tadao Uchida, ed., Nihon Keizai o Kangaeru [Thinking of the Japanese Economy] (Tokyo: Japan Productivity Center, 1966), p. 204.

8. Hisao Kanamori, Nihon no Boeki [Japanese Foreign Trade] (Tokyo: Shisei Do, 1961), p. 248.

9. Tomomitsu Ohba, "Hogo Boeki Shugi to Jiyuka" [Trade Protectionism and Liberalization], Boeki to Kanzei (January, 1969), p. 61.

10. Sakae Akamatsu, "Boeki Jiyuka no Genkai" [Limits of Trade Liberalization], Boeki to Kanzei (June, 1956), p. 14.

11. Editorial in Tsusho Seisaku (July, 1968), p. 3. Tsusho Seisaku [Foreign Trade Policy] is published by the trade-policy study group of MITI officials.

12. See William W. Lockwood, ed., The State and Economic Enterprise in Japan (Princeton, N.J.: Princeton University Press, 1965).

13. A systematic treatise on the subject by a MITI official is: Yoshihiko Ryokaku, Sangyo Seisaku no Riron [The Theory of Industrial Policy] (Tokyo: Nihon Keizai Shimbun Sha, 1966).

14. Shigeru Sahashi, "Kanmin Kyocho ni Yoru Tekisetsu na Seisaku Unei o Kitai" [Expectations for Appropriate Execution of the Policy of Government-Business Cooperation], Toyo Keizai (December 11, 1968), p. 37.

15. For the government views on free trade and trade liberalization, see: the special issue on "Progress of Liberalization and the

Japanese Economy," Tsusho Sangyo Kenkyu, No. 109 (1962); the special
issue on "Trade Liberalization and Industrial Policy," Tsusho Sangyo
Kenkyu, No. 87 (1960); MITI, Tsusho Hakusho [Foreign Trade White
Paper] 1960, pp. 97-123; Isamu Miyazaki and Takekuni Ebihara, "Boeki
Kawase no Jiyu-ka to Keizai Seicho" [Trade and Exchange Liberali-
zation and Economic Growth], Keizai Hyoron (March, 1960); and Shunji
Arima, "Boeki Jiyuka no Yukue" [Future of Trade Liberalization],
Sekai Keizai Hyoron (October, 1959), pp. 15-20.

5

**THE FRAMEWORK
OF
FOREIGN CAPITAL
CONTROL**

PREWAR PERIOD

The first major inflow of foreign capital into Japan during the prewar period occurred in 1870 when the Meiji government sold a 9 percent bond in London to raise capital for financing construction of a railroad between Tokyo and Yokohama. The same government floated, also in London, a 6 percent bond to finance redemption of the stipend certificates (Roku-ken) in 1873. The inflow of foreign capital became more conspicuous after 1879, the year in which Japan adopted the gold standard, and particularly during the periods from the Russo-Japanese War to World War I, and from around 1920 to 1935. The first of these periods (1895-1914) was the time when Japan was in tremendous need of capital to pay the direct and indirect costs of the Russo-Japanese War as well as to finance development of the domestic heavy industries that were then in the embryonic stage. The large-scale influx of foreign capital during the second period was induced by the strong demand for capital in the electric power, chemical, and other modern basic industries that were then rapidly expanding and by the emergency need for reconstruction after the Great Earth-quake of 1923 that caused extensive damage in Tokyo and other parts of the Kanto district.

A characteristic of the inflow of foreign capital into Japan during the prewar period is that there was a heavy reliance upon floatation of bonds in the overseas money markets—especially of national bonds issued by the Japanese government. Prior to the Taisho period (1912-1925) the weight of national bonds the Japanese government sold overseas in Japan's total external borrowings was approximately 80 percent. During the decade from 1926 to 1935 the

weight remained as high as about 60 percent. In short, the Japanese
government was the major borrower of foreign capital before World
War II.

Prior to 1897 there had been little direct private investment
by foreign enterprises in Japan. However, the volume of foreign
private investments in Japan began to increase steadily after the
reform of the Japanese commercial code in 1899. Foreign capital
was invested in Nippon Electric in 1899 and in Osaka Gas in 1902.
Many of the newly emerging industries such as oil refining and electric
appliances absorbed varying amounts of foreign capital and technology.
Prior to 1911 seven joint ventures had been formed in Japan; eleven
and nineteen were established during the Taisho period and the period
1926-1941, respectively.

After the Manchurian Incident of 1931 the view that foreign
investments in Japan should be placed under direct control and supervision of the Japanese government in order to protect and foster the
military and other strategic industries in the nation gained popularity.
A series of laws was legislated in this direction. The Important
Industries Control Law of 1931 authorized the government to supervise
practically all phases of operations of the twenty-four designated
industries—from production and inventory to sales and marketing.
Similarly, the Petroleum Business Law of 1934 and the Automobile
Manufacturing Business Law of 1936 laid the legal bases for government control over private activities of the petroleum and automobile
industries.

In 1937 Japan moved into the period of a semi-war economy.
Machinery, airplanes, ship building, and many other industries were
placed under direct government control, one after another. Japan
quickly became an unattractive market to foreign enterprises. On
legal grounds the entry of new foreign capital into Japan as well as
continuation of business by foreign interests in Japan were made
increasingly difficult and risky. The exodus of foreign investments
began. Symbolic of the trend during the years preceding the outbreak
of the Pacific War, Japan Ford and Japan General Motors retreated
from Japan in 1939.

POSTWAR DEVELOPMENTS

Japan's war economy came to an end in August, 1945, with her
unconditional surrender to the Allied Forces. The cessation of the
Pacific War was followed by several years of chaos and turmoil as

Japan struggled to rehabilitate and recover from the devastations of the war. All aspects of external economic transactions were placed under strict control of SCAP (Supreme Commander for the Allied Powers). In 1947 private trading was partially reopened. In 1949 the single rate of exchange for yen ($1 to 360 yen) was established for the first time since the war. In the same year the Foreign Exchange and Foreign Trade Control Law was promulgated. In 1950 the Foreign Investment Law was enacted. These two laws constituted the fundamental, legal framework of control over foreign trade, exchange, and capital transactions in postwar Japan.

In 1952 the San Francisco Peace Treaty was brought into force, and Japan became a member of the IMF and the World Bank. With respect to liberalization of trade and capital transactions in accord with the postwar, global trend, Japan lagged several years behind West European countries. It was after 1959 that Japan began to take major steps to liberalize her trade. In 1961 the IMF charged during its annual consultation with Japan that her liberalization was unwarrantedly too slow. The IMF brought similar charges against Japan in the following years. In April, 1964, Japan finally began to comply with Article 8 of the IMF Charter. Compliance with Article 8 meant, inter alia, that it was no longer legitimate for Japan to impose restrictions on payments and transfer of funds related to her external, economic transactions. In 1964 Japan also became a member of the Organization for Economic Cooperation and Development (OECD). Japan was now formally obliged to proceed to liberalize her capital transactions in accordance with the provisions of the OECD's Code of Liberalisation of Capital Movements.

The extent of her capital liberalization prior to joining the OECD was modest. The specific measures of import that had already been taken were limited to the following: 1. authorization of Japanese private firms' issuance and sale of foreign currency bonds abroad and ADRs (American Depositary Receipts) in the United States as well as of foreign investors' purchase of national bonds issued by the Japanese government (1961); 2. relaxation of restrictions on foreign investors' collection of principals and capital gains on Japanese stocks that they had initially purchased in a foreign currency (April, 1963); 3. termination of the "yen base" investment system (to be explained later) because of its problematical prohibition of external remittances of earnings to foreign investors (April, 1964); 4. partial relaxation of restrictions on withdrawals from the blocked (nonfree) yen funds (April, 1964); and 5. authorization of external transfer of dividends and other earnings originating from foreign investments in Japan under the "yen base" system (April, 1964).

The OECD's Code of Liberalisation of Capital Movements cites categories of foreign capital transactions under List A and List B. Of these, those items in List A are irreversible once a member country declares its decision to liberalize them. The decision to liberalize items in List B may be reversed subsequently for compelling reasons. As of July, 1964, (the year in which Japan became a member of the OECD) Japan lodged a total of eighteen reservations, equally divided in Lists A and B. This number was much larger than those lodged by the advanced West European countries and was par with Spain and Portugal. The official explanation given by the Japanese government was that Japan's foreign exchange reserve was not yet sufficiently large relative to the size of her total imports, and many (small) firms in Japan were so vulnerable as to be unable to withstand the pressure of capital liberalization because of low productivity and inadequate capital accumulation. Notwithstanding the Memorandum of Understanding Between the OECD and the Government of Japan (July 26, 1963) in which the Japanese government expressed its intent to cooperate with the spirit of the OECD and to liberalize her capital transactions as soon as feasible, the reaction of the West was one of irritation and discontent which led to the growing pressure against Japan to accelerate her capital liberalization in subsequent years.

FOREIGN INVESTMENT LAW

During the postwar period foreign investments in Japan have been regulated by the Foreign Investment Law and the Foreign Exchange and Foreign Trade Control Law (FEFTCL). The former has assumed the status of a particular law relative to the general coverage of the latter. The intent of the Foreign Investment Law has been to regulate the inflow of foreign capital from the standpoint of its desirability for the Japanese economy and to provide legal protection for those foreign investments which have been approved by the government as well as guarantee external remittances related with those approved investments.[1]

During the early postwar years FEFTCL was designed to regulate external economic transactions in general in light of the then prevailing acute shortage of foreign exchange. As a supplement to FEFTCL the Foreign Investment Law was promulgated in 1950 in order to fulfill the specific need of encouraging a more active inflow of high-grade foreign capital that was in critical demand for reconstruction of the national economy. At first the general vulnerability of the Japanese economy and the precarious foreign exchange reserve position of the country led the government to adopt and apply severe

standards in selecting foreign investments for approval with emphasis
on. "positive" criteria as stipulated in Article 8 of the Law; in later
years, as the Japanese economy continued to grow at accelerated
rates and the increasing number of foreign enterprises became interested in the Japanese market, the government has been gradually relaxing
its validation standards.

Both the Foreign Investment Law and FEFTCL have their own
jurisdictions. If and where conflicts, inconsistencies, and the need
for interpretations exist regarding their jurisdictions, the adjustments
are made in accordance with the provisions of those two laws as well
as by a series of special Cabinet Orders. Theoretically, all foreign
investments of significance in Japan are to be regulated by either the
Foreign Investment Law or FEFTCL. The design of the legal system
is such that the Foreign Investment Law is applied first, and those
foreign investments to which the said Law may not apply come under
FEFTCL. In practice there has been a good deal of confusion on the
part of the Japanese government as well as foreign investors.

The stated objective of the Foreign Investment Law is "to create
a sound basis for foreign investments in Japan by limiting the induction
of foreign capital to that which will contribute to the self-support and
sound development of the Japanese economy as well as to the improvement of the international balance of payments, by securing remittances
arising from foreign investments and by providing for adequate protection of such investments." (Article 1)

In order to achieve this objective the Law specifies various
categories of foreign investments to which the Law applies, prohibits
those foreign investments which are not validated under the Law, and
defines standards and procedures of approving the foreign investments.
The jurisdiction of the Law covers the following categories of foreign
investments: 1. stocks; 2. beneficiary certificates; 3. corporate
bonds; 4. loans; and 5. technical assistance. However, each of
these categories must meet certain specified conditions before it
becomes applicable, and not all foreign investments are subject to
the Law.

Validation of foreign investments by the competent Minister
under the Law implies permission of external transfer of returns on
those investments, principals withdrawn, compensations for technical
assistance, and the like. But such permission is by no means automatic. For instance, as of 1967, external transfer was approved if it
was of the following kinds: 1. stock dividends and receipts from sales
of assets provided that two years had passed since the acquisition of

such assets and that the receipts from sales of such assets were to
be remitted over five years; 2. profit shares and refunds on beneficiary
certificates provided that such refunds were to be made over five
years; 3. compensations for technical assistance; and 4. interest
on and redemptions of corporate bonds and loans.

When assets legally owned by foreign investors or assets of
juridical persons that are controlled by foreign investors are purchased
or expropriated by the Japanese governments, national or local, the
Foreign Investment Law guarantees approval of remittance of compensations for such transactions.

Those foreign investments which are not subject to the Foreign
Investment Law are regulated either by FEFTCL or by one of the
Japanese laws. Corporate bonds as defined by the Foreign Investment
Law do not include foreign currency bonds, namely, those bonds which
are issued and sold abroad. Consequently, foreign currency bonds
are regulated under FEFTCL. Similarly, national bonds, local-government bonds, and bonds issued by public corporations are subject to
FEFTCL. Financial transactions related with operations of the
branch offices and branch factories of foreign corporations normally
require validation under FEFTCL. The following transactions are
also subject to approval under FEFTCL: corporate bonds which
mature in less than one year; those loans which are repayable in
less than one year and which are for the settlement of international
commercial transactions; compensations for technical assistance
that are payable in less than one year; loans for which foreign investors demand the guarantee of Japanese banks; service charges and
the like in connection with foreign investments through ADRs (American
Depositary Receipts) and EDRs (European Depositary Receipts).

The Foreign Investment Law spells out two sets of validation
standards, positive and negative, both of which are expected to be
satisfied before contemplated foreign investments are approved
under the Law. The positive criteria for those foreign investments
which may be approved are that they will: 1. contribute to improvement
of the balance of payments; 2. contribute to development of important
industries or public works; and 3. be necessary for continuation,
renewal, and/or associated changes of technical contracts for the
important industries and public works. The negative criteria for
those foreign investments which may not be approved under the Law
are as follows: 1. contracts are unfair and illegal; 2. contracts
involve fraud, coercion, or undue pressure; 3. those foreign investments which will have an adverse effects on the recovery of the
Japanese economy; and 4. the acquired foreign currencies lack
sufficient convertibility.

The severity of these criteria reflects the precariousness of the Japanese economy at the time the Law was promulgated. The Law itself does not regard them as permanent and rigidly fixed; instead, the Law states that these criteria will gradually be relaxed as the need for stiff control diminishes. In practice predominant attention was given to the positive criteria in the years immediately following the promulgation of the Law, whereas in the later years emphasis was shifted to the negative criteria.

FEFTCL does not mention the positive criteria. However, it lists the following as the negative criteria: 1. The balance of payments will be adversely affected; 2. recovery of the national economy will be hampered; 3. capital movements in question are believed to be for the purpose of evading the existing laws and regulations; and 4. capital movements in question are deemed undesirable in light of the condition of the foreign exchange reserves.

DIRECT INVESTMENT

Direct investments refer to those foreign investments in stocks whose main purpose is to exert influence on the management of the corporations concerned. Stock purchases by foreign investors without intent to participate in or control the management are usually classified as portfolio investments. In the case of direct investments the Cabinet Order concerning Special Provisions of the Foreign Investment Law (Gaishi Ho Tokurei Seirei) designates as competent Ministers the Minister of Finance and the Head of that Ministry whose jurisdiction covers activities of the corporations in question. In the case of portfolio investments the Minister of Finance alone assumes the role of competent Minister.

Whether or not a given foreign investment is "direct" is ultimately determined by the very intent of the foreign investor. His intent may or may not be ascertainable by the objective criteria such as the stock ratio, whether or not the purchase was made through the stock market and the presence or absence of foreign officers in the corporation after the investment took place. Conceptually it is possible to make a clear distinction between direct and portfolio investments, but in practice the distinction is often blurred by diverse situations and is sometimes impossible to make. There has been no internationally agreed definition of direct investments; various international organizations and national governments have employed different criteria and definitions of their own. Varying ratios (commonly ranging between 10 to 30 percent) of foreign-owned shares have been used. The Japanese government has used ratios not only for total

shares owned by foreign investors at large but also ownership ratios
for single foreign investors. These, however, are hardly foolproof
methods of distinguishing direct investments from portfolio investments
inasmuch as there are cases whereby higher ratios do not necessarily
mean managerial control and lower ratios do not preclude the possibility of effective participation in the management of the firms.

The purchase of stocks of Japanese corporations by foreign
investors is subject to approval under the Foreign Investment Law
irrespective of whether the purchase constitutes a "direct" investment
or not. If the investment is classified as a "managerial-participation"
type, in principle each application is examined by the Minister of
Finance and the competent Minister in charge of that industry to
which the firm belongs who, before validating the application, consult
with and respect the view of the Foreign Investment Council. With
respect to the direct investment in a new firm that belongs to a
liberalized industry, the competent Minister alone may grant an automatic approval. Direct investments in new firms that belong to unliberalized industries are subject to separate and individual examinations.

The following kinds of stock purchases need not be approved
under the Foreign Investment Law: 1. those stocks which were
acquired from another foreign investor; 2. those which were acquired
through donation or inheritance; 3. those which were transferred
between foreign investors as a result of merger or combine; 4. shares
acquired by foreign investors of a new firm that was established as
a result of merger or reorganization of older firms; 5. shares
acquired by foreign investors that were issued as a result of the
firm's dividend policy, stock split, transfer of reserves to the capital
account, and the like; 6. new shares that were legitimately converted
from corporate bonds; and 7. stocks that were assets of the Allied
Forces and are being recovered under the special laws.

In connection with foreign capital control the Japanese government makes a distinction between restricted and unrestricted businesses. Restricted businesses are those which are protected more
heavily against the inflow of foreign capital because of their public
nature. In restricted businesses all stock purchases by foreign
investors need to be validated. As of 1968 businesses classified as
restricted included the Bank of Japan, mutual banks, long-term trust
banks, foreign exchange banks, local railways, surface transportation
other than railways, air transportation, electricity, gas, city water,
mining, fishing, and broadcasting. The Japanese government also
makes a distinction between designated and undesignated foreign

investors. The competent Minister designates those countries to
which it is necessary for Japan to provide the most-favored-nation
treatment and the like in order to fulfill the existing treaty obligations.
Designated foreign investors are investors from the designated countries. Undesignated foreign investors are subject to more restrictions
in Japan.

Prior to July, 1963, there had been two main routes through
which foreign capital could move into Japan. One was in the form of
foreign investments to be validated under the Foreign Investment Law
or FEFTCL in exchange for a guarantee of external transfer of dividends, profits, principals withdrawn, and the like. The other route
available for foreign investors was to invest in Japanese stocks with
no legal requirement of approval under the above two laws provided
that dividends, profits, etc. were to be retained within Japan. The
latter was commonly known as the "yen base" system. The logic of
the system was to encourage the inflow of foreign capital into Japan
and at the same time to effectively control its outflow, all within the
domain of domestic laws. The "yen base" system was established in
October, 1956, but was abolished in July, 1963, in anticipation of the
irreconcilable difficulties that would arise in connection with Japan's
compliance with Article 8 of the IMF Charter to be effected in April,
1964.

OTHER KINDS OF FOREIGN INVESTMENT

Portfolio Investment

Unlike the OECD's Code of Liberalisation of Capital Movements
the Japanese Foreign Investment Law makes no explicit distinction
between direct and portfolio investment. The Cabinet Order concerning
Special Provisions of the Foreign Investment Law uses the expression
"managerial-participation type," and those foreign investments which
are not "managerial-participation type" are interpreted to correspond
to what is defined as portfolio investment in the OECD's Code of
Liberalisation. As of 1968 foreign portfolio investments were to be
automatically approved by the Bank of Japan provided that a single
foreign investor's share did not exceed 7 percent of total shares and
the combined shares of all foreign investors did not exceed 15 percent
(20 percent) of total shares of a restricted business (an unrestricted
business).

The Foreign Investment Law does not apply to those foreign

portfolio investments in Japanese corporations that are classified as
unrestricted businesses provided that shares are purchased in yen.
Similarly, the Law does not apply to the purchase in foreign currencies
of shares of unrestricted Japanese businesses by resident foreign
investors or branch offices of foreign corporations located in Japan
if there is no intent to transfer abroad profits or principals withdrawn
from such investments.

American Depositary Receipt (ADR)

An attempt to sell stocks of one country directly in another
country without making special arrangements is bound to face difficulties because of differences in languages, customs, conventions, laws,
and regulations. An ADR (American Depositary Receipt) is a substitute
stock sold in the United States in place of the original stock of a
Japanese corporation. It is a device through which Japanese firms
have attempted to promote sales of their stocks abroad. Typically
a Japanese bank acts as an agent for a Japanese firm issuing shares
of an original stock. An American bank in turn assumes the role of
an agent for the Japanese bank, and issues ADR on the bases of the
original stock deposited in the Japanese bank. American buyers of
ADR are serviced by the American bank with respect to dividends,
change of ownership, and notices from the Japanese corporations.
The Japanese bank functions as an intermediary between the Japanese
firm and the American bank. Besides managing the deposit of the
original stock, the Japanese bank receives dividends and notices
from the Japanese firms and forwards them to the American bank.
One advantage of the ADR system is that Americans interested in
investing in Japanese stocks may forego all the restrictions and complications under the Foreign Investment Law by simply purchasing
ADR in the United States. The system is said to have been advantageous
to the Japanese side as well in that it has helped publicize the worth
and attraction of the Japanese firms.

Issuance and sale of ADR by an American bank are subject to
laws and regulations in the United States. Arrangements made in
Japan pertaining to ADR come under the jurisdiction of both FEFTCL
and the Foreign Investment Law. FEFTCL interprets ADR as the
equivalent of a resident attempting to sell stocks abroad, and such an
attempt must be validated under FEFTCL. The Foreign Investment
Law requires that all the original stocks for ADR be those stocks
which have been approved under the Law.

Loans

As a rule all loans issued by foreign investors in Japan are subject to restrictions under the Foreign Investment Law. However, those loans which are repayable in less than one year, those loans which are issued for settlement of short-term international commercial transactions and the yen loans are outside the jurisdiction of the Law, and are instead regulated by FEFTCL. Import credit is a typical example of what is meant by "settlement of short-term international commercial transactions." If the term of import credit is longer than five years, it is interpreted to be in the nature of "foreign investment" and is subject to the Foreign Investment Law.

The following categories of loans require no validation under the same Law: 1. Creditor rights are acquired through donation or inheritance; 2. creditor rights are acquired from another foreign investor who legally owned those rights; and 3. creditor rights are acquired by a new corporation that was established as a result of merger or combine of the other corporations which previously owned those rights.

Bonds

Foreign investors' purchase of corporate bonds whose terms of maturity exceed one year normally require validation under the Foreign Investment Law, regardless of whether the foreign investors desire a guarantee of external transfer of interests and principals withdrawn. The Law mentions only corporate bonds, and all other bonds such as national bonds, local-government bonds, bonds issued by public corporations, are covered by FEFTCL. Approval of the purchase of corporate bonds does not imply approval of external transfer of interests and principals withdrawn. Purchase of those bonds which mature in less than a year is to be approved under FEFTCL. Application is submitted to the Minister of Finance via the Bank of Japan; but if the term of maturity is less than six months, the Bank of Japan alone may validate the application.

Purchase of corporate bonds is free of restrictions in the following circumstances: 1. Bonds are acquired from another foreign investor; 2. bonds are acquired through donation or inheritance; 3. bonds are acquired by a new corporation formed as a result of merger or combine of the other corporations that previously owned those bonds; 4. bonds are purchased by resident foreign investors in a medium of exchange other than foreign currencies; 5. bonds are purchased by resident foreign investors in a foreign currency and without an intent to remit abroad interests and principals withdrawn; and 6. bonds are purchased in a foreign currency by branches of foreign corporations located in Japan without an intent to remit abroad interests and principals withdrawn.

Beneficiary Certificates

Beneficiary certificates as defined by the Foreign Investment Law refer to beneficiary certificates of the securities investment trust and of the loan trust. Foreign investors' purchase of the certificates normally require validation under the Law irrespective of whether external transfer of related funds is desired. The foreign investors are required to use the convertible yen in purchasing the certificates. The Bank of Japan grants validation, but the Bank follows the policy of not validating those certificates which are redeemable within six months. Foreign investors' purchase of certificates in yen withdrawn from the nonresident deposit account may be approved by the Bank of Japan under the provisions of FEFTCL rather than the Foreign Investment Law.

Foreign Currency Bonds

Issuance and sale abroad of corporate bonds denominated in a foreign currency by Japanese residents are regulated by FEFTCL. Those residents who desire to acquire foreign capital through this medium must submit application to the Minister of Finance for approval. However, nonresidents' purchase or sale of these bonds (known as foreign currency bonds) abroad is free of restrictions under the Japanese laws. On the other hand, residents attempting to purchase foreign currency bonds are normally required to have their transactions validated under FEFTCL. Approval of the Minister of Finance is not necessary in the case of issuance of national bonds or government-guaranteed bonds denominated in foreign currencies.

NOTE

1. There are numerous works in Japanese that deal with the legal framework of foreign capital control in postwar Japan. A partial list includes: Yoshio Kanazawa, Keizai Ho [Economic Laws] (Tokyo:

Yuhikaku, 1968); MITI, ed., Tsusho Sangyo Roppo [Laws Concerning
Foreign Trade and Industry] (Tokyo: Tsusho Sangyo Chosa Kai, 1968);
Gaikoku Kawase Kenkyu Kyokai, Gaikoku Kawase Sho Roppo [Foreign
Exchange Laws] (Tokyo: 1968); Kokusai Toshi Kenkyu Sho, Gaishi
Donyu Kankei Hoki Shu [Laws and Regulations Concerning the Induction
of Foreign Capital](Tokyo: 1967); and Fujio Yoshida, Shihon Jiyuka to
Gaishi Ho [Capital Liberalization and the Foreign Investment Law]
(Tokyo: Zaisei Keizai Koho Sha, 1967). Available in English are:
U.S. Department of Commerce, Investment in Japan (Washington,
D.C.: 1956); Ministry of Finance of the Japanese Government, Guide
to Laws Relevant to Foreign Investment in Japan (Tokyo: 1954), IMF,
Annual Report on Exchange Restrictions (Washington, D.C.), and OECD,
Code of Liberalization of Capital Movements (Paris: various years).

6

THE CONTROL
OF
TECHNOLOGY
IMPORTS

BACKGROUND

During the Meiji period the Japanese government sent abroad a large number of promising young men to study science, technology, and other subjects, the understanding and absorption of which were vital to the social, economic, and political development of the country, and at the same time numerous foreign engineers, scientists, technicians, and experts in other areas were invited to come to Japan to serve as teachers in the art and technique of building a modern state. Many of these foreign experts were hired at extraordinarily high salaries, but few of them were given the permanent, executive positions that would enable them to control segments of Japanese society. They were aliens, temporarily employed in Japan, who would return to their homelands once their contracts expired. This was not an accident but a result of the deliberate policy objective of the Meiji government, motivated by its brand of nationalism and a desire to preserve Japan's cultural hegemony while absorbing Western technology and technical know-how. Whether or not some form of colonization of Japan would have taken place in the absence of this posture of occidental phobia is debatable and hard to verify empirically.

As we turn to the postwar period, we observe a certain parallel to the Meiji development. Japan after World War II was in tremendous need of catching up with the advanced West. On the part of the Japanese government, however, a strong sense of occidental phobia prevailed. Every inflow of foreign capital was, as it were, considered a potential instrument of the Western enterprises to take over Japanese firms. The overall pattern of Japan's induction of foreign capital during the period 1950-1970 is clear. The government has held a basic policy of caution toward any kind of foreign capital moving into

Japan. Foreign loans and debentures have been preferred to direct (managerial-participation type) investments. Induction of foreign technology has been most favored as the safest, quickest, simplest means of accelerating Japan's catching up. The Japanese government's cautious attitude was manifest even in this last category as, for example, it continued to lodge ten reservations concerning technical assistance in the OECD's Code of Liberalisation of Nontrade Transactions as late as 1967 and a major liberalization of technology imports did not occur till 1968. The reservations were justified on the grounds of "demerits" that go along with "merits" of technology imports; these "demerits" could not presumably be ignored in the light of the internal problems such as the vulnerability of small-business sectors and "excessive" competition within the Japanese markets.

The often cited "merits" of liberalization of technology imports are: 1. The Japanese firms become able to acquire necessary technical know-how sooner and in the manner they desire; 2. inter-firm competition will be stimulated by the imported, advanced technology, and greater competition will promote technological development in general in the nation; 3. Japan's image abroad will improve, given the fact that many Western countries have been highly critical of Japan's restrictive policy toward technology imports; and 4. the observed inconsistencies between liberalization of foreign investments in Japan with respect to select industries and that of technical assistance to those industries—particularly in the case of direct investment which often accompanies technical assistance—will be dissolved. These favorable effects, however, are presumably mixed with the following "demerits": 1. Some Japanese firms may become unfairly controlled by the Western firms supplying technological aid, and attention is called to the fact that Japan's postwar Anti-Monopoly Law is ambiguous concerning the monopolizing impact of foreign technology; 2. the outflow of foreign exchange due to the payment of royalties and fees that are associated with borrowed technology may become so large as to cause balance-of-payments difficulties; 3. excessive dependence upon foreign technology may lead to laxity on the part of the Japanese firms and to insufficient research and development (R&D) projects in the nation; 4. a sudden induction of foreign technology into some vulnerable sectors of the Japanese economy may cause undue disruptions, generating conflicts with the economic policy of the Japanese government.

Prewar Japan was a conspicuous importer of foreign technology. The technological gap between Japan and the West (particularly the United States) was widened during World War II. In the United States—a country which escaped from the war-caused devastation

within the homeland and which was endowed with a well developed
foundation of basic research in science and technology even before
the war—significant progress was made in atomic energy, electronics,
chemicals, etc. during the war years. The same was not true of Japan.
Before the war she may have had a sufficient capacity to borrow and
absorb foreign technology, but she lacked the foundation of basic research and the capacity to develop autonomously her own technology
relative to the advanced Western countries. The wartime isolation,
together with extensive destruction of production and research facilities, resulted in a greater technological gap after the war. This was
one of the fundamental reasons for Japan's intensive demand for foreign technology during the postwar period. In the words of a Japanese
author:

> Japan has tended to lessen the technological gap with de-
> veloped countries by the importation of foreign techniques
> rather than by improving the standards of industry, science
> and technology through research done by Japanese them-
> selves. This tendency may have been inevitable, consider-
> ing the historical backwardness of science and technology
> in Japan. Much of the importation of foreign technique in
> the heavy electrical machine industry in the postwar period
> (for example) could be considered as part of the historical
> process of technical cooperation with foreign enterprises
> since the Meiji period.[1]

The bulk of Japan's heavy and chemical industries before and
during the war was dependent upon production of war goods. The
market for military production expanded tremendously from the late
1930's on, only to collapse with the cessation of the war. The leading
firms in these industries found themselves after the war in acute
need of discovering and developing new markets. In order to find
new markets for their outputs and to cope with rising competition
within the domestic economy as well as in the overseas markets,
many firms considered the induction of Western technology to be
the quickest, the least costly and most rational alternative to take in
the context of the time. Autonomous research and development was
too time-consuming, risky, and expensive to undertake. It was more
expedient to borrow Western technology whose usefulness had already
been proven. The borrowed technology might not be the best and the
most advanced available, but it could be improved and adapted to the
Japanese needs and conditions. A typical case of technology import
involved the payment of an initial fee which was presumably much
less than the cost of developing independently the comparable technology, and the payment of royalty expressed as a percentage of

production or sale. The cost was to be paid over time as the firm
realized benefits from such borrowed technology.

There is yet another reason for Japan's extensive and intensive
borrowing of Western technology, which may be called the "dependency effect." Namely, once a firm acquires a habit of borrowing
foreign technology rather than cultivating its own, it is prone to touch
off and perpetuate a cycle of more borrowing, and this propensity was
notable especially during the early phase of the postwar period. The
capacity to develop a series of new products presupposes the presence
of extensive layers of basic research, a cumulative stock of knowledge
and information, a corps of scientists and engineers experienced in
testing and exploring the feasibility of commercial application of new
technology and know-how. If a firm becomes accustomed to borrowing
foreign technology, it is bound to neglect the development and maintenance of a fluid pool of technical skills and data from basic research
to the final stage of production of new goods. All that the firm does is
to absorb and apply the borrowed technology and produce only those
goods which are prescribed by the technology. Since the independent
capacity to develop new products is lacking, the firm is compelled to
seek a further round of borrowing technology from abroad as the
present good becomes obsolete. This "dependency effect" was intensified by the fact that during the postwar period the Japanese government has been a modest contributor to the total R&D expenditures
in the country (about 33 percent) compared with other nations such
as the United States (65 percent), France (60 percent) and Western
Germany (55 percent). The relatively low figure for Japan is, in
part, a reflection of the small weight of defense expenditures in postwar Japan, and the large figure for the United States is indicative
of heavy military-oriented expenditures by the U.S. government.
Equally true, however, is the fact that much of the fruit of what was
originally defense-oriented research becomes available for private,
peaceful applications after a lag of several years.

LEGAL ASPECTS

There are three categories of technological assistance contracts
as the term is used in the Foreign Investment Law and FEFTCL:
1. those contracts which involve transfer of rights to use certain
production techniques (e.g., purchase or lease of patents) and related
technical know-how (including the right to use trade-marks); 2. those
contracts which pertain to technical instructions for factory management given by foreign engineers in Japan or through the training of
Japanese engineers overseas; and 3. those contracts which refer

to the induction of foreign technical know-how concerning management of the firms belonging to those industries which are designated by the competent Ministers.

Technological assistance is classified as Type A if the term of contract or of payment of compensation lasts longer than one year; all others are classified as Type B. All Type A contracts are to be approved under the Foreign Investment Law, but guarantees of external transfer of compensations are granted only to those cases in which applicants specify their desire to transfer compensations abroad. Technology imports by a branch of a foreign enterprise in Japan from its parent corporation abroad are regulated by FEFTCL even if the terms of contracts or of payments of compensations last longer than one year.

The Foreign Investment Law requires, unless exempted by Cabinet Orders, a foreign investor and his Japanese partner to obtain approval of the competent Minister with respect to the following transactions: 1. renewal or change of the existing, Type A technological assistance contract; and 2. revision of the existing Type B technological contract which changes the said contract to Type A. In the cases of stocks, bonds, loans, and beneficiary certificates, only the foreign investor is to apply for approval; however, both the foreign investor and his Japanese partner are required to apply for validation if the contract involves technological assistance.

The following transactions are exempted by Cabinet Orders from the Foreign Investment Law: 1. resident foreign investors (i.e., foreign investors who are neither natural nonresidents nor foreign juridical persons) who attempt to initiate or revise Type A contracts without an intent to transfer compensations abroad or to change the existing Type B contracts into Type A contracts; and 2. nonresident foreign investors (i.e., natural nonresidents or foreign juridical persons) who attempt to let their branch offices located in Japan initiate, revise, or renew contracts concerning technology, either developed by those branch offices or imported from their main offices outside Japan, without an intent to transfer earned compensations abroad.

For approval of Type A technological assistance contracts and revisions thereof, applications are to be submitted, via the Bank of Japan, to the competent Ministers (the Minister of Finance and Head of a relevant Ministry) who in turn consult with and respect the view of the Foreign Investment Council.

The Type B technological assistance contracts, regulated under FEFTCL, must be validated by the Minister of International Trade and Industry or the Minister of Finance. The former is in charge of those contracts which pertain to industrial property rights, and the latter approves the rest of the contracts. As a rule validation by the Director of the Agency of Science and Technology is also required. If the value of a contract is less than $30,000, only the Bank of Japan's approval may be required.

Japan's joining the OECD in April, 1964, obliged her to comply with its Code of Liberalisation of Capital Movements and Code of Liberalisation of Current Nontrade Transactions. Technological assistance is covered by the latter Code along with patents, foreign travel, transportation, repairs, insurance, films, investment income, personal income, personal expenditures, public revenue, public expenditure, etc. As of early 1968 Japan was the only member nation that retained reservations on those contracts of technological assistance or patents whose terms lasted longer than one year or whose values exceeded $30,000. In its memorandum of understanding to the OECD (July, 1963) the Japanese government explained its position that while it duly recognized the importance of foreign technology as a stimulant for economic expansion the government was compelled to lodge those reservations as a safeguard against sudden disruptions in the small-business sectors beset by "excessive" competition. The OECD has been highly critical of Japan's conservativism in this area. In actuality there have been few reported cases of notable disruptions among small businesses in Japan on account of the induction of foreign technology, and practically all applications for technical assistance to the small-business sectors have been validated. However, the same has not been true of major technical assistance contracts with large firms. About 80 percent of joint ventures and other forms of foreign direct investments in the advanced sectors have involved some kind of technical assistance as part of general contracts, and technology imports have been effectively regulated to the extent that foreign direct investments have been controlled by the Foreign Investment Law or by the Government-Business Coordinating Conferences (Kan-min Kyocho Kondai Kai), an instrument of administrative control that MITI has frequently employed in order to stabilize investments in plant and equipment in major industries such as machinery, electronics, and chemicals.

The highlights of change in the rules and regulations of technology imports were as follows. On May 10, 1950 (time of promulgation of the Foreign Investment Law) only those contracts with terms lasting longer than one year and involving external remittances were then brought under the jurisdiction of the Foreign Investment Law, and emphasis was placed on "positive" criteria such as contribution to Japan's balance-of-payments equilibrium, growth and development of the important industries and public works. On July 21, 1959, the government adopted the Conditional Approval System, namely, those applications which failed to obtain unconditional approval might still be granted conditional validations. On May 21, 1961, the government switched to "negative" criteria, i.e., technology imports became free in principle except for those cases which were believed detrimental to the Japanese economy. On April 1, 1964, changes were made in the Foreign Investment Law and the Foreign Exchange Order so as to comply with Article 8 of the IMF Charter. On August 1, 1966, the government adopted the so-called one-month rule, i.e., each application as a rule was to be processed through the executive committee of the Foreign Investment Council and competent Ministers within one month. On November 15, 1966, the application and validation procedures were substantially simplified. About one-third of the previous check items were deleted. It was further decided that no revisions were to be imposed by the government on the following kinds of contracts: those in which the compensation is a fixed fee not exceeding $50,000; those contracts related to Japan's plant exports; and those contracts pertaining to the purchase of technical know-how, in which the initial sum is less than $50,000, the royalty is less than 5 percent for machinery and less than 3 percent for "others," and the term of contract does not last longer than seven years. In 1968 and 1969 most of the reservations with respect to the provisions of the OECD's Code of Liberalisation of Current Nontrade Transactions were partially or totally withdrawn.

PATTERN OF TECHNOLOGY IMPORTS

The number of new Type A technological assistance contracts validated continued to show a rising trend from 1950, the year in which the Foreign Investment Law was promulgated. The numbers of contracts validated in various years were: 101 (1951); 133 (1952); 103 (1953); 82 (1954); 72 (1955); 144 (1956); 118 (1957); 90 (1958); and 153 (1959). A major relaxation of validation standards in 1960 led to a sizable increase of new contracts in the subsequent years. They numbered: 327 (1960); 320 (1961); 328 (1962); 564 (1963); 500 (1964); 472 (1965); 601 (1966); and 638 (1967). There was another major liberalization of technology imports in June, 1968. The number of new contracts increased to 782 (1968), 1,099 (1969), and 1,218 (1970).

For the period 1950-1967 about 50 percent of the contracts were in the category of machinery and approximately 20 percent were in chemical industries. The United States was the major source of Japan's technology imports (2,568 cases), followed by Western Germany (469), Switzerland (314), Great Britain (257) and France (157). The United States alone accounted for 60 percent of the total and the OECD countries excluding the United States and Canada supplied 35 percent of the total.

Throughout the postwar period the number of technology imports was much larger than that of direct investments approved under the Foreign Investment Law. Of direct investments in the form of new joint ventures, about 80 percent were accompanied by technology imports. On the other hand, roughly 30 percent of foreign direct investments in the existing Japanese firms involved some kinds of technical assistance.

The value of Japan's technology imports (payment) persistently far exceeded that of her technology exports (receipt). In 1966 Japan's payment was $190 million in contrast to her receipt of $15 million. The receipt/payment ratio was only 8.3 percent. Similar ratios for the same year were: 38 percent for Western Germany; 80 percent for France; and 70 percent for Denmark.

Japan's payment for technology imports in 1966 was $190 million or 70 billion yen. Assuming that the average royalty for technical assistance is 4 percent of sales, the implied amount of total sales related with technical assistance is roughly 1.8 trillion yen. Inasmuch as 50 percent and 20 percent of technical assistance are in machinery and chemicals, respectively, we may estimate the sales of machinery and chemicals that are induced by the imported foreign technology to be 1.4 trillion yen, which was approximately 20 percent of Japan's total output in the same commodity categories in the same year. Namely, as a matter of rough estimate, 20 percent of Japan's production of machinery and chemicals was generated by the imported foreign technology.

It is nearly impossible to measure precisely the impact of technology imports upon the Japanese economy. The impact runs in all directions, touching various aspects of the economy. A technology import may lead to a significant degree of import substitution. There may be secondary as well as tertiary effects on Japanese imports as the effects of the initial borrowed technology spill over into the related sectors. It is possible, however, that even in the absence of borrowed technology, the same product will be developed independently by the Japanese firms after some time lags. The technical assistance may first result in productivity gains and output expansion on the homefront—then sufficient externalities may be generated so that exports of the related goods will increase. What all this means to Japanese exports, imports, overall balance of payments, level of employment, etc. is hard to answer in precise terms. At best, we may find it difficult to deny that the borrowed technology has had a far-reaching effect on the expansion of the domestic economy and exports in postwar Japan.

During the decade of 1950's total royalty payments for imported technology (inclusive of both Type A and Type B) rose steadily. The total, which was $7 million in 1951, increased to $16 million in 1954, to $42 million in 1957 and to $95 million in 1960. Inasmuch as most technological assistance contracts stipulate that the royalty be paid as a percentage of production and/or sales, the above increase was a combined effect of the growing number of contracts validated and the expansion of imported-technology-using goods. During the same decade the indexes of the number of unexpired Type A technological assistance contracts as well as of royalty payments for the use of foreign technology of the same category continued to increase but the latter index rose faster than the former. Treating 1951 as the base year the former index reached 915 in 1960 whereas the latter index was as large as 1,660 in 1960. This may be construed as indicative of the relatively greater concentration of productivity gains in those industries which heavily depended upon imported technology (e.g., electrical machinery and chemicals) than elsewhere in the Japanese economy.

According to a survey conducted by the Bureau of Enterprises of MITI, the total foreign-technology-using production accounted for 5.3 percent of total industrial production in 1955. The impact of foreign technology in particular industries was naturally much greater than is suggested by this overall average. The weights of foreign-technology-using output in total output in particular sectors were: 30.9 percent (electrical machinery); 6.6 percent (general machinery); 6.9 percent (metals and metallic goods); 4.6 percent (chemicals) and 7.2 percent (rubber, leather).[2]

One of the "demerits" of liberalization of technology imports, often cited by the Japanese government, is that the liberalization would adversely affect the nation's balance of payments. This claim cannot be empirically substantiated. The weight of royalty payments for Type A technology imports in Japan's total foreign exchange payments for imports and nontrade transactions remained small throughout the postwar period. It was merely 0.5 percent in 1953, rose modestly to 0.8 percent in 1955 and to 1.0 percent in 1957. In 1960 it was still as small as 1.8 percent.[3]

The weight of "new" technology imported to Japan (i.e., technology of the kind that has not been imported previously) has shown a steady decline. The weight of such technology imports was 70 percent of the total in 1961. It decreased to 43 percent in 1965 and to 33 percent in 1966. The similar declining trends have been observed with respect to major industrial categories such as chemicals, machinery, metals, electrical equipment, and textiles.[4]

Another trend has been a decline of the large-scale technology imports. In 1961 about 40 percent of total technology imports of Type A was unaccompanied by foreign direct investments, whereas the percentage rose to 60 percent in 1966. Similarly, in 1961 approximately 31 percent of technology imports was linked with foreign direct investments worth more than 100 million yen; but the weight of the said technology imports fell to 14 percent in 1966. Of those technology imports linked with foreign direct investments, the average investment value per technology import was 490 million yen in 1961, and this value decreased to 240 million yen in 1966. Reflecting the rising level of technology within the Japanese industries (and the declining relative need to import new foreign technology) as well as the increasing hesitancy on the part of the foreign firms to engage in technical assistance contracts with the Japanese firms, the numbers of cross-licenses and joint research projects showed an upward trend during the second half of the 1960's.[5]

Japan remained a net technology importer throughout the postwar period. However, Japan's technology exports rose persistently. Most of these exports first went to the developing countries, and more recently an increasing number of them were contracted with the advanced countries. In 1966 there were 84 cases of Japan's technology exports, of which 28 were in chemicals and 19 in electrical machinery. In terms of their geographic distribution 31 cases were to Europe, 24 to Asia and 21 to North America (the United States and Canada). During 1956-1964 the average weight of the OECD countries in Japan's total technology exports was 11 percent. The weight rose to 58 percent in 1966.[6]

RETROSPECT

Many observers, Japanese as well as Western, have pointed out that Japan's conspicuous dependence upon Western technology

constitutes a problematical aspect of her economic growth. The conventional wisdom that underlies the familiar remarks about the imi-
tative propensity of Japanese seems to assume that there is something intrinsically virtuous about a nation's autonomous capacity to
develop modern technology. It has often been said that, since the
Western enterprises never sell the latest, most advanced technology
but instead provide only what has become second-rate, Japan's chronic
dependence upon foreign technology means that she is forever doomed
to be a second-rate technological power in the world.[7] As we look
back over some two decades of developments in postwar Japan, however, it seems that the conventional view requires some modifications.

During the first ten years or so after the war Japan was in
acute need of closing the technological gap vis-à-vis the Western
countries. In addition to the fact that the gap that had existed before
the war was widened during the war years, Japan faced another problem of keeping up with the much faster tempo of innovations in the
postwar world. It is said that the successful innovation of locomotives
took one hundred years from the time of discovery of the principles
involved. The time interval from invention to innovation of vacuum
tubes was some fifteen years. In the postwar context the transistor
became commercially producible in four years.

In order to accelerate the process of catching up it was quickest
and least costly (hence most rational) for Japan to borrow Western
technology. During 1950-1954 it was not uncommon for the Japanese
firms to produce a wide range of products that were 100 percent or
nearly 100 percent based upon the imported technology.[8] If it is an
advanced technology, the sheer act of "imitating" or borrowing it
alone requires an enormous reservoir of scientific-technological
knowledge and understanding on the part of the recipient. We are
not speaking of learning how to use simple, primitive tools but of
handling highly complex and sophisticated equipment and machinery.
It is well to remember that all the underdeveloped countries in the
world have had no less access to Western technology than Japan has
but the same sort of technological catching up has not occured in those
countries because of their insufficient technology-absorbing capacities.

One learns by doing, and the first step of doing is imitating. It
is misleading and even erroneous to say, however, that all that Japan
has done is to borrow and imitate foreign technology. While the act
of imitating modern, advanced technology itself presupposes an ability
meritorious in its own right, Japan went much farther than that. Particularly during the second decade of the postwar period Japan demonstrated, with increasing frequency, her unique ability to digest, adapt,
and improve the imported technology and to produce higher-quality

products than was possible with the original technology. The transistor
was not developed by the Sony Corporation. Sony discovered a commercially feasible method of producing transistors, whereas the idea
itself had been discovered several years earlier in the United States
but had been discarded, for the cost of production was believed to be
prohibitively high. The kind of technological breakthroughs witnessed
in the Japanese automobile industry from 1965 on has been little short
of amazing. According to a survey conducted in Japan the majority
of 68 products whose production rose rapidly and involved imported
foreign technologies for the period 1954-1964 was found to have been
significantly improved in quality by the supplementary technologies
developed by the Japanese firms; only 8 products depended solely
upon imported technologies.[9]

It is a curious fact to note that while few people question the
irrationality of autarchy or economic self-sufficiency as a matter of
economic policy, the same people often regard technological self-
sufficiency as inherently good and desirable. The doctrine of economic
nationalism—rather than the principle of comparative advantage—
gains greater popularity as far as technology is concerned. From
a practical standpoint it seems foolhardy, if not literally impossible,
to try to increase R&D efforts on all fronts in Japan so as to make
her technology status more or less comparable to that of an advanced
Western country. It is to be noted that even the most advanced countries of Western Europe have by and large been net importers of technologies. It is puzzling that the same people who point out the folly
of duplicating research projects within one country react differently
when there is duplication internationally, which is what the national
policy of technological self-sufficiency implies.

What has been happening in postwar Japan is that, through the
process of vigorous catching up and intensive as well as extensive absorption of Western technology, her own capacity to develop technology
matured and rose steadily as indicated by the increasing numbers of
cross-licenses and technology exports to the Western countries. If a
country is less developed, there is room (by definition) for that country
to exploit the comparative advantage in absorbing technology from the
more advanced countries. In other words, there is nothing irrational
about borrowing foreign technology as an effective means of promoting
the nation's economic growth. There has been at work a circular causa-
tion of cumulative development in postwar Japan. The large, expanding
economy of a hundred million people generated tremendous demand
for new innovations, and at the same time the growth of the economy
was enhanced by the waves of new innovations. However, the required

pace of new innovations could not possibly have been sustained without swift and skillful absorption of the Western technology.

NOTES

1. Akira Uchino, "Technological Innovation in Postwar Japan," Developing Economies (December, 1969), p. 421.

2. See Toyoro Ikuta, "Gijutsu Donyu to Royalty Shiharai" [Technology Imports and Royalty Payments], Tsusho Sangyo Kenkyu, No. 98 (1961), pp. 67-79.

3. Ibid.

4. Kagaku Gijitsu Cho, Kagaku Gijitsu Hakusho [White Paper on Science and Technology] (Tokyo: 1967), pp. 240-241.

5. Ibid., pp. 242-243.

6. Ibid., p. 245. See also U.S.-Japan Trade Council, The Growth of Japanese Technology (Washington, D.C.: December, 1967), pp. 8-15.

7. See for instance Kazuhiro Kikuchi, "Boeki Jiyuka to Gijutsu Shinko" [Trade Liberalization and Technological Progress], Tsusho Sangyo Kenkyu, No. 87 (1960), pp. 83-92.

8. MITI, Sangyo Gorika Hakusho [White Paper on Industrial Rationalization] (Tokyo: Nikkan Kogyo Shimbun Sha, 1957), pp. 132-33.

9. Economic Planning Agency, Keizai Hakusho [Economic White Paper] (Tokyo: 1967), p. 86.

7

**CAPITAL
LIBERALIZATION**

BEFORE 1967

The first major liberalization of capital transactions took place on July 1, 1967. This does not mean, of course, that there had been no inflow of foreign capital into Japan prior to that date. For the period from 1950 (promulgation of the Foreign Investment Law) to July, 1967, the cumulative total of about $5.1 billion worth of foreign capital moved into Japan. Of this amount 67.8 percent consisted of loans, and 18.3 percent was foreign investment in Japanese stocks. The sort of foreign capital that has been deemed problematical from the standpoint of the national interest refers to foreign investors' purchases of Japanese stocks that break down into three categories— direct investment, portfolio investment, and "others." Foreign direct investments in Japanese stocks between 1950 and July, 1967, amounted to approximately $300 million or 33 percent of total foreign investments in Japanese stocks. Portfolio investments that are intended for capital gains and dividends tend to fluctuate sensitively, depending upon conditions of the securities market in Japan; their cumulative sum for the same period was about $400 million but the real net balance as of the spring of 1967 was presumably much smaller. "Others" mainly refer to the afore-mentioned ADR and foreign investors' purchase of new shares issued as expansion of the already validated portfolio investments.

In contrast to portfolio investments, direct investments are bound to stay in the country more or less permanently. Prior to 1967 few cases of validated direct investments had been withdrawn from Japan. Consequently, the above figure of $300 million might be interpreted to represent the cumulative total as well as the net balance of direct investments in Japan as of early 1967. This figure is strikingly small in comparison with other countries. In 1965 alone the amount of foreign direct investments in Great Britain was $450 million. Similarly, the direct investments in the same year were: $640 million in Western Germany; $430 million in France; and $330 million in Italy. In 1965 foreign direct investments in Japan amounted to only $40 million or about one-tenth of what was absorbed by an advanced West European country. Even allowing for historical and geographic differences, one is struck by the modest figure for Japan. This impression is only strengthened when one notes that the foreign direct investments of $40 million accounted for less than 1 percent of gross capital formation in Japan during the same year.

Prior to June, 1963, practically all cases of foreign investments with the 100 percent foreign capital ratio were in the form of the so-called "yen base" companies, namely, those foreign-owned companies which did not have to be approved under the Foreign Investment Law, provided that principals and earnings were to be retained within Japan. The majority of well-known, early entrants such as Mobile, Esso, Shell, Coca-Cola, and Pepsi-Cola made their initial entries into Japan as "yen base" companies. From 1950 through June, 1963, the "yen base" companies numbered 316. In April, 1964, Japan joined the OECD and officially began to comply with Article 8 of the IMF Charter. Japan was now obliged to remove the categorical ban on external transfer of profits and principals in the case of "yen base" foreign investments. In anticipation of this international obligation the "yen base" system was dissolved in July, 1963, and from April, 1964, all direct foreign investments became subject to validation under the Foreign Investment Law. For the period from 1950 through 1966 the total number of joint ventures established in Japan under the Foreign Investment Law was 431, the majority of which came into being after 1963. Of this figure, about 50 cases refer to those which initially started out as "yen base" firms and later, through expansion and/or reorganization, became subject to validation under the Foreign Investment Law.

Of 669 foreign investments approved between 1950 and March, 1966, 453 cases (70 percent) were of American capital, and 58 were of Swiss origin. The majority of the Swiss firms investing in Japan are actually controlled by American capital. Therefore, it may be held that close to 80 percent of the inflow of foreign capital during the period consisted in substance of American capital. Total value of direct foreign investments during the same period was $272 million. In terms of industrial categories the three most important industries were: petroleum ($89 million); chemicals ($68 million); and transport equipment ($62 million). The last category absorbed the highest number of cases (247 out of 669), whereas the number of cases in petroleum was only 34, indicating that foreign investments in the petroleum industry were represented by "big" foreign concerns.

According to the straight, Western-style argument in favor of capital liberalization it is the weak, backward sectors of the domestic economy that should encourage the induction of foreign capital because foreign investments often imply not only supply of financial resources but also introduction of new products, technology, technical know-how, managerial skills, the latest marketing methods, and the like that would contribute to the nation's economic development. This viewpoint distinctly has not been held by the Japanese government. The approach adopted by the government on the eve of the first capital liberalization was to check which industries in Japan were still too weak to withstand the impact of foreign direct investments and to proceed with utmost caution in liberalizing those sectors which were assuredly so developed as not to be overwhelmed by the invading foreign enterprises. In 1966 MITI conducted an extensive survey of Japanese industries concerning their preparedness for liberalization, the results of which were published in November of the same year.[1] The survey covered 104 industries, of which 40 were heavy industries, 19 chemicals, 31 textiles and sundries, and 14 mining. Its main findings were as follows.

With respect to the state of technology, about 50 out of 104 industries were found to be in need of improvement. Electronic computers, electronics, and petrochemicals were cases in which rapid technological progress was urgently required. Atomic power plants, heavy (thermo) generators, data processing, electronic telephone exchange, space communications, wireless communications, and construction machinery were cases whereby major breakthroughs were strongly desired so that the Japanese firms would remain competitive in the world market over the future years.

About 50 industries were cited as problematical in terms of industrial organization. Larger scales of production were recommended for 10 (e.g., automobiles and petrochemicals). Greater specialization was deemed desirable for 30 (including cables, synthetic dyes, tires, machinery, electronics). Excess capacities were reported in 10 cases (e.g., cotton, rayon staple).

Consumer credit and the marketing-distribution methods were found to be critically underdeveloped in such areas as computers, automobiles, electrical appliances, oil refining, and construction machinery.

Brand was cited as a potential source of "problems" for cosmetics, fountain pens, cigarette lighters, razor blades, paints, synthetic dyes, and specialized tires.

The overcrowding of small firms and technical backwardness
were cited as critical problems in such sectors as shoes, beds, and
frame metals.

In addition to the findings about specific industries the MITI
survey also identified the following to be the general problems associated with the capital liberalization: 1. the greater likelihood of
"take over" of Japanese firms in the case of foreign direct investments
in the existing (as against new) firms; 2. the tremendous financial
resources possessed by world enterprises that may overwhelm the
Japanese markets; 3. the possibility of critical disruptions of Japanese
money as well as labor markets through large-scale borrowings,
sudden plant closures, and the like by the Western enterprises; and
4. the possibility that Western firms' behavior in Japan may seriously
conflict with the economic policy of the Japanese government (e.g.,
Western firms may launch a series of new investments when the
government is pursuing a deflationary policy or they may not adhere
to the government's administrative guidance). The implied recommendations of the MITI survey were duly incorporated into the safeguard
provisions of the first liberalization in 1967.

FIRST LIBERALIZATION

Prior to 1967 all foreign investments had theoretically been
subject to case-by-case examinations by the Japanese authorities.
The first round of capital liberalization took place on July 1, 1967,
as the Japanese government put into effect a new explicit framework
of regulating the inflow of foreign capital.[2] All industries were classified into three groups: Category I; Category II; and "Others."
Category I refers to those industries in which foreign direct investments that involve the foreign-capital ratio of up to 50 percent and
that result in establishment of new enterprises in Japan are to be
automatically approved. Category II includes those industries in
which foreign direct investments that involve the foreign-capital
ratio of up to 100 percent and that result in establishment of new
enterprises in the country are to be automatically validated. "Others"
are those industries in which all foreign direct investments must be
individually examined. Those under Categories I and II need be
examined separately if foreign investments involve managerial participation in the existing Japanese firms. The normal criterion for

distinguishing direct investment from portfolio investment is whether the foreign enterprise in question is sending its representative(s) to Japan.

The first liberalization covered portfolio investment as well. A single foreign investor was now allowed to purchase up to 7 percent (instead of the previous 5 percent) of total shares of the stock of a Japanese company. Similarly, the automatically approvable ratio of shares owned by all foreign investors was raised from the previous 15 to 20 percent in general and from 10 to 15 percent in the case of restricted industries such as utilities and banking. All portfolio investments within these bounds could now be approved directly by the Bank of Japan. Those exceeding the prescribed limit remained subject to case-by-case examinations by the Minister of Finance. The new general limits of 7 percent (for a single foreign investor) and 20 percent (for all foreign investors) were lower than those recommended (10 percent and 25 percent, respectively) by the OECD. The reason was that according to the Japanese Commercial Code the 25 percent share ratio enables foreign investors to send in their representatives who may account for more than 25 percent of all representatives, and the share ratio of a major Japanese stockholder seldom exceeded 8 to 9 percent. A single foreign investor's holding as much as 10 percent of the shares of a company was therefore deemed undesirable.

What appears to be a peculiar aspect of the first liberalization is the fact that it refers to liberalization of foreign direct investments in "new" enterprises only, and the designated industries under Categories I and II remained unliberalized if foreign investments in question were in the existing enterprises. Namely, the latter continued to be individually examined rather than automatically validated. The basic reason for this oddity is the attitude of extreme caution on the part of the Japanese government. The pre-liberalization surveys on the preparedness of Japanese industries revealed that even among those industries which were regarded as "ready" for liberalization there was much apprehension not so much about the coming of new foreign-controlled firms as about the existing Japanese firms being suddenly taken over by foreign interests. From the Japanese viewpoint there was a rational basis for this phobia. Unlike prewar Japan the stock ownership in postwar Japan became relatively more diffused. Seldom did a single stockholder own more than 10 percent of total shares of a major corporation. In addition, Japanese corporations during the postwar period became heavily dependent upon debt financing (loans from city banks) rather than equity financing (sales of stocks). Consequently, at the time of the first liberalization of

capital transactions the average owned-capital ratio among major
corporations was about 20 percent—a low figure relative to those in
the United States and Western Europe. It was believed that these
elements of vulnerability made it facile for foreign interests to take
over Japanese enterprises.

The new enterprise, as distinguished from the existing enterprise
was defined as referring to the following cases: 1. A foreign investor
purchases shares of a newly established corporation; and 2. a foreign
investor purchases shares from a Japanese investor within one month
after a new corporation is established. A newly formed corporation
would be classified as an existing enterprise if the Japanese co-inves-
tor(s) supplied corporate properties other than land, e.g., factories,
stores, warehouses, machines, and equipment. Similarly, if the
ownership transfer of industrial properties, mergers, combines, and
the like are scheduled immediately after the establishment of a new
firm, such a firm would be regarded as an existing enterprise.

The main emphasis of the first capital liberalization was on
those industries which were liberalized up to the 50 percent foreign-
capital ratio. This "50 percent" approach was unprecedented among
the member nations of the OECD except for Spain. The Japanese
government took every possible precaution to minimize disruptions
that might result from the liberalization. Whenever there was some
doubt about their preparedness, industries were placed in Category I
instead of Category II. The equal partnership of U.S.-Japanese investors was considered to be the most desirable format for introducing
foreign capital to Japanese soil where customs, mores, and conventions
in running businesses were presumably very different from those
in the West and where the coming of corporations wholly owned and
operated by foreigners was believed incompatible with the general
sentiment among Japanese. The solution was to design a framework
of capital liberalization that would assure an environment of "live
and let live" and economic co-prosperity for foreign as well as
Japanese investors.

The rule of automatic approval (Jido Ninka) was not quite
"automatic." Before a foreign investment in a new enterprise in
Category I was approved, there were still several conditions that
had to be met in order that the principle of equal partnership be followed not as a mere formality but in terms of the substance of corporate management. These conditions, explicitly stated rather than
left to discretionary interpretations of the government, were as follows: 1. more than a half of Japanese shares be owned by the Japanese
investors who are engaged in the same business as that of the newly

formed enterprise, and at least one Japanese investor own more than
one-third of total shares; 2. the ratio of Japanese executive directors
be larger than the ratio of shares owned by the Japanese investors;
3. the method of corporate decision-making employed within the new
enterprise be consistent with the Japanese Commercial Code, and
no particular director or stockholder be given a veto power.

Those applications which fail to fulfill these conditions are
transferred to separate examinations. Even when these conditions
are not met, approval may be granted providing that there is no reason
to believe that the principle of equal partnership will be violated.
Before validating the application the government may make recommendations concerning revisions of the proposed contract. Unlike case-
by-case examinations of foreign investments in unliberalized industries, the government as a rule does not raise questions as to what
(adverse) effects a new foreign investment may have upon the industry
concerned in the case of evaluation of foreign direct investments in
liberalized industries.

The foreign investor who is interested in direct investment in
a new enterprise that belongs to one of the liberalized industries in
Category I and who has fulfilled the above three conditions faces yet
another hurdle to pass if the foreign-capital ratio exceeds one-third.
Namely, there are two additional subconditions to be met by the
applicant. They are: 1. He shall seek approval of the competent
Minister when he later moves into a new business different from that
for which the initial validation was granted; and 2. he shall seek
approval of the competent Minister when he later attempts a reorganization of the firm, combine, merger, etc., that is not stipulated in
the initial contract. The first of these was a measure to prevent the
foreign investor from moving into a restricted industry after he had
first established himself in a liberalized industry, and the second
was designed to prevent the new enterprise from taking over existing
firms.

Within the bounds of the OECD Code of Liberalisation the
Japanese government reserved yet another line of defense against
foreign direct investments in the liberalized industries. The application could be blocked if there was sufficient evidence to believe that
the foreign investment would have "exceptionally adverse effects on
the Japanese economy." Similarly, the Japanese government reserved
the right, under extraordinary circumstances, to regulate the firms
with foreign managerial participation as regards output, range of
products, the time to commence production, and the like. "Extraordinary circumstances" were interpreted to refer to conspicuous

disruptions in Japanese industries induced by: 1. introduction of the
scale of production by foreign interests that far exceeds the Japanese
standards; 2. introduction of new or radically different, advanced
technology to which the Japanese firms are not yet accustomed; and
3. major influx of foreign investment at a time when excess capacities
are observed in the industry concerned.

Given all the above qualifications associated with "automatic"
approval of foreign investments, one feels that the official expression,
Jiyuka (liberalization), was a gross misnomer. Nonetheless, a total
of 50 industries was "liberated" on July 1, 1967. Of these, 33 industries were in Category I and 17 in Category II. Those industries
under the jurisdiction of MITI numbered 30, of which 20 were in
Category I and 10 in Category II. These 30 industries accounted for
roughly 25 percent of total output of industries under MITI. The
actual scope of liberalization was narrower than the pronounced list
would suggest, inasmuch as many problematical items belonging to
the liberalized industries continued to be restricted as exceptions.
The international competitive position of a Japanese industry in terms
of technology, financial capital, and resources was used as the selection criterion. Those industries whose overall competitive position
was as strong as that of the advanced Western industries were included
in Category II. If some gaps were believed to exist in favor of foreign
enterprises, industries were given the Category I classification. The
small-business sectors, characterized by low efficiency and technological backwardness, were precluded. The marketing-distribution
sectors such as supermarkets, wholesaling, retailing, and advertising
were exempted on account of their alleged backwardness and vulnerability. Those industries which were in the process of reorganization
toward greater specialization and larger scale of production (e.g.,
machinery, electronic parts, automobiles) under the provisions of the
Machinery Industry Promotion Act and the Electronics Industry Promotion Act were excluded. Likewise, those industries noted for the
then prevailing technological gaps (e.g., electronic computers, color
films, petrochemicals) were also exempted from the liberalization.
These industries were to be liberalized in later years as they would
develop a sufficiently high degree of preparedness. In contrast, it
was assumed that the strategic industries from the standpoint of
national defense and security such as weapons, gunpowder, aircraft,
utilities, and atomic energy would remain unliberalized more or less
permanently.

The major industries in Category I included: electric appliances
for private uses (excluding electronic range, air conditioner, and
battery-operated appliances); radio and television (excluding color

television and integrated circuits); tape recorders and record players; telephone and telephone exchange equipment (excluding push-button or automatic dial phones); cameras (including parts and attachments); watches (excluding decorative clocks and alarm clocks); printing ink (including newspaper ink); and synthetic textiles.

The main industries in Category II were: ordinary steel; two-wheel vehicles; cement; rayon; piano; organ; shipbuilding; beer; hotel; and travel service.

A branch office in Japan of a foreign enterprise may resemble, in terms of its activity, a wholly controlled subsidiary of a foreign corporation. However, a branch office is regulated only by the Foreign Exchange and Foreign Trade Control Law and this has often been cited as a loophole of the Foreign Investment Law. A foreign corporation may open a branch office in Japan merely by submitting a notice to the competent Minister. Transfer of funds from the parent corporation abroad to the branch in Japan is regulated under FEFTCL. The general principle that had been followed by the Japanese government was to approve only transfer of funds for communication and commercial purposes and not to validate transfer of funds to build new plants or factories or to engage in any form of manufacturing activity in Japan. The 1967 liberalization introduced a new administrative rule of approving on an ad hoc basis a branch office's manufacturing activity if it was sufficiently small and insignificant so that no adverse effects might be anticipated.

According to the OECD Code of Liberalisation loans of longer than five years maturity with intents of managerial participation are classified as direct investments. However, not infrequently it is difficult to classify foreign loans in terms of industrial categories in the manner stock investments may be so classified. For example, a loan from abroad may be to supplement a revolving, consumer-credit fund of a trading company catering to various businesses rather than to a specific manufacturing firm in a specific industry. For this reason the Japanese government did not undertake liberalization of loan investments as such in 1967, and instead left the matter to case-by-case examination. However, the Japanese government has been most lenient toward foreign loans, and there has been a de facto liberalization of foreign loan investments throughout the postwar period.

For many years the Japanese government had been criticized by foreign investors for its bureaucratic red tape, maze-like rules and regulations which no one even within the government seemed able to understand, and strange administrative conventions, such as not giving the applicant an explicit negative reply but rather remaining in silence indefinitely till the applicant gave up the whole idea of investing in Japan, or revising the proposed contract to the government's liking, and so forth. In response to these complaints the government formulated a new working rule, as part of the 1967 liberalization, to complete the processing of each application and make a decision on the validation within one month in the case of liberalized industries, and to announce the government's opinion of the proposed investment also within one month in the case of unliberalized industries. The intent of the government is one thing; materialization of that intent is another. Noritake Kobayashi gives the following description of what it was like for a Western investor to approach Japan around 1968.

Let us begin with an imaginary situation—but one that is by no means unfamiliar. Let us suppose that an American wishes to invest both money and technology in Japan. He consults his lawyer, who almost certainly advises him that because of Japanese law, the establishment of a wholly-owned foreign company is virtually impossible, and that the only practicable way to operate a business in Japan is by means of a joint venture with a Japanese partner. Our American investor, therefore, goes to Japan, finds a reliable partner, and begins negotiations toward the establishment of a joint venture and the granting of technological licenses.

During the course of the negotiations, the representative of the American investing company is perplexed by the fact that his Japanese partner makes regular 'informal inquiries' of government officials in an effort to determine whether or not he should agree with the American partner on such important issues as equity division, royalty rate, and sales territory division. These are all matters that the American partner feels should be kept secret, at least until the signing of the agreement.

Once the agreement has been signed, the contracts have to be sent to the government for official validation (required by existing foreign exchange and investment control laws) before the American partner has the right to bring his technology and money into Japan, with the right of remittance. Usually, because of language difficulties, it is only the representative of the Japanese partner who goes to the indicated government office to apply for the necessary validation. The American partner, at this point, is further perplexed by the fact that, in spite of all the 'informal inquiries' the Japanese partner had made during the 'private' negotiations prior to the signing of the contract, the government now makes the validating process still more difficult by offering a great deal more 'informal guidance.'

The American partner now discovers that government officials never turn down an application with an explicit 'no.' Rather, they make suggestions for amendments to the agreement. The implication is that unless the suggestions are complied with, the government will withhold its validation. In attempting to grapple with this problem, the American will now ask to see the 'suggestions' and have them translated; whereupon, he will be told that they have all been made orally from government official to Japanese partner. Nothing has been written down.

The American's perplexity increases when he attempts to discuss with his Japanese partner ways of making the 'suggested' amendments more favorable. The latter, reluctant to argue with the government official, merely asks his American partner to agree to the government's 'suggestions.' Unless he acquiesces, the American learns, the necessary validation will rarely, if ever, be granted. At this stage (unless he just gets mad and goes home) he will probably throw up his hands and agree to all the government's 'suggestions,' however unsatisfactory he may consider them. He realizes that this is his only hope of extracting any profit from the joint venture.[3]

The Western investor would have received neither comfort nor encouragement had he read a statement issued on July 6, 1967 by the Secretary General of the Cabinet—caricatured by some as the "Ten Commandments"—in which he advised foreign investors to: 1. uphold the principles of coexistence, co-prosperity and equal partnership by choosing joint ventures as a form of direct investment in Japan; 2. avoid moving into a given sector in a sudden, disruptive manner; 3. refrain from engaging in activities that would disturb small businesses; 4. cooperate with Japanese business and industry concerning their autonomous efforts to develop and maintain order in the domestic market; 5. restrain from making discriminatory or exclusive agreements with parent corporations abroad that would constitute unfair

competition in Japan; 6. strive to contribute to autonomous technological progress in Japan; 7. cooperate with Japan's efforts to promote
exports and improve her balance of payments; 8. employ as many
Japanese as possible for managerial positions; 9. respect Japanese
conventions and mores in the employment area and refrain from mass
layoffs, sudden plant closures, etc. that would cause confusion and
disorder in the Japanese labor market; and 10. cooperate with the
Japanese government concerning pursuit of its economic-policy
objectives.

SECOND LIBERALIZATION

The Japanese government requested the Foreign Investment
Council on October 17, 1968, to study and make recommendations
concerning the second liberalization of capital transactions. The
Council continued its deliberations through the fall and winter, and
submitted its report to the government on February 5, 1969. The
Cabinet decision to accept the Council recommendations contained in
the report without alterations was made two days later (February 7),
and the second liberalization was put into effect on March 1, 1969.
The basic framework of the first liberalization (1967) was retained.
The second liberalization meant, in effect, increasing the number of
liberalized industries in both Categories I and II. All the industries
liberalized in 1967 had been reexamined. Some of the exemptions
and qualifications made in 1967 were deleted or revised. The total
of 155 industries was newly added to the list of liberalized industries,
of which 135 were to Category I and 20 to Category II. Nine industries,
included in Category I in 1967, were shifted to Category II. Adjusting
for overlappings, the second liberalization raised the total number
of liberalized industries to 204, of which 160 were in Category I and
44 in Category II. These figures refer to 4-digit industries (gyoshu)
in the Japanese Standard Industrial Classification Table.

Among the main items newly added to Category I in 1969 were:
textile manufacturing machines, paper manufacturing machines,
elevators, escalators, springs, boilers, troubles, electric generators,
motors, electric lighting equipment, broadcasting equipment (for
radio as well as television), electronic microscopes, X-ray equipment,
batteries, cameras (8 and 16 mm), clocks, tires, rubber belts, cement
products, pulp, glass products, ceramics, toys, lead pipes, lead plates,
electric wires, insurance, theatres, meat products, canned fruits,
instant coffee, cornflakes, oatmeal, plywood, rolling stock, and salvage.
Among those newly added to Category II were: electric home appliances
(excluding air conditioners and electronic ranges), radios, television

sets (including color TV), tape recorders, watches, record players, hotels, barbershops, beauty shops, restaurants, ship building, and architectural consulting.

To the Japanese government capital liberalization has meant not so much an opportunity to encourage and welcome foreign direct investments as a matter of fulfilling international obligation. Every precautionary step was taken in order to minimize disruptions among Japanese firms. As far as the protectionist objective of the government is concerned, the result has been satisfactory. Between the first and second liberalizations (July 1, 1967-March 1 1969) only 4 joint ventures (CBS-Sony, Showa-Diamond Chemicals, Daiichi-Radio Isotope and Toyobo Pet Chord) were established in Japan through Category I. In preparing for the second liberalization the Japanese government followed the same procedures as for the first liberalization. Industries to be liberalized had to meet the criterion of having a sufficiently strong competitive position relative to Western enterprises in terms of scale of production, size of invested capital, quality of products, price factor, technology, R&D capability, marketing network and the like. Liberalization was postponed whenever there was some indication that foreign direct investment might hinder industrial reorganization in progress or threaten the autonomy of the nation's technology. Similar considerations were given to those industries in which the Japanese firms suffered disadvantages relative to the Western enterprises as regards access to the supply of industrial materials.

As was the case in 1967, the distribution sector—allegedly backward, overcrowded, and hence vulnerable to the invasion of foreign capital—received special attention. As part of preparation for the second liberalization, MITI requested the Industrial Structure Council (Sangyo Kozo Shingikai) to study the problem via the Council's ad hoc committee on the distribution sector. The committee formulated general principles of extra caution, gradualism, and coordination with related, liberalized industries. It gave top priority for liberalization to trading firms in general, followed by wholesaling, and retailing. With respect to retailing the order recommended was: 1. single good-single store; 2. multiple goods-single store; 3. single good-multiple stores; and 4. multiple goods-multiple stores.

In the case of wholesale distributors the emphasis was placed upon those who deal with products of liberalized industries. Convertors and rack jobbers were excluded because their activities would presumably generate serious conflicts with the traditional methods of wholesale distribution in the country. As for retailing the 1969 liberalization covered only the category of specializing, single-store companies whose floor space did not exceed 500 square meters.

THIRD LIBERALIZATION

On May 18, 1970, the Japanese government asked the Foreign Investment Council to study and report on the third capital liberalization. The Council continued its deliberations through the summer of the same year, and released its report on August 17, 1970. On the basis of the Council's recommendations contained in the report the Japanese government put into effect the thrid liberalization as of September 1, 1970. The basic framework of the first as well as second liberalizations was retained. What the third liberalization did was to expand the coverage of Categories I and II. With respect to 42 industries already included in Category I the hitherto existing partial and conditional restrictions were removed. Similarly, greater coverage of liberalization was extended to 2 industries in Category II. Twenty-seven industries were shifted from Category I to Category II. The total of 323 industries was newly added to the list of industries officially classified as liberalized, of which 315 were to Category I and 8 to Category II. The third liberalization raised the numbers of industries included in Categories I and II to 447 and 77, respectively, making the grand total 524. In the area of portfolio investments the only notable change that was made as part of the third liberalization was to raise up to 25 percent the automatically approvable foreign-capital ratio for all foreign investors per enterprise in the category of unrestricted industries.

Among those newly added to Category II (100 percent liberalization) were newspaper, news service, private employment service, job training facilities, special public baths, playgrounds, and recreation centers. Some of the important additions to Category I (50 percent liberalization) in the nonmanufacturing area were ordinary banks (including savings banks), long-term trust banks, money exchange, securities service, securities investment trust, department stores, and supermarkets (single-store companies only). Despite mounting pressures from the United States, automobiles and electronic computers were not liberalized. However, the Foreign Investment Council recommended the liberalization of the former by the fall of 1971. Political pressure from the United States continued, and the automobile industry was placed in Category I in the spring of 1971, about a year earlier than originally scheduled by the Japanese government.

FOURTH LIBERALIZATION

The fourth round of capital liberalization took place on August 4, 1971. The measures called for liberalization of some 800 items, a large number of which were newly placed in Category I. However, seven industries such as oil refining, real estate, sales-distribution, agriculture-forestry-fishery, and electronic computers remained subject to case-by-case screening by the authorities. The Japanese government announced its plan to include the information-processing industry in Category I within three years. One hundred and fifty-one industries were added to Category II, raising the total number of industries in this category to 228.

The fourth round also increased the limit for automatic approval of portfolio investment by a single foreign investor from 7 percent to 10 percent of the outstanding stock of a company.

NOTES

1. MITI, Tainai Chokusetsu Toshi ni Kansuru Jittai Chosa [Survey of Problems concerning Direct Foreign Investments in Japan] (Tokyo: November 28, 1966).

2. Numerous books have been written about Japan's liberalization of capital movements. The list includes: Toshihiko Yoshino, Shinon no Jiyuka to Kinyu [Capital Liberalization and Finance] (Tokyo: Iwanami Shoten, 1969); Shin-ichiro Shimojo, ed., Shihon Jiyuka no Genjo to Tembo [Capital Liberalization: Present Condition Outlook] (Tokyo: Kinyu Zaisei Jijyo Kenkyu Kai, 1967); Masao Kamino, ed., Shihon Jiyuka to Kokusai Kyosoryoku [Capital Liberalization and International Competitive Strength] (Tokyo: Shiseido, 1968); Nihon Keizai Shimbun Sha, ed., Shihon Jiyuka to Nihon Keizai [Capital Liberalization and the Japanese Economy], Tokyo, 1967; Tetsuo Sugioka, ed., Shihon Jiyuka to Sangyo Saihensei [Capital Liberalization and Industrial Reorganization] (Tokyo: Tokuma Shoten, 1967); Hidezo Inaba and Tetsuo Sakane, eds., Shihon Jiyuka to Dokusen Kinshi Ho [Capital Liberalization and the Anti-Monopoly Law] (Tokyo: Shiseido, 1967); and Yuji Hirayama, Kokkyo no Nai Keizai [The Economy without National Borders] (Tokyo: Diamond Sha, 1967).

3. T. F. M. Adams and Noritake Kobayashi, The World of Japanese Business (Tokyo and Palo Alto: Kodansha International, 1969), pp. 230-231.

8

JAPANESE VIEWS
ON
FOREIGN
CAPITAL

EAST AND WEST

Contrary to the widely held impression in the West, it is not true that Japan has pursued a closed-door policy toward foreign capital throughout the postwar period. The need to receive capital from abroad as a supplement to the fund for internal development has always been recognized. One of the alleged intents of the Foreign Investment Law (1950) was to encourage induction of high-quality foreign capital that would contribute to the reconstruction and growth of the Japanese economy. However, Japan has been extra cautious about the manner in which foreign capital is brought into the country. Debt financing in the forms of loans and debentures has been given the top priority. Induction of advanced technology of the West has also been favored. But equity financing (particularly direct foreign investment) has been subjected to what looks to Westerners to be xenophobic (or more precisely, occident-phobic) restrictions and regulations.

Prior to the end of the 1950's the amount of direct foreign investment in Japan had been insignificantly small, not so much as a result of Japan's restrictive policy but rather because Japan, despite her impressive recovery from World War II, had not yet become an attractive enough market to the eyes of Western enterprises. Consequently, the particular policy posture of the Japanese government did not become an object of heated controversy in the arena of international politics. In later years the situation began to change. As the attractiveness of the Japanese market grew, so did the intensity of desire on the part of Western enterprises to penetrate one of the fastest expanding economies in the world. Their desire, however, was met by what seemed to be an irritatingly rigid and incomprehensively irrational attitude of the Japanese government. The rising frustration among Western enterprises in the early 1960's is illustrated by the following statement of the (American) Committee for Economic Development.

> There seems to be fear in some quarters in Japan that the increase of direct foreign investment would compromise the independence of Japan. This fear is groundless. On the contrary, it is the foreign investor who gives hostages and subjects himself to the control of the government of the country he enters. The assurance the foreign investor has of fair treatment—an assurance now inadequate in much of the world—comes not from the power of the investor or of his native country but from the host country's awareness of the benefits it derives from foreign investment.

> We regard Japan's hesitancy to permit entry of foreign enterprise in its economy as a major deficiency of Japanese foreign economic policy, and as a major obstacle to the full inclusion of Japan as a partner in the free world economic system. We recommend that Japan dismantle its barriers to equity investment in Japan by foreign firms, and that it permit foreign investors freedom to establish wholly owned and managed branches in Japan comparable to the freedom which Japanese investors enjoy in the United States.[1]

After Japan became a member of the OECD in the spring of 1964 the Western criticism of Japan's policy became increasingly open and direct. The OECD is said to be a club of the advanced nations, and each member is expected to behave like a mature nation. Each member is obliged to comply with its Code of Liberalisation of Capital Movements. However, Japan, after acquiring the coveted status, immediately moved to lodge an astounding number of reservations in the Code, and showed no sign of quickly removing barriers against the entry of foreign firms.

At the OECD conferences and elsewhere the Western countries began to register their complaints about Japan's policy toward direct foreign investment. Japan's rules and regulations were found to be too cumbersome, complicated and time-consuming to understand. Too much restriction, it was pointed out, was placed upon transfer of funds to and from branches of foreign firms situated in Japan. The

Western observers felt that the Japanese government was too inflexible about its preference of joint ventures based upon the principle of equal partnership, and intervened excessively with the affairs of Japanese private businesses. Japan fondly cited her balance-of-payments disequilibrium as a reason for the protectionism, but her external balance looked to be one of the soundest among the OECD countries. Japan seemed unable to understand that the alleged demerits of capital liberalization (e.g., major market disruptions caused by the flood of foreign capital) were more often than not based upon exceptional instances that had occured in Europe, and that foreign enterprises were mainly interested in profitability of their investments in Japan rather than "take over" or gaining managerial control of the Japanese firms. Apparently, Japan could not see that the "backward and vulnerable" sectors exist in any country and therefore their presence hardly constitute a legitimate argument against capital liberalization. In short, Japan was viewed as a misbehaving infant who, despite her adult status as a member of the OECD, needed a lot of growing up.

What were Japan's replies to these Western charges? At the official level and in direct dialogues with the West, her reply tended to be mild and restrained as indicated by the following statement of the Japan Committee for Economic Development.

In liberalizing the capital inflow from abroad, a few questions should be considered. First, there is a question of how liberalization should proceed and of its timing. Second, there is a question of preference of one form of capital inflow relative to another. Advanced countries seem to have provisions regulating outflow rather than inflow of capital and the movement of short-term rather than long-term capital. There is also an inevitable presentiment among Japanese businessmen that too rapid an enforcement of capital liberalization by the Japanese government might invite a certain amount of confusion in the Japanese economy and in the industries affected.

Though these questions will have to be answered in relation to particular situations, we firmly believe that Japan's liberalization of capital transactions should be effected and that the present regulatory arrangements should be simplified. It is strongly hoped that not only the government but also Japanese industrialists themselves will take appropriate measures to solve various problems arising in the process of removing the existing barriers to the movement of foreign capital in and out of Japan.[2]

Diplomatic statements aside, Japanese feel that there is much hypocrisy and self-righteousness in the Western accusation of Japan. They feel that the OECD has been discriminatory in that it has shown much leniency toward the older members, tolerating the infamous interest equalization tax of the United States as well as the special import taxes of Great Britain, while demanding a lot from Japan, a new entrant, irrespective of her internal problems. As late as 1967 France continued to maintain import quotas against 71 Japanese products. The numbers of Japanese products that continued to be discriminated against by other countries of Europe in the same year were: 104 by Italy; 19 by Western Germany; 28 by Benelux; 57 by Great Britain; and 11 by Denmark. These countries at first justified their import quotas on the grounds that low-priced Japanese goods, based upon Japanese "cheap labor," would be disruptive to their domestic markets. Later their justification was switched to Japan's refusal to fully liberalize her capital transactions. If the international, free movement of factors (of which capital is an example) is good because it results in a more efficient allocation of resources on a global scale, then the argument must apply to all the factors including labor. As Japanese point out, however, the same Western countries that criticize Japan's hesitancy to accelerate capital liberalization remain curiously silent on the virtue of liberalizing international movements of labor.[3]

The feeling among many Japanese about Western ethnocentrism is expressed in the following remarks by a Japanese economist.

If we examine the chronology and statistics with care, we note that Japan carried out her trade liberalization in about half the time which it took Western European countries. When allowance be made for per capita income differences and for the fact that Japan is an isolated economy in Asia without access to the benefits of regional integration such as the European Common Market, the speed of Japanese liberalization might be considered fastest in history. Did the world applaud Japan? No. Japan has been criticized instead that her liberalization has been too slow. Now the United States, Great Britain, France and Western Germany are attacking us concerning our capital liberalization. Their political pressure on Japan adds to our internal strain, and those Western countries in the role of critics are well aware of it. They should show more of the virtues of patience and tolerance. It might be added, however, that their vigorous protest and criticism are another way of expressing what an attractive market Japan has become to them.

A power organization called government anywhere
tends to be self-centered and self-righteous. The U.S.
government has introduced the interest equalization tax,
regulations over American bank loans to foreign firms,
etc. as means of slowing down the outflow of capital from
the United States; at the same time that same country has
been preaching to other countries that capital liberalization is the obligation of all modern states, and represents
the new spirit of international cooperation with which each
nation has to abide.[4]

Sometimes, even while writing to the Western audience, the
Japanese authors carry themselves to the point of mixing their caustic
remarks with a bit of chauvinism. Concerning the maze-like rules
and regulations and the mysterious, extra-legal ways of getting things
done in Japan that are all too perplexing to the Westerners, Noritake
Kobayashi wrote:

It is useless for the foreign investor to decry the (Japanese) system or to point out that this is not the way things
are done in his country. It is the way things are done in
Japan—and the only sensible solution for the foreigner who
wants to do business in Japan is to accept that fact and to
cope with the difficulties arising from it as best he can.
He really has no choice.

....

In Japan . . . the purpose of law is to express minimum protection of national interest. Whenever the force
of law diminishes, administrative action must increase.
The Westerner may find this system unsatisfactory (just
as the Japanese might find the Western way unsuitable),
but the fact remains that if the Westerner wants to do
business in Japan, he must do it the Japanese way. Only
after he accepts that fact will he be able to find practical
means of meeting the situation.[5]

Not all Western observers, of course, have indulged in ethnocentrism while evaluating the Japanese situation. The following,
seasoned analysis was offered by a private, American consulting
group.

The Japanese government has come under severe criticism
from both foreign governments and foreign businessmen

for the maze of obstacles which are put in the way of the
foreign investor as well as the importer to Japan. Obviously this is characteristic nationalism to some extent.
Not so obvious, but more important, is the fact that this
may be essential to the Japanese growth, at least for the
present. Japan, as an economy, is walking a tightrope.
It has a democratic form of government. This means that
it is subject to popular emotions and pressure for short
term consequences. It must be a trading nation because
it has virtually no raw materials. Therefore, it must
maintain price levels and foreign exchange flows which
are consistent with this while it is doubling its raw material requirement about every seven to ten years. It must
maintain internal price levels which keep internal consumption low enough to permit the massive capital formation required by the high growth rate.

All of this must be done in an external environment
which is politically very complex. The major potential
market is Red China. The major potential raw material
supplier is Russian Siberia. The major potential customer
is the U.S. All of these are vitally important; all are in
conflict with each other; all use their foreign business
activities as an arm of foreign policy.

It is not surprising that the Japanese government,
with full business support, feels that it must keep under
control every possible one of the interlocking factors
which affect their economy. It is not likely that this attitude will change in the foreseeable future. It seems obvious that Japan will give the fewest possible hostages to
a foreign government. It is also obvious that the Japanese government wants no undisciplinable foreigner to be
in a position to seriously upset this intricate balancing
act.[6]

FOREIGN CAPITAL PHOBIA

That there exists in the minds of many Japanese almost an
instinctive fear of foreign capital, and that this fear has been a not
insignificant, psychological factor in Japan's policy toward capital
liberalization, cannot be denied. As with any other phobia, the phobia
among Japanese of foreign capital may appear to be groundless and
irrational to outsiders, and yet it may have not so irrational origins

and even a logical basis. A Westerner would argue that direct foreign investments in Japan mean more employment, introduction of advanced management techniques, marketing of new and better products, and higher wages. A Japanese would reply that, while no one denies the positive consequences of foreign investments on the part of the capital-receiving country, to say that foreign capital brings no problems is an exercise in oversimplification.

Japan was a late starter in the global race of economic development. Ever since the Meiji period Japan's development has been essentially a process of catching up by borrowing foreign technology and, to a much less extent, foreign capital. But it is the Japanese themselves who have absorbed, digested, and applied them to their own cause. Now that Japan has become an enormous and rapidly growing market, the increasing number of Western enterprises has become interested in direct investments in Japan. The Japanese would argue that, inasmuch as the prime motive of those Western enterprises is profit-making in Japan, what they do may or may not be desirable from the standpoint of Japan's national interest.

It may be said that the history of Japan makes the said phobia of foreign capital almost inevitable. Japan, an island country located in a far corner of Asia, was isolated from the West for centuries. Her cultural homogeneity helped produce a strong sense of self-pride, independence, and respect for group loyalty. At the same time, her long-lasting isolation resulted in a profound ignorance and misconception on the part of Japanese about the Western world. It was no surprise that, when Japan's capital liberalization was formalized in 1967, the matter was fondly referred to in Japan as the second coming of the black ships—alluding to Commodore Perry's fleet of black warships that approached the shores of Japan in 1853.

The Meiji Restoration produced a varied and far-reaching set of reforms directed toward political, economic, and social modernization of the country. But those reforms were imposed from above. Much of the traditional Japanese mentality leaning toward authoritarianism and hierarchical cohesiveness remained unchanged.

After World War II a political democracy was introduced to Japan, but it was something artificially transplanted by the occupation forces. The Japanese economy has been characterized as one huge conglomerate or, as James Abbeglen puts it, Japan Incorporated. It is the economy where the government and (big) businesses form a formidable coalition, where what may be called enterprise nationalism or entrepreneurial nationalism flourishes, and where "national

interest" more often than not is business interest, and consumer
sovereignty and welfare have, to a large extent, been ignored. It is
the economic society where the consumers are conditioned to endure
if not suffer, for a higher cause, and where many people uncritically
believe that what is good for Japanese producers is necessarily good
for them, whereas what is good for foreign businesses in Japan is
likely to be bad to their welfare. Many Japanese would feel a strong
psychological resistence to the picture of Japanese corporations controlled and managed by the "blue-eyed" executives. This may be a
case of sheer provincialism, but it will be of interest to speculate
about the reverse situation, e.g., how an average Swede will feel if
Japanese enterprises move in and take over some of the key industries
in Sweden.

Hisao Kanamori has suggested that the influence of Marxism
might be one of the causes of the Japanese phobia of foreign capital.
In Japan about 50 percent of academic economists is either Marxist
or of Marxist orientation. Many articles in the leading influencial journals and magazines are written by leftist intellectuals. Consequently,
according to Kanamori, many Japanese who themselves are not Marx-
ists may unconsciously become conditioned to the Marxist terminology and mode of thinking, thus associating the word "foreign capital" with "exploitation," "monopolization" and the like.[7]

VARIATIONS ON THE THEME

In pure theory capital moves from country A to country B because the rate of return is higher in B than in A. The marginal productivity of capital becomes greater when it is invested in B instead
of A; thus the international movement of capital increases the total
output of the world economy. However, if the question is whether or
not the movement of capital from A to B is always in the (national)
interest of B, we are not sure of the definitive answer. Economists
have thus far not succeeded in developing a general theory of international capital movements that is capable of answering questions
of this sort.

In the case of international trade the theory of comparative advantages, after modifications and refinements since Ricardo, remains
to be the theoretical foundation for arguing in favor of free trade.
Even if two countries, A and B, are at different stages of economic
development wherein the absolute levels of productivity in producing
different goods in A are universally higher than those in B, the two
countries can still benefit from trading as each country exports those

goods in which its relative advantages lie and imports those goods whose production is relatively disadvantageous.

The same concept of comparative advantage may be applied to the case of international movements of capital between two countries both of which are sufficiently developed. For example, it does not require much hard thought to see the benefits of letting an Italian enterprise with its superior technical know-how in manufacturing typewriters move into Western Germany while this Italian direct investment is reciprocated by a German firm's producing precision machinery of a superb quality in Italy. Less clear is the case whereby capital moves from a developed to a developing country. Capital moves only in one direction—from the capital-rich to the capital-poor country. The foreign investment in this case becomes a unilateral act. There is much uncertainty as to whether or not the developing country can, always and unconditionally, derive benefits from activities of the enterprises that are controlled and managed by the foreign investors. Japan, like a huge sponge, has been absorbing Western technology, technical know-how and capital—but without letting the Western investors assume managerial control of the Japanese firms. It is not difficult to understand that the Japanese policy-makers have felt that the capital liberalization that included the liberalization of direct foreign investments in Japan presented to them a new set of qualitatively different problems.

The debates and discussions that preceded the 1967 liberalization tended to be ad hoc and without a solid theoretical foundation. One of the most popular approaches then taken might be termed the "merit-demerit argument." Many authors listed large numbers of presumed merits and demerits of liberalizing capital transactions. The liberalization was to be approved if the alleged merits sufficiently exceeded the demerits. Aside from the analytical validity of this sort of exercise in taxonomy, the following list of merits and demerits of capital liberalization that were debated at the meetings of the Foreign Investment Council in 1966 and 1967 provides a useful insight into Japanese thoughts on the matter.

Merits and Demerits of Capital Liberalization

Production, Distribution, Management

Merits:

1. It will help raise the level of technology in Japan.

2. It will encourage modernization of industries through greater competition, increase in the scale of production and introduction of advanced industries to Japan.

3. It will reduce the cost of capital.

4. It will encourage more modern, rational management.

5. It will improve the distribution system.

Demerits:

1. It will increase Japan's dependence upon foreign technology.

2. It may aggravate excessive competition, causing many Japanese firms to go bankrupt; the foreign enterprises may monopolize many sectors of the Japanese economy.

3. Japanese money market may come under too much influence of powerful foreign enterprises that are armed with enormous, financial resources.

4. Managerial control by foreign investors may become excessive.

5. Many Japanese firms may not be able to compete with foreign firms in Japan in terms of the capacity to finance sales.

6. Foreign enterprises may interfere too much with the interfirm harmony in Japan.

7. Foreign enterprises may disrupt the implementation of Japan's industrial policy.

Foreign trade

Merits:

1. Japanese exports will increase through greater productivity gains.

2. Japanese exports will increase through greater access to the global marketing system associated with the world enterprises.

3. It will encourage import substitution.

Demerits:

1. Some Japanese exports may be restricted at the mercy of foreign enterprises in Japan.

Labor and Consumer Welfare

Merits:

1. It will raise the level of employment.

2. It will raise wages and help rationalize the Japanese wage system.

3. The greater efficiency in production and distribution will have the anti-inflationary effects.

4. It will help rationalize labor-management relations in Japan.

5. New and better products will improve consumer welfare.

Demerits:

1. Frictional unemployment may increase.

2. The foreign enterprises in Japan may practice administered pricing.

3. There may be considerable social frictions.

Money Market

Merits:

1. It will help mitigate capital shortage in Japan.

2. A greater supply of capital will help raise the owned-capital ratio among Japanese corporations.

Demerits:

1. The conduct of foreign enterprises may conflict with Japan's monetary policy.

Economic Diplomacy

Merits:

1. It will induce closer economic cooperation between Japan
   and other countries.

2. It will provide a wider and stronger basis for Japan's overseas investments.[8]

Protectionism begins in the mind of man. In understanding
Japan's foreign-capital policy, it is helpful to turn to the minds of the
government officials who are responsible for the formulation of that
policy. In 1968 Naohiro Amaya of MITI expressed his view on the
concept of free competition in the following way.

> If the system of free competition is to work, a precondition
> must be met—and that precondition is that the firms prac-
> tice economic rationalism in their behavior. The merits
> of free competition will be realized provided that the firms
> do not indulge in a maddening scramble for greater market
> shares and refrain from violating the market rules. There-
> fore, it is problematical to insist that we should liberalize
> capital transactions now when we are aware that the rules
> of competition are not fully adhered to.
>
> How should we steer ourselves? In which direction
> should we move? If we liberalize the inflow of foreign
> capital as well as technology too fast now, it is probable
> that many Japanese firms will fall under the excessive in-
> fluence of foreign capital. . . . On the other hand, if the
> government initiates mergers and consolidations in Japa-
> nese industries as a defensive measure, this will likely
> generate the harm of monopoly in the near future. The
> best road we can take is the middle road. Like traffic con-
> trol we should regulate what otherwise will be a chaotic
> pattern of behavior of the firms. It does the nation more
> harm than good to introduce free competition when the
> structures of industry and finance provide only a less than
> satisfactory environment in which free competition can
> flourish. It is duly acknowledged, however, that the sys-
> tem of governmental regulations and administrative guid-
> ance is a device that is hard to design and harder yet to
> implement.[9]

Noahiro Amaya's candid disclosure of the following thought is not what one would expect to hear at international economic conferences.

Japan is a country that needs the free world as well as free trade. But MITI has often been criticized for its protectionist posture. The free world is one in which the stronger survives. For Japan to survive in the free world, her economy must be made strong first. That is why we have strategically operated under the free-enterprise system mixed with the tactically adopted protectionist policy. Universal and perpetual protectionism cannot obviously be expected. MITI's basic approach has been to gain time as long as the opponents are not too angry. Frustration of the United States, however, has of late been rising noticeably. We have reached a point where an early liberalization of capital transactions becomes mandatory.[10]

Shintaro Hayashi, another outspoken MITI official and theoretician, summarizes his views on capital liberalization in the following manner.

Capital liberalization means that Japan lets foreign corporations come into the Japanese market freely. In Japan there is a fairly large number of people who hold an optimistic view that there is nothing to worry about—on the grounds that her economy continues to grow at an accelerated rate, that the competitive position of the Japanese firms has substantially risen, and that there is still much vitality among Japanese producers.

The problem we face, unfortunately, is not so simple. Those Western firms—especially American firms—which are anticipated to come in have the backing of advanced technology and fantastically large, financial resources that constitute their formidable, overall competitive strength. The wages they have to pay in their home country are about 4 to 5 times as high as those in Japan. The weight of total personnel cost is very large, and much of that cost will be saved by operating in Japan. This will further improve their competitive strength. By coming to Japan the Western enterprises can combine their technology and capital with high-quality (but cheaper) labor in Japan, thus enhancing their position not only vis-à-vis their parent firms in the home country but also relative to the Japanese firms that have no access to foreign capital and technology.

The above is not the whole story. Technology and capital have far-reaching implications beyond whay they do as determinants of production cost. Technology is the engine of economic development. The long range prospect of economic development of a country largely, depends upon how much of technology in use originates in that country. To be sure, technology is mobile across national boundaries; hence short-term growth is possible with borrowed technology. However, the chronic and excessive dependence upon borrowed technology destroys the internal capacity to develop new technology and dims the hope for the nation's playing a leading role in global development. The world enterprise typically lets its parent corporation in the home country concentrate on the R and D efforts. If we allow world enterprises with this sort of behavioral pattern to come and operate in Japan as they please, we will likely suffer a critical slow down of technological progress on our own footing.[11]

The structure of Japanese society is said to be very different from those in the West—particularly with respect to labor-management relations and the wage-employment system. Elements of traditional society linger on even among the modern firms engaged in production of advanced products in Japan. Because of this difference many Japanese have opined that the uncontrolled entry of foreign enterprises will cause undue strain in Japanese society. The Japanese government's administrative guidance, even when it has little or no legal justification, is presumed to work effectively mainly because of the we-feeling (or the ethos of enterprise nationalism) that prevails among Japanese. There may exist much tension and attrition of all kinds within Japanese society; but the Japanese have been noted for their strong sense of unity and self-identity vis-à-vis the outside world. On the other hand, it is doubtful that in-coming Western enterprises will readily conform to the mores of the country. In the case of trade liberalization Japan is still left with the defensive weapon of adjustive changes in her tariff rates. It has been widely held in Japan, however, that the capital liberalization poses a much greater threat to the nation because the Anti-Monopoly Law and all other laws of the land are somehow assumed to be impotent and incapable of restraining the unwanted behavior of the monsterous foreign enterprises once they establish themselves on Japanese soil.[12]

The variations on the theme of foreign capital phobia evolve around the Japanese brand of nationalism which is a mixture of self-pride, self-confidence, and basic distrust of the West. It provides a certain frame of reference that inevitably involves preconceptions. The fact that the majority of so-called world enterprises actually consists of relatively small firms simply interested in profitable markets anywhere in the world is ignored. Instead the Western enterprises are conceived as giant corporations with magical power to engulf the Japanese economy which is now the third largest in the entire world. The bigness of Western firms is feared because it is believed that with bigness the overall competitive power of the firm increases, which includes everything from managerial efficiency to productivity, bargaining power, the capacity to raise capital, the ability to influence the governments, the R&D capability, the power to monopolize the market and so on. Attention is paid not to the fact that profitability of the firm is not correlated with its size but rather to the impressive statistics of total assets and outputs of the giant Western corporations.

It is feared that capital liberalization will invite a flood of foreign capital in the Japanese market, contrary to the verifiable fact that foreign enterprises not uncommonly raise capital in the host countries. Then one encounters a bewildering view that either way it is bad for Japan. It is often maintained that the in-coming American corporations have been heavily subsidized by the U.S. government in that their advanced technology originates in defense-related, federally financed research, and therefore their entry constitutes unfair competition to the Japanese firms. Those who argue along this line of thought do not consider the fact that the corporation tax rates in the United States are higher than in Japan, with much of the tax revenue going into financing the research projects of the federal government, and that something similar can be done in Japan through raising her corporate income tax rates and/or sizably reducing the presently tax-deductible expense accounts of astronomical magnitudes specifically for the purpose of expanding government-sponsored research in science and technology.

It is easy to attack the irrationality of Japanese nationalism solely from the standpoint of economic analysis. The fact remains, however, that economic gains are not the only gains that matter to a society, and human motives are frequently irrational. In pure economic theory a free flow of capital between nations is good for each national economy. But this statement fails to carry much weight in the country where the rate of economic growth has been fastest in the world despite (because of?) the protectionist policy toward foreign investments. Whether or not the particular foreign capital policy pursued by the Japanese government has been the best alternative in terms of its economic, social, and political implications is a value-oriented question that must be answered by the Japanese themselves.

NOTES

1. Committee for Economic Development, Japan in the Free World Economy (New York: 1963), pp. 51-52.

2. Ibid., Supplement Section, p. 37.

3. See Masao Kanno, "BIAC ni okeru Nippon no Shihon Jiyuka Rongi" [Controversies on Japan's Capital Liberalization at BIAC], Boeki to Kanzei (February, 1967), pp. 30-35; and Toshiro Ohishi, "Nichi-Bei Keizai no Shin Jidai" [New Era for the U.S.-Japan Economic Relations], Boeki Seisaku (September, 1969), p. 6.

4. Masao Kanno, "Seifu no Jiyuka to Minkan no Jiyuka" [Liberalization: Governmental versus Private Versions] Keizai Hyoron (November, 1965), p. 94.

5. T. F. M. Adams and Noritake Kobayashi, The World of Japanese Business (Tokyo and Palo Alto: Kodansha International, 1969), pp. 248 and 254.

6. The Boston Consulting Group, What Makes Japan Grow? (Boston: 1968), pp. 5-6.

7. Hisao Kanamori, Chikarazuyoi Taiyo: Nihon Keizai no Ko Seicho Ryoku [The Strong Sun: Growth Capacity of the Japanese Economy] (Tokyo: Diamond Sha, 1968), pp. 149-150. See also Shiro Osada, "Nihon no Jiyuka Seisaku" [Japan's Liberalization Policy], Keizai Seminar (August, 1968), pp. 12-16; and Noboru Kamakura and Kazuo Noda, "Kigyo Seicho no Mittsu no Jyoken" [Three Conditions for Growth of the Firm"], Chuo Koron (May, 1966), pp. 213-216.

8. Fujio Yoshida, Shihon Jiyuka to Gaishi Ho [Capital Liberalization and the Foreign Investment Law] (Tokyo: Zaisei Keizai Koho Sha, 1967), pp. 32-34.

9. Naohiro Amaya, "Jiyu Kyoso e no Kisogatame o" [Building a Foundation for Free Competition], Japan Economic Research Center Report (July 15, 1968), p. 35.

10. Naohiro Amaya, "Atarashii Sangyo to Sangyo Seisaku" New Industry and Industrial Policy], Japan Economic Research Center Report (September 1, 1969), p. 50.

11. Shintaro Hayashi, "Shihon Jiyuka to Keiki Chosei Saku" [Capital Liberalization and Counter-Cyclical Policy], Boeki to Kanzei (November, 1967), pp. 10-11. See also Shintaro Hayashi, "Shihon Jiyuka to Keizai Seisaku" [Capital Liberalization and Economic Policy], in Japan Economic Policy Association, ed., Shihon Jiyuka to Keizai Seisaku [Capital Liberalization and Economic Policy] (Tokyo: Keiso Shobo, 1969), pp. 1-11; and Yoshihiko Ryokaku, Sangyo Seisaku no Riron [Theory of Industrial Policy] (Tokyo: Nihon Keizai Shimbun Sha, 1966), pp. 124-136.

12. See, for example, Kiichi Miyazawa, "Shihon Jiyuka to Nihon no Taido" [Capital Liberalization and Japan's Attitude], Chuo Koron [Management Series](Spring, 1967), pp. 68-69.

Of all the existing arguments in favor of protection, the "infant industry" (or "young economy") argument is said to be the only one that meets the test of economic validity and is consistent with the dynamic interpretation of Ricardo's doctrine of comparative advantages. However, the contemporary economic literature tends to caution policy-makers of less developed countries that even this argument is subject to pitfalls and qualifications, and the costs of protection may far exceed the benefits of free competition. If the choice is between protection or competition, the conventional economic wisdom suggests that the latter is the better alternative.[1] This principle of dichotomy is seriously challenged by the experience of the Japanese economy.

The phenomenal growth of the Japanese economy during the postwar period has rested upon elements of both protectionism and competition. World War II and the postwar economic and social reforms (perhaps the most important of which was the Zaibatsu dissolution) destroyed the established order of business and industry. As a result, the market environments in all major sectors of the Japanese economy became significantly more competitive than during the prewar years. It was, however, not a case of the laissez-faire economy in the sense of Adam Smith, but rather was a carefully controlled and purposefully guided sort of competition. The system of control was taken for granted during the period of rehabilitation from the war; but even during the post-recovery period the Japanese government continued to practice its subtle art of regulating and guiding the activities of the private sectors. Through public loans, preferential tax treatments and the foreign exchange allocation system the government has heavily subsidized those industries whose growth was deemed

137

of strategic importance for Japan's future in light of the global trends
in modern industry and technology. Administrative guidance has
frequently been invoked to condition the behavior of the firms to suit
the government's objectives. The Anti-Monopoly Law was reformed
to pave the way for the rise of bigger firms. The exchange allocation
system was skillfully manipulated as an incentive measure to encourage
private investment in plant and equipment. The Bank of Japan used the
so-called low-interest-rate policy to keep the Japanese economy in a
state of excess demand for investment credit, while the vigorous,
deflationary policy was adopted whenever the overheating of the domestic economy caused an import surplus of undesired proportions. However, the occasional use of such deflationary policy did not result in
reversing the trend of accelerated growth.[2]

One arm of Japan's "industrial policy" was the import policy
whose logic and objectives were simple and straightforward. The
imports were to be carefully regulated in order to achieve the triple
objectives: 1. to maintain the balance-of-payments equilibrium;
2. to make available sufficient quantities of raw materials from
abroad to the Japanese industries, and to favor the import of investment goods at the expense of consumer goods and 3. to protect the
Japanese industries from foreign competition. Similarly, the foreign-
capital policy was aimed at protecting domestic firms (particularly
those which belonged to what the government regarded as strategic
industries) by postponing as long as politically feasible the liberalization of direct foreign investments.

In retrospect it looks as though Japan's industrial policy has
worked almost like magic. The Japanese economy has remained
highly competitive internally, which in turn has acted as a powerful
stimulant to growth. At the same time the economy has been sufficiently protected from the outside world so that the internal process
of moving onto higher stages of development has not been disturbed.
To conclude from this that the brilliant growth of the Japanese economy
is the result of industrial policy is to oversimplify the whole picture.
It is hard to believe that major industries such as automobiles,
electronics, computers, petrochemicals, synthetic textiles, and electrical machinery in Japan could have developed without protection in
the form of subsidies as well as barriers against the entry of foreign
goods and foreign enterprises. It is equally hard to believe that the
overall effectiveness of the industrial policy was possible without
the competence and superb professionalism of the Japanese bureaucracy
which draws in a large number of the top brains each year from among
Japanese university graduates.

And yet the proper mix of protection and competition would have failed without the sustained boom of the world economy during the postwar period. Without the external boom Japanese exports would have stood stagnant, and without sufficient exports Japan could not have imported enough materials to supply the expanding domestic industries. The policy mix of protection and competition managed to ride, as it were, the upward growth trend supported by the world boom. Internal stagnation would have killed the vigorous competition, and in the context of stagnation the protectionism, in all probability, would have yielded only negative results. Similarly, no matter how capable and dedicated the policy-makers might be, Japan's postwar growth is unthinkable in the absence of entrepreneurial nationalism, hard work and discipline of Japanese workers and the apparent willingness on the part of Japanese consumers to bear the costs of protection and to forego much of their present economic gains for the sake of the welfare of future generations of Japanese.

Thus we are led to a paradoxical conclusion that the Japanese economy has grown because of as well as in spite of the protectionism. The lesson to the developing countries is clear. While those countries can learn a great deal from the Japanese experiences, the mere fact of duplicating the particular protectionist policy pursued by Japan of and by itself would provide little assurance of positive results. In the case of Japan it has been a necessary but not a sufficient condition. In another context it may be neither necessary nor sufficient. Indeed, we cannot preclude the possibility of a disaster resulting from the premature and careless adoption of a protectionist policy.

NOTES

1. See, for example, Gerald M. Meier, The International Economics of Developments (New York: Harper and Row, 1968), p. 212; and Leland B. Yeager and David G. Tuerck, Trade Policy and the Price System (Scranton, Pennsylvania: International Textbook Company, 1966), pp. 227 and 230.

2. For a lucid discussion and appraisal of Japan's postwar industrial policy, see Takafuse Nakamura, "Sengo no Sangyo Seisaku" [Industrial Policy in Postwar Japan] in Hiroshi Niida and Akira Ono, eds., Nihon no Sangyo Soshiki [Industrial Organization in Japan] (Tokyo: Iwanami Shoten, 1969), pp. 303-315.

PART

III

**SOURCE
MATERIALS**

(Law No. 228, December 1, 1949)

---

*What is reproduced here is an English translation of Gaikoku
Kawase oyobi Gaikoku Boeki Kanri Ho as it stood in January, 1968.
The word "Ho" may be translated into "Act" or "Law," alternatively.
I have chosen the latter for ease of cross-references in this Source

CHAPTER I. GENERAL PROVISIONS

(Purpose)

Article 1. The purpose of this Law is to provide for the control of foreign exchange, foreign trade and other foreign transactions in order to assure, for the sake of rehabilitation and expansion of the national economy, the proper development of foreign trade, safeguarding of the balance of international payments, stability of the currency and the optimal use of foreign currency funds.

(Review)

Article 2. The provisions of this Law and orders issued thereunder to implement this Law shall be reviewed for the objective of gradually relaxing and eliminating the restrictions established by this Law or the orders issued thereunder as the need for those restrictions diminishes.

---

and elsewhere in the book. There have been many changes in the Law since its promulgation in 1949 though its tenor has remained the same. Many of these changes, relevant to our subject, are mentioned in the text. Those interested in details of the changes are referred to the following Amendments: Law No. 52, March 31, 1950; Law No. 56, March 30, 1951; Law No. 270, July 31, 1952; Law No. 299, August 5, 1952; Law No. 259, September 1, 1953; Law No. 67, April 10, 1954; Law No. 138, June 1, 1954; Law No. 140, August 6, 1955; Law No. 156, May 15, 1958; Law No. 140, May 16, 1962; Law No. 161, September 15, 1962; Law No. 33, March 31, 1964.

Article 3 and Article 4. [Omitted.]

(Scope of Application)

Article 5. This Law shall apply to acts performed outside Japan by representatives, agents and employees of legal persons having their head offices or main places of business in Japan provided that those acts pertain to the property or business of such legal persons. The same shall apply to acts performed outside Japan by persons residing in Japan, their representatives, and employees provided that those acts pertain to the property or business of such persons.

(Definitions)

Article 6. In order to make uniform the application of the Law and orders issued thereunder the following definitions shall be employed:

(1) "Japan" shall mean Honshu, Hokkaido, Shikoku, Kyushu, and adjacent islands thereof as stipulated by orders;

(2) "Foreign countries" shall mean territories outside Japan;

(3) "National currency" shall mean the currency whose unit of account is Japanese yen;

(4) "Foreign currency" shall mean any currency other than the national currency;

(5) "Residents" shall mean all natural persons who have their place of permanent residence or customarily live in Japan, and also legal persons having their place of business in Japan. Branches and offices in Japan of nonresidents are considered to be residents irrespective of whether or not they are jurisdictionally independent in Japan and even if their main place of business and headquarters are located abroad;

(6) "Nonresidents" shall mean persons, natural or legal, other than residents;

(7) "Means of payment" shall mean bank notes, Treasury notes, small paper money, coins, checks, bills of exchange, money orders, letters of credit, and other orders for payment;

(8) "Foreign means of payment" shall mean money in foreign currency and other means of payment which are expressed in foreign

currency or payable abroad irrespective of the currency in which they are expressed;

(9) "Domestic means of payment" shall mean any means of payment other than foreign means of payment;

(10) "Precious metals" shall mean gold, alloy of gold, gold coins withdrawn from circulation and all goods principally composed of gold;

(11) "Securities" shall mean bonds, stocks, certificates giving title to bonds or stocks, debentures, Treasury bills, mortgage bonds, profit certificates and similar documents as well as interest and dividend coupons, irrespective of whether or not they are registered;

(12) "Foreign securities" shall mean securities which are payable abroad or expressed in foreign currency;

(13) "Assets" shall mean time deposits, demand deposits, insurance policies and claims, balances in current account and claims on loans or bids, that are expressed in terms of money and are not embodied within the meaning of the preceding items of this Article;

(14) "Foreign assets" shall mean those assets which are payable abroad or expressed in foreign currency;

(15) "Goods" shall mean movable assets other than gold and other precious metals, means of payment, securities and certificates giving title to assets;

(16) "Property" shall mean property included under items (7), (10), (11), (13), (15) and any other property.

2   The Minister of Finance shall make a decision whenever the distinction between resident and nonresident is not clear.

(Rate of Exchange)

Article 7. There shall be a single rate of exchange of the national currency for all transactions, and the Minister of Finance shall determine the rate with approval of the Cabinet.

2   The orderly cross rates of exchange with foreign currencies shall be determined by the Minister of Finance.

3   The Minister of Finance may determine the buying and selling rates of exchange at which authorized foreign exchange transactions as well as commissions related thereto may be executed.

4   After the Minister of Finance has determined, in accordance with the provisions of the preceding three paragraphs, the basic rate, cross rates, and the buying and selling rates for foreign exchange transactions or commissions related thereto, no person may perform transactions at rates other than those determined by the said Minister.

(Designation of Currency)

Article 8. Transactions authorized under this Law may be effected only with currencies prescribed by the Minister of Finance.

(Emergency Suspension of Transactions)

Article 9. In the case of a sudden change in the international economic situation the competent Minister may, as provided for by Cabinet order, suspend transactions governed by the provisions of this Law for a period of time specified in Cabinet order.

2   The suspension under the provisions of the preceding paragraph shall not result in default of those payments which were already authorized under provisions of this Law, and the possible delay of those payments shall be limited to the extent of the suspension period specified in Cabinet order.

CHAPTER II. AUTHORIZED FOREIGN EXCHANGE BANKS AND MONEY CHANGERS

(Authorization of Foreign Exchange Business)

Article 10. Any bank which intends to perform foreign exchange business shall obtain authorization of the Minister of Finance concerning its designated offices where business shall be performed (including offices in foreign countries of banks which are legal persons established under Japanese law) as well as the scope of such business.

2   The Minister of Finance shall not give authorization under the preceding paragraph if he deems that the bank concerned will fail to entertain sufficient international trust or it does not have a sufficient staff capable of effectively performing foreign exchange transactions.

3   The bank which has obtained the authorization under paragraph 1 shall apply for approval of the Minister of Finance when it intends to establish new offices performing foreign exchange business, alter the name or location of such offices or alter the contents of foreign exchange business.

4   The bank which has obtained the authorization under paragraph 1 shall notify the Minister of Finance in advance when it intends to relinquish foreign business at all or any of the offices performing such business.

(Business Arrangements)

Article 11. The bank which has obtained authorization under paragraph 1 of the preceding Article or a foreign exchange bank authorized under the Foreign Exchange Bank Law (Law No. 67, 1954) shall apply for approval of the Minister of Finance before concluding arrangements to transact business under the provisions of this Law with banks or other financial institutions abroad.

(Duty of Confirmation by Authorized Foreign Exchange Banks)

Article 12. The authorized foreign exchange bank shall not, when it intends to perform transactions with clients concerning business under the provisions of this Law, perform such business until after it has confirmed that the clients concerned have obtained, or are not required to obtain, approval in accordance with the provisions of this Law.

Article 13. If the authorized foreign exchange bank has violated or attempted to violate the provisions of this Law, or any order or measure issued under this Law, the Minister of Finance may cancel the authorization under paragraph 1 of Article 10 or suspend the business conducted at that office which has committed such violation and/or restrict the scope of such business for a period not exceeding one year.

(Money Changers)

Article 14. Any person who intends to perform money exchange business shall obtain authorization of the Minister of Finance concerning the designated office where the business shall be performed as well as the scope of such business.

2   The provisions of paragraphs 3 and 4 of Article 10, Article 12 as well as the preceding Article shall apply to money changers authorized under the provisions of the preceding paragraph.

(Duty to Report)

Article 15. The authorized foreign exchange banks and money changers shall submit reports to the competent Minister as provided for by Cabinet order concerning business transacted under the provisions of this Law.

CHAPTER III. [OMITTED.]

Articles 16 through 20. [Omitted.]

CHAPTER IV. CONCENTRATION
OF FOREIGN EXCHANGE

(Concentration of Foreign Means of Payment)

Article 21. Any person in Japan may, as provided for by Cabinet order, be required to deposit or register the properties mentioned below at the specific place or by specific procedures, or to sell the same for national currency to the Foreign Exchange Fund Special Account, the Bank of Japan, authorized foreign exchange banks or other persons at the official price determined by the Minister of Finance or, if no official price exists, at the market price:

(1) Foreign means of payment situated in Japan,

(2) Precious metals situated in Japan.

Article 22. Any resident may, as provided for by Cabinet order, be required to deposit or register the properties mentioned below at the specific place or by specific procedures, or to sell the same for national currency to the Foreign Exchange Fund Special Account, the Bank of Japan, authorized foreign exchange banks or other persons at the official price determined by the Minister of Finance or, if no official price exists, at the market price:

(1) Foreign means of payment,

(2) Precious metals,

(3) Foreign assets,

(4) Foreign securities.

Article 23. Any nonresident may, as provided for by Cabinet order, be required to deposit or register the properties mentioned below at the specific place or by specific procedures:

(1) Domestic means of payment,

(2) Assets expressed in national currency,

(3) Securities expressed in national currency.

(Special Rules of Concentration)

Article 24. The Cabinet orders issued under the preceding three Articles shall determine the manner in which the rules prescribed in those Articles will apply to authorized foreign exchange banks and money changers.

Article 25. The provisions of Article 22 shall apply to non-Japanese residents only insofar as they pertain to those transactions of such non-Japanese residents which are governed by this Law and orders issued thereunder.

(Duty to Collect Assets)

Article 26. Any person who acquired assets claimable against non-residents shall collect the same without delay as they become due unless otherwise authorized by Cabinet order.

2   No person shall frustrate such claimable assets by discarding them in whole or in part, receiving less than the full value or conniving in delay of payment.

CHAPTER V. RESTRICTIONS AND PROHIBITIONS

Section I. Payments

(Restriction and Prohibition of Payment)

Article 27. Unless authorized under this Law or ordinances issued thereunder, no person in Japan shall:

(1) Make any payment to a foreign country;

(2) Make any payment to a nonresident or receive any payment from a nonresident;

(3) Make any payment to a resident on behalf of a nonresident or receive such payment;

(4) Place any sum to the credit of a nonresident or receive any sum for credit from a nonresident.

2   The provisions of items (2) through (4) of the preceding Article shall not apply:

(1) To a nonresident's payments in national currency to cover the cost of living or normal purchases of goods and services during such nonresident's stay in Japan;

(2) To a nonresident's payments made in national currency and in the course of such nonresident's business transactions in Japan which are authorized under this Law.

Article 28. Unless authorized under this Law or orders issued thereunder, no person in Japan and no resident abroad shall make any payment to or for another resident if such payment is associated with profits accruing to anyone abroad or with acquisition of property abroad.

Article 29. Unless authorized under this Law or orders issued thereunder, no person in Japan and no resident abroad shall receive any payment from or on behalf of another resident if such payment is associated with the transfer of ownership of property located abroad.

Section II. Assets

(Restriction and Prohibition concerning Claimable Assets)

Article 30. Unless authorized by Cabinet order, no person shall become a party to creation, modification, liquidation, settlement, direct or indirect transfer of the following items:

(1) Assets expressed in national currency and claimable between nonresidents;

(2) Foreign assets claimable between residents;

(3) Assets claimable between a resident and a nonresident.

Section III. Securities

(Securities Located in Japan)

Article 31. No person may sell, purchase, donate, exchange, lend, borrow, deposit, pledge or transfer in any way securities located in Japan or transfer any rights to such securities without being duly authorized or obtaining a license under provisions of Ministry of Finance ordinance.

2   The provisions of the preceding paragraph shall not apply to transactions of domestic securities between residents.

Article 32. No resident may sell, buy, donate, exchange, lend, borrow, deposit, pledge or transfer in any way securities located abroad or transfer any rights to such securities without being duly authorized or obtaining a license under the provisions of Ministry of Finance ordinance.

2   The provisions of the preceding paragraph shall apply to non-Japanese residents only insofar as they pertain to those securities transactions by such non-Japanese residents which are governed by the provisions of this Law and ordinances issued thereunder.

(Safekeeping of Securities)

Article 33. Unless licensed under the provisions of Ministry of Finance ordinance, no person may become a party to an arrangement of safekeeping securities except for safekeeping domestic securities for residents or safekeeping for nonresidents foreign securities located abroad.

(Issuance of Securities)

Article 34. Without being duly authorized or obtaining a license under the provisions of Ministry of Finance ordinance:

(1) No person may issue abroad securities payable in national currency;

(2) No resident may issue any securities abroad;

(3) No nonresident may issue foreign securities in Japan.

(Subscription to Securities)

Article 35. Without being duly authorized or obtaining a license under the provisions of Cabinet order:

(1) No resident shall subscribe to foreign securities;

(2) No nonresident shall subscribe to domestic securities.

Section IV. Real Estate

(Real Estate Located Abroad)

Article 36. Unless authorized under the provisions of Ministry of Finance ordinance, no resident shall acquire real estate located abroad or rights thereto.

Article 37. Unless authorized under the provisions of Ministry of Finance ordinance, no resident shall dispose of this real estate located abroad, or surrender all or any part of his right thereto.

(Real Estate Located in Japan)

Article 38. Unless authorized under the provisions of Cabinet order, no resident shall dispose of real estate located in Japan or any right thereto on behalf of a nonresident.

Article 39. Unless authorized under the provisions of Cabinet order, no nonresident shall acquire real estate located in Japan or rights thereto from another nonresident.

Article 40. Unless authorized under the provisions of Cabinet order, no nonresident shall dispose of real estate located in Japan, or surrender all or any part of his right thereto.

(Exceptions)

Article 41. The provisions of Articles 36 and 37 shall apply to non-Japanese residents only insofar as they pertain to real estate acquired in connection with those transactions which are governed by the provisions of this Law and ordinances issued thereunder.

Section V. Others

(Services)

Article 42. Unless authorized under the provisions of Cabinet order, no person shall engage in services involving payment, settlement or any other transactions governed by the provisions of this Law.

Article 43. Unless authorized under the provisions of Cabinet order, no resident shall render services to a nonresident without an adequate payment provided in accordance with this Law.

Article 44. Under the provisions of Cabinet order any person or resident as specified in the preceding two Articles may be required to obtain prior approval from, or present a certification of adequate payment to, the competent Minister.

(Export or Import of Means of Payment)

Article 45. Unless authorized under the provisions of Cabinet order, no person may export or import means of payment, precious metals, securities or documents embodying rights to claimable assets.

Article 46. The Cabinet order cited in the preceding Article shall prescribe the manner in which the provisions of the preceding Article shall apply to persons entering or leaving Japan.

CHAPTER VI.   FOREIGN TRADE

(Principles of Exports)

Article 47. Exports of goods from Japan shall be permitted with minimum restrictions thereon as long as those exports are consistent with the purpose of this Law.

(Approval of Exports)

Article 48. Any person desiring to export goods from Japan may be required to obtain approval of the Minister of International Trade and Industry concerning types and destinations of those exports and/or methods of transactions or payments as provided for by Cabinet order.

2   The restrictions specified in the preceding paragraph shall be within the limit of necessity for maintaining a balance-of-payments equilibrium, and promoting a sound development of international trade and national economy.

(Certification of Payments Method)

Article 49. Under the provisions of Cabinet order the Minister of International Trade and Industry may require from any person desiring to export goods an adequate certification of satisfactory payments method.

Article 50. (Deleted)

(Emergency Suspension of Shipment)

Article 51. The Minister of International Trade and Industry may, by ordinance, suspend the shipment of exports, or designate the articles and/or destinations of such exports for a period not exceeding one month when he deems it necessary as a matter of grave emergency.

(Approval of Imports)

Article 52. In order to ensure the sound development of international trade and national economy any person desiring to import goods may be required to obtain approval from the competent Minister as provided for by Cabinet order.

(Sanction)

Article 53. The Minister of International Trade and Industry may prohibit any exporter or importer, who has violated the provisions of this Law or ordinances and measures based thereon, from engaging in export or import transactions for a period not exceeding one year.

(Direction and Supervision over Customs Chief)

Article 54. The Minister of International Trade and Industry shall direct and supervise the customs chief regarding export and import of those goods which are under the said Minister's jurisdiction as provided for by Cabinet order.

2   Under the provisions of Cabinet order the Minister of International Trade and Industry may delegate to the customs chief a part of his authority based upon this Law.

(Presentation of Collateral)

Article 55. Under the provisions of Cabinet order any person desiring to import goods may be required to furnish deposit, securities or other forms of collateral in order to assure effectuation of the import concerned.

2   If the person who obtained an import license has failed to effectuate such import, the deposit, securities or other forms of collateral cited in the preceding paragraph may be forfeited to the national treasury in accordance with the provisions of Cabinet order.

CHAPTER VII. MOTION FOR COMPLAINT

(Hearing Procedures concerning Motion for Complaint)

Article 56. A competent Minister shall, upon receiving from any person an objection to or a request for investigation of the action taken under the provisions of this Law or ordinances issued thereunder, afford such person an opportunity of public hearing after a reasonable advance notice.

2   The notice shall state the time, place and issues involved.

3   At the hearing, opportunity shall be afforded the person raising objection or requesting investigation and all other interested persons to present evidence and arguments concerning the issues involved.

4   Matters concerning the hearing procedures in addition to those which are provided for in the preceding three paragraphs shall be prescribed by Cabinet order.

(Relation between Motion for Complaint and Lawsuit)

Article 57. The lawsuit for cancellation of the action as provided for in paragraph 1 of the preceding Article shall not be initiated until after a decision or ruling concerning the objection or request for investigation with respect to said action has been made.

Articles 58 through 64. (Deleted)

CHAPTER VII-II. THE FOREIGN EXCHANGE COUNCIL

(Establishment)

Article 64-2. In order to investigate and deliberate on important matters concerning control of foreign exchange, the Foreign Exchange Council shall be established as a subordinate organ of the Ministry of Finance.

(Organization and Operation)

Article 64-3. The Foreign Exchange Council shall consist of the Minister of Finance and not more than seven other members.

2   The Minister of Finance shall be the chairman of the Council and preside over the affairs of the Council.

3   The members of the Foreign Exchange Council shall be appointed by the Minister of Finance from among officials of concerned administrative agencies of the Government and experts outside the Government.

4   The term of office of the member of the Foreign Exchange Council shall be two years, and that of a member who fills a vacancy in the membership shall be the unexpired portion of that of his predecessor.

5   The member of the Foreign Exchange Council may be reappointed.

6   The member of the Foreign Exchange Council shall be in part-time service.

7   Necessary matters concerning the organization and operation of the Foreign Exchange Council other than those prescribed in the preceding six paragraphs shall be provided for by Cabinet order.

CHAPTER VIII. MISCELLANEOUS

(Power of the Fair Trade Commission)

Article 65. Nothing in the provisions of this Law shall be construed to repeal, modify or affect application of the Law concerning Prohibition of Private Monopoly and Preservation of Fair Trade (Law No. 54, 1947) or the power of the Fair Trade Commission with respect to actions taken by said Commission under any circumstances.

(Actions of Government Agencies)

Article 66. Those provisions of this Law or ordinances issued thereunder which stipulate that a license, approval or other measures of the competent Minister, the Bank of Japan or the authorized foreign exchange banks be required, shall not apply to a government agency which, in accordance with the provisions of Cabinet order, performs acts requiring a license, approval or other measures concerned.

Article 67. In addition to those reports which are stipulated under this Law, the competent Minister may require, as provided for by

Cabinet order, other reports from any person conducting those transactions which are governed by this Law or any other related persons whenever such reports are considered necessary in enforcing this Law.

(Spot Inspection)

Article 68. The competent Minister may permit appropriate officials to enter the places of business or offices of the authorized foreign exchange banks, money changers and others who engage in those transactions which are governed by this Law, and inspect books, documents and other articles or interrogate the persons concerned whenever such inspection and interrogation are considered necessary in enforcing this Law.

2   In conducting spot inspection in accordance with the provisions of the preceding paragraph, the official shall carry and present to the persons concerned a certificate of his identification.

3   The authority to conduct spot inspection or interrogation in accordance with the provisions of paragraph 1 shall not be construed as being approved for criminal investigation.

(Delegation of a Part of Official Business)

Article 69. As provided for by Cabinet order the competent Minister may delegate a part of his official business pertaining to the execution of this Law to the Bank of Japan or authorized foreign exchange banks.

2   When a part of official business is entrusted to the Bank of Japan in accordance with the provisions of the preceding paragraph, expenses for handling such business may be borne by the Bank of Japan.

3   Those employees of the Bank of Japan and authorized foreign exchange banks who perform business in accordance with the provisions of paragraph 1 shall be regarded as officials engaged in public service insofar as application of the Penal Code (Law No. 45, 1907) and penal provisions of other laws is concerned.

CHAPTER IX. PENALTY PROVISIONS

Article 70. Any person who comes under any one of the following items shall be liable to penal servitude not exceeding three years or to a fine not exceeding 300,000 yen, or to both, and if three times the value of the goods concerned exceeds 300,000 yen, the fine shall not exceed three times the value of such goods:

(1)   Any person who violated the provisions of Article 7, paragraph 4;

(2)   Any person who violated the provisions of Article 8;

(3)   Any person who engaged in foreign exchange transactions without obtaining a proper authorization under Article 10, paragraph 1;

(4)   Any person who violated the suspension or restriction under Article 13 (as well as under Article 14, paragraph 2);

(5)   Any person (excluding authorized foreign exchange banks) who engaged in money exchange business without obtaining a proper authorization under Article 14, paragraph 1;

(6)   Any person who violated the provisions of Article 26, paragraph 1 or 2;

(7)   Any person who violated the provisions of Article 27, paragraph 1;

(8)   Any person who violated the provisions of Article 28;

(9)   Any person who violated the provisions of Article 29;

(10) Any person who violated the provisions of Article 30;

(11) Any person who violated the provisions of Article 31;

(12) Any person who violated the provisions of Article 32, paragraph 1;

(13) Any person who violated the provisions of Article 36;

(14) Any person who violated the provisions of Article 37;

(15) Any person who violated the provisions of Article 38;

(16) Any person who violated the provisions of Article 39;

(17) Any person who violated the provisions of Article 40;

(18) Any person who violated the provisions of Article 45;

(19) Any person who violated the provisions of Article 51;

(20) Any person who violated the prohibition of export or import under the provisions of Article 53;

(21) Any person who violated the ordinances issued under the provisions of Articles 9, 21 through 23, 48 or 52.

Article 71. Any person who comes under any one of the following items shall be liable to penal servitude not exceeding one year or to a fine not exceeding 100,000 yen, or to both:

(1) Any person who established a new office performing foreign exchange business or money change business, altered the name or location of the office performing foreign exchange business or money change business, or altered the scope of foreign exchange business or money change business, without obtaining a license under Article 10, paragraph 3 or under the same paragraph to be applied mutatis mutandis in case of Article 14, paragraph 2;

(2) Any person who violated the provisions of Article 33;

(3) Any person who violated the provisions of Article 34;

(4) Any person who violated the provisions of Article 35;

(5) Any person who violated the provisions of Article 42;

(6) Any person who violated the provisions of Article 43;

(7) Any person who failed to obtain a prior approval in violation of the provisions prescribed by Cabinet order under Article 44.

Article 72. Any person who comes under any one of the following designations shall be liable to penal servitude less than six months or a fine not exceeding 50,000 yen:

(1) Any person who relinquished his foreign exchange business or money change business without making a report or with a false report under the provisions of Article 10, paragraph 4 or under the same paragraph to be applied mutatis mutandis in case of Article 14, paragraph 2;

(2) Any person who concluded an arrangement under Article 11 without obtaining a proper approval under the same Article;

(3) Any person who violated the provisions of Article 12 or the same Article to be applied mutatis mutandis in case of Article 14, paragraph 2;

(4) Any person who failed to make a report or made a false report under the provisions of Article 15;

(5) Any person who failed to present a certification or presented a false certification in violation of the provisions of ordinances issued under Article 44;

(6) Any person who failed to present a satisfactory certification or presented a false certification in violation of the provisions of ordinances issued under Article 49;

(7) Any person who failed to make a report or made a false report in violation of the provisions of ordinances issued under Article 67;

(8) Any person who refused, obstructed or evaded the inspection under Article 68;

(9) Any person who failed to respond or made a false response to the interrogation under Article 68.

Article 73. When a representative of a legal person, or an agent, employee or other worker engaged by a legal person or a natural person, violated the preceding three Articles in regard to the business or property of such legal or natural person, the legal person or the natural person concerned shall be liable to a fine specified in each Article in addition to the punishment of the offender.

SUPPLEMENTARY PROVISIONS

1   The effective date of this Law shall be prescribed for each Article by Cabinet order, provided that such date shall not be later than June 30, 1950.

2   Laws and ordinances stated below shall be repealed: The Foreign Exchange Control Law (Law No. 83, 1941); The Ordinance concerning the Restriction and Prohibition of Importing Bullion, Alloy of Gold,

Silver or Platinum (Imperial Ordinance No. 578, 1945); The Ordinance concerning Exceptional Measures for Penal Provisions of the Foreign Exchange Control Law (Imperial Ordinance No. 615, 1945); The Ordinar concerning Temporary Measures for Foreign Trade (Imperial Ordinanc No. 328, 1946); the Cabinet Order concerning Control of Exports and Imports of Properties and Commodities (Cabinet Order No. 199, 1949); the Cabinet Order concerning Temporary Measures for Foreign Exchange Banks (Cabinet Order No. 353, 1949).

[Other supplementary provisions have been omitted.]

THE LAW CONCERNING FOREIGN INVESTMENT

---

*What is reproduced here is an English translation of Gaishi ni Kansuru Horitsu, commonly known as "Gaishi Ho" or the "Foreign Investment Law," as it stood in January, 1968. Many changes in the Law have been made since its promulgation; but the tenor has remained the same. Those interested in details of the changes are referred to the following amendments: Cabinet Order No. 6, January 22, 1951;

CHAPTER I. GENERAL PROVISIONS

(Purpose)

Article 1. The purpose of this Law is to create a sound basis for
foreign investments in Japan, by limiting the induction of foreign
capital to that which will contribute to the self-support and sound
development of the Japanese economy as well as to the improvement
of the international balance of payments, by securing remittances
arising from foreign investments, and by providing for adequate protection of such investments.

(Basic Principle)

Article 2. Foreign investments in Japan shall be permitted as freely
as possible, and the system of validation pursuant to the provisions
of this Law shall be relaxed and eliminated gradually as the necessity
for such system diminishes.

(Definitions)

Article 3. In order to make uniform the application of this Law and
orders issued thereunder, the following definitions shall be employed.

(1) "Foreign investors" shall mean:

   a. "Nonresidents" (excluding juridical persons) as defined in
       Article 6, paragraph 1 of the Foreign Exchange and Foreign
       Trade Control Law (Law No. 228, 1949);

   b. Any juridical person established under foreign law, or having
       its seat or place of administration in foreign countries, ex-
       cept for those which were designated by the Minister of
       Finance;

   c. Any juridical person whose stock or proprietary interest is
       wholly owned, directly or indirectly, by a person or persons
       as specified in either item a. or b. above;

Law No. 127, April 3, 1951; Law No. 195, June 14, 1952; Law No. 223,
July 1, 1952; Law No. 270, July 31, 1952; Law No. 259, September 1,
1953; Law No. 67, April 10, 1954; Law No. 140, May 16, 1962; Law
No. 161, September 15, 1962; Law No. 33, March 31, 1964; Law No. 83,
June 14, 1966.

    d. Any juridical person which is de facto controlled by a person or persons as specified in either item a. or b. above;

    e. In addition to those which are specified in any one of the items a. through d., any person as mentioned in Article 2, paragraph 1 of the Cabinet Order concerning the Acquisition of Properties and/or Rights by Foreign Nationals (Cabinet Order No. 51, 1949).

(2) "Japan," "foreign countries," "national currency," "foreign currency," "residents," "foreign means of payment," "domestic means of payment" and "property" shall mean "Japan," "foreign countries," "national currency," "foreign currency," "residents," "foreign means of payment," "domestic means of payment" and "property" as defined in Article 6, paragraph 1 of the Foreign Exchange and Foreign Trade Control Law.

(3) "Technological assistance contracts" shall mean contracts concerning the transfer of rights relating to technologies such as industrial property rights, license agreement thereof, assistance of techniques for factory management and others designated by the competent Minister (hereafter referred to as "technological assistance").

(4) "Proprietary interest" shall mean the proprietary interest of member of a limited partnership, unlimited partnership or limited company, and other proprietary interests of juridical persons as provided for by Cabinet order.

(5) "Beneficiary certificate" shall mean the beneficiary certificate of the securities investment trust as mentioned in Article 2 of the Securities Investment Trust Law (Law No. 198, 1951) or of the loan trust as mentioned in Article 2 of the Loan Trust Law (Law No. 195, 1952).

(6) "Fruit" shall mean the dividend arising from stock or proprietary interest, the income arising from the trust relative to the beneficiary ownership represented by the beneficiary certificate of the securities investment trust such as is distributed in proportion to the number of the beneficiary ownership concerned, the income arising from the trust relative to the beneficiary ownership represented by the beneficiary certificate of the loan trust, the interest arising from debentures (exclusive of those which are floated abroad and the payment of which may be made abroad; hereafter the same), or the interest arising from the claimable loan assets.

(7) "Principal withdrawn" shall mean the proceeds arising from the sale of stock or proprietary interest, money delivered to the stockholder as a result of the redemption of the stock through profits in the case that the stock concerned is issued in accordance with the provisions of Article 222, paragraph 1 of the Commercial Code (Law No. 48, 1899) and has the statement of time of the redemption concerne (hereafter referred to as "redeemable stock"), the refundment of trust relative to the beneficiary ownership represented by the beneficiary certificate of the securities investment trust such as is distributed in proportion to the number of beneficiary ownership concerned, the refundment of trust relative to the beneficiary ownership represented by the beneficiary certificate of the loan trust, and the repayment of principal of debentures or claimable loan assets.

2   In case of doubt as to whether a juridical person comes under Item (1) c. or (1) d. above, the classification shall be determined by the Minister of Finance.

(Statement on External Assets and Liabilities, and Balance of Payments) Article 4. The Minister of Finance shall, as provided for by Cabinet order, prepare and maintain a statement concerning the external balance of payments, assets and liabilities.

2   The Minister of Finance shall periodically submit to the Cabinet the statement prescribed in the preceding paragraph.

3   The Minister of Finance may, as provided for by Cabinet order, request the Government agencies and others concerned to submit data necessary for drafting the statement prescribed in paragraph 1.

(Measures to be Taken When External Liabilities Become Excessive or When There is Danger of Default)

Article 5. In the event that the amount of external liabilities relative to external assets becomes excessive and there arises, as a consequence, a danger that the necessary payment to a foreign country (including payment through foreign means of payment, and hereafter the same) in connection with new foreign investment cannot be made, the Minister of Finance shall report the situation to the Cabinet.

2   In the event that the report mentioned in the preceding paragraph is made, the competent Minister shall not license, validate, approve or take any other administrative action to cause new obligations to foreign investors or new payment to a foreign country arising

from such new obligations, until the Cabinet decides the policy to be followed with regard to the said report.

3   In the event that the Cabinet has decided its policy based upon the report prescribed in paragraph 1, the competent Minister shall follow such policy while licensing, validating, approving or taking any other administrative action to cause new obligations to foreign investors or new payment to a foreign country arising from such new obligations.

4   The provisions of the preceding two paragraphs shall not be construed to impair the rights acquired by foreign investors on the bases of license, validation, approval and/or any other administrative action granted or taken by the competent Minister in accordance with the provisions of the existing laws and regulations.

Article 6. (Deleted)

(Announcement of Desired Technological Assistance)

Article 7. The Minister of Finance and the Minister of International Trade and Industry shall, in accordance with the Ministry of Finance ordinance and the Ministry of International Trade and Industry ordinance, make public a list of the kinds of desired technological assistance from foreign investors.

2   The Minister of Finance and the Minister of International Trade and Industry may revise from time to time the list made public in accordance with the provisions of the preceding paragraph.

(Standards of Validation and Designation)

Article 8. The competent Minister shall apply the following standards in validating contracts prescribed in this Law, and the priority shall be given to those which will most effectively contribute to an improvement of the international balance of payments:

(1) Directly or indirectly contributing to the development of important industries or public enterprises;

(2) Directly or indirectly contributing to improvement of the international balance of payments;

(3) Necessary for continuation, alteration and renewal of the existing technological assistance contracts in the important industries or public enterprises.

2   The competent Minister shall not validate those contracts prescribed in this Law which fall under any one of the following items:

(1) Contracts whose provisions are not fair, or are in violation of laws and regulations;

(2) Contracts whose conclusions, alterations or renewals are deemed to have been made in a manner not free of fraud, duress or undue influence;

(3) Contracts which are deemed to have an adverse effect upon recovery of the Japanese economy;

(4) Unless otherwise provided for by Cabinet order, in the event that the payment concerned for acquisition by a foreign investor of stock, proprietary interest, beneficiary certificate, debentures or claimable assets arising from loans is not made in any of the following manners—

a. Payment is made with domestic means of payment which have been legally converted from the foreign means of payment, or others equivalent in value to the foreign means of payment;

b. Payment is made with domestic means of payment which have been obtained by the foreign investor through his sale of stock, proprietary interest or beneficiary certificate (provided that the payment to a foreign country of the fruit or the principal withdrawn of such stock, proprietary interest or beneficiary certificate is deemed to have been authorized pursuant to the provisions of Article 15-(2), paragraph 1), exclusive of the domestic means obtained through such sale as was made one month or more earlier than the day of filing an application for validation of the acquisition concerned;

c. Payment is made, in connection with the stock or proprietary interest as mentioned in the preceding paragraph b., with domestic means of payment which have been obtained by the foreign investor as surplus assets distributed, as money paid to the stockholder or the member in case of amalgamation, as money delivered to the stockholder or the member in case of the stock (exclusive of the redeemable stock) or the proprietary interest being redeemed by profits, as money delivered to the stockholder or the member pursuant to the provisions of Article 379, paragraph 1 of the Commercial Code (inclusive of those cases wherein these provisions apply mutatis mutandis

for Article 379, paragraph 3 and Article 416, paragraph 3 of
the same Code, and Articles 58 and 63 of the Limited Company
Law of 1938), as money paid in return for the rights to the
allotment of new stock in case of the said rights being transferred to others in accordance with the provisions of Article
17-(2), as money paid in return for the transfer of rights to
the allotment of the new stocks in those cases wherein the
company has issued new stock through crediting of the revaluation reserves to the stated capital as prescribed in the provisions
of Article 109 of the Assets Revaluation Law (Law No. 110,
1950), or as money delivered to the stockholder due to request
as provided for by the provisions of Article 10 of the Law concerning Crediting Revaluation Reserves to the Stated Capital
(Law No. 143, 1951) and as others as provided for by Cabinet
order (hereafter referred to as surplus assets distributed),
these provisions excluding the case wherein the day of payment
of the said surplus assets distributed is one month or more
earlier than the day of filing an application for the acquisition
concerned;

d. Payment is made with domestic means of payment which have
been obtained by the foreign investor as the principal withdrawn
of the beneficiary certificate as provided for in b. above, exclusive
of the case wherein the day of payment of the said principal
withdrawn is one month or more earlier than the day of filing
an application for the acquisition concerned;

e. Payment is made with domestic means of payment which have
been obtained by the foreign investor through inheritance, bequest or amalgamation from another foreign investor and which
come under b., c., or d. above, provided that the "foreign investor" in b., c., or d. reads "another foreign investor as mentioned
in e.";

f. Payment is made with domestic means of payment which have
been withdrawn from the Foreign Investors Deposit Account by
the foreign investor for the purpose of the acquisition concerned
as provided for in Article 9-(2), paragraph 1 on or after the day
of validation of the acquisition concerned.

3   The provisions of the preceding two paragraphs shall be applied
mutatis mutandis in the event that the Minister of Finance designates
pursuant to the provisions of this Law, or that the Foreign Investment
Council expresses its opinions concerning license, validation, approval
or other administrative actions pursuant to the provisions of this Law.

(Statement concerning Remittance Stipulation)

Article 9. In the event that a foreign investor desires to receive compensation for technological assistance, fruit or principal withdrawn of debentures or claimable assets arising from loans in the form of payment to a foreign country, the said effect shall be so stated in the contracts concerning technological assistance, subscription to debentures, or loans.

2   In the event that a foreign investor desires to receive payment of fruit or principal withdrawn of stock, proprietary interest, beneficiary certificate or debentures in the form of payment to a foreign country, the said effect shall be so stated in the applications to the competent Minister for validation of acquisition of the said stock, proprietary interest, beneficiary certificate or debentures.

(Foreign Investors Deposit Account)

Article 9-(2). The Foreign Investors Deposit Account shall be a special deposit account, expressed in national currency, with the authorized foreign exchange banks (meaning the authorized foreign exchange banks as provided for in Article 11 of the Foreign Exchange and Foreign Trade Control Law; hereafter the same), and shall be established for the foreign investors.

2   A foreign investor may deposit in his Foreign Investors Deposit Account the following:

(1) Proceeds arising from the sale of stock or proprietary interest which has been legally owned by the foreign investor as provided for in Article 15-(2), paragraph 1, item (3)—exclusive of the proviso— provided that not more than three months have passed since the date of the sale concerned;

(2) Principal withdrawn of the beneficiary certificate which has been legally owned by the foreign investor as provided for in Article 15-(2), paragraph 1, item (4)—exclusive of the proviso—provided that not more than three months have passed since the date of withdrawal of the said principal;

(3) Surplus assets distributed to the foreign investor on the strength of the stock or proprietary interest which has been legally owned by the foreign investor concerned, provided that the payment to a foreign country of the principal withdrawn is deemed to have been authorized pursuant to the provisions of Article 15-(2), paragraph 1 and that not more than three months have passed since the date of the said payment;

(4) Proceeds arising from the sale of stock or proprietary interest, principal withdrawn of beneficiary certificate or surplus assets distributed, the confirmation of which was made on behalf of the foreign investor pursuant to the provisions of Article 13-(3) (hereafter referred to as "proceeds, etc." in this item), or proceeds, etc. arising from the claimable assets provided that not more than three months have passed since the date of confirmation of the acquisition by the foreign investor of the said claimable assets, or proceeds, etc. which have been legally deposited in the Foreign Investors Deposit Account by another foreign investor in the case where more than three months have passed since the date of confirmation of payment of proceeds, etc. arising from the claimable assets acquired by the foreign investor concerned (since the date of sale in case of the proceeds, etc. arising from the sale of stock or proprietary interest).

3   No one shall deposit, or accept a deposit of, any item other than those which may be deposited pursuant to the provisions of the preceding paragraphs in Article 9-(2) in the Foreign Investors Deposit Account.

4   Other than those which are specified in the preceding paragraphs in Article 9-(2), the necessary matters concerning the Foreign Investors Deposit Account, such as opening of a new account, depositing in or withdrawal from the account shall be provided for by Cabinet order.

CHAPTER II. VALIDATION OF FOREIGN INVESTMENT AND DESIGNATION OF FOREIGN CAPITAL INVESTED

(Validation of Technological Assistance Contracts)

Article 10. In the event that a foreign investor and the other party desire to conclude a technological assistance contract for a period of contract or payment in excess of one year (hereafter referred to as "Type A technological assistance contract"), or to renew the Type A technological assistance contract, or otherwise to alter the articles of the said contract, or in the event that they desire to renew a technological assistance contract other than Type A technological assistance contract (hereafter referred to as "Type B technological assistance contract"), or otherwise to alter the articles of the said contract with the result that the Type B technological assistance contract becomes a Type A technological assistance contract because of the said renewal or alteration of the articles of the contract, the validation of conclusion of such technological assistance contract or renewal or alteration of the articles of such contract shall, excluding those cases which are prescribed by Cabinet order, be obtained from the competent Minister as provided for by Ministerial ordinance.

(Validation of Acquisition of Stock or Proprietary Interest)

Article 11. A foreign investor desirous of acquiring stock or proprietary interest of a juridical person established under the Japanese laws and ordinances shall obtain validation of the acquisition concerned from the competent Minister as provided for by Ministerial ordinance.

2   The provisions of the preceding paragraph shall not apply to the following situations:

(1) Where a foreign investor acquires stock or proprietary interest through transfer from another foreign investor who has legally owned the said stock or proprietary interest;

(2) Where a foreign investor acquires stock or proprietary interest through inheritance or bequest;

(3) Where, in the case of a merger of juridical persons, a foreign investor who continues to be a juridical person after the said merger or who has become a juridical person as a result of the said merger acquires stock or proprietary interest of those juridical persons which performed the said merger;

(4) Where a foreign investor who legally owns stock or proprietary interest of a juridical person acquires, after the said juridical person performs a merger, new stock or proprietary interest of that juridical person which continues to exist after the said merger or which was established as a result of the said merger on the strength of his legal ownership of the said stock or proprietary interest before the said merger;

(5) Where a foreign investor who legally owns stock of a juridical person acquires new stock of the said juridical person allotted to the investor on the strength of his ownership of the said stock when the said juridical person issues the new stock through crediting of the reserve fund to its stated capital;

(6) Where a foreign investor who legally owns stock of a juridical person acquires new stock allotted to the investor on the strength of his ownership of the said stock when the said juridical person issues the new stock (excluding the new stock whose valuation is provided for in Article 4, paragraph 1 of the Law concerning Crediting

Revaluation Reserves to the Stated Capital) through crediting of the revaluation reserves to its stated capital;

(7) Where a foreign investor who legally owns outstanding stock acquires new stock issued through split or consolidation of the said outstanding stock;

(8) Where a foreign investor who legally owns outstanding stock acquires new stock distributed to the investor in place of dividends on the said outstanding stock;

(9) Where a foreign investor who has legally owned outstanding convertible stock or convertible debentures acquires new stock through conversion of the said convertible stock or debentures;

(10) Where a foreign investor restores stock or proprietary interest pursuant to the provisions of the Cabinet Order concerning Restoration of United Nations Shares (Cabinet Order No. 310, 1949), the German Property Custory Order (Cabinet Order No. 252, 1950) or the Cabinet Order concerning the Restoration of United Nations Property (Cabinet Order No. 6, 1951);

(11) Other cases which are provided for by Cabinet order.

3   The provisions of the preceding paragraphs in Article 11 shall not in any way affect restrictions pursuant to the provisions of the Foreign Exchange and Foreign Trade Control Law.

(Validation of Acquisition of Beneficiary Certificate)

Article 12.   A foreign investor desirous of acquiring beneficiary certificate shall obtain validation of the acquisition concerned from the Minister of Finance as provided for by Ministry of Finance ordinance.

2   The provisions of the preceding paragraph shall not apply to those cases which come under Article 11, paragraph 2, items (1) through (3), provided that "stock or proprietary interest" in the said items reads "beneficiary certificate," and to other cases which are prescribed by Cabinet order.

3   The provisions of the preceding paragraph shall not in any way affect the restrictions pursuant to the provisions of the Foreign Exchange and Foreign Trade Control Law.

(Validation of Acquisition of Debentures or Claimable Assets Arising from Loans)

Article 13. In the event that a foreign investor desires to acquire debentures of a juridical person established under the Japanese laws and orders or to acquire claimable assets arising from loans, validation of the acquisition thereof shall be obtained from the competent Minister in accordance with ordinance of the competent Ministry; the same shall not apply, however, in the case where the period from the day of acquisition of the said debentures or claimable assets arising from loans to the day of amortization of the principal thereof is not longer than one year and in other cases where the acquisition concerne is deemed to have been made for the purpose of settling short-term commercial transactions through application of the provisions of orders issued under the Foreign Exchange and Foreign Trade Control Law.

2   The provisions of the preceding paragraph shall not apply to those cases which come under Article 11, paragraph 2, item (1) through (3), provided that "stock or proprietary interest" in the said items reads "debentures or claimable assets arising from loans," and to other cases prescribed by Cabinet order.

3   The provisions of the proviso in paragraph 1 above and the preceding paragraph shall not in any way affect the restrictions pursuant to the provisions of the Foreign Exchange and Foreign Trade Control Law.

(Designation of Foreign Capital Invested)

Article 13-(2). In the event that a foreign investor desires to receive, by way of payment to a foreign country, the fruit or principal withdrawn of any of the below-mentioned stock, proprietary interest, beneficiary certificate, debentures or claimable assets arising from loans (hereafter referred to as "stock, etc." in this Article) and the day of payment (in the case where the acquisition concerned is through inheritance or bequest, the day when the foreign investor concerned came to know the commencement of the said inheritance or bequest; hereafter the same in the Article) is not earlier than the day of acquisition by the foreign investor concerned of the said stock, etc., designation of the said stock, etc. may be obtained through filing an application with the Minister of Finance in accordance with the Ministry of Finance in accordance with the Ministry of Finance ordinance within three months after the day of acquisition of the said stock, etc.:

(1) In those cases which come under Article 11, paragraph 2, item (1) (including the cases which hold if "stock or proprietary interest" in the said item reads "beneficiary certificate, debentures or claimable assets arising from loans"), the stock, etc. which have been acquired by the foreign investor concerned and the payment for which has been made as provided for in Article 8, paragraph 2, item (4), sub-items a. through f.—provided that in the above cases "one month or more earlier than the day of filing an application for the acquisition concerned" in Article 8, paragraph 2, item (4), sub-items b. through d. reads "three months or more earlier than the day of acquisition concerned," and "on or after the day of validation of the acquisition concerned" in the same paragraph, item (4), sub-item f. reads "less than one month earlier than the day of acquisition concerned";

(2) In those cases which come under Article 11, paragraph 2, items (1) through (3) (including the cases which hold if "stock or proprietary interest" in those items reads "beneficiary certificate, debentures or claimable assets arising from loans"), the stock, etc. which have been acquired by the foreign investor through transfer from another foreign investor (exclusive of the transfer the payment for which was made with domestic means of payment), inheritance, bequest or merger— provided that the payment to the said another foreign investor, inheritee, legator or the juridical person dissolved because of merger (including the persons who acquired the stock through inheritance, bequest or merger as provided for by Cabinet order) is deemed to have been authorized in accordance with the provisions of Article 15 or Article 15-(2), paragraph 1;

(3) In those cases which come under Article 11, paragraph 2, items (4) through (8), stock or proprietary interest which have been acquired by the foreign investor on the strength of his legal ownership of the outstanding stock or proprietary interest, provided that the payment to a foreign country of the fruit or principal withdrawn thereof is deemed to have been authorized in accordance with the provisions of Article 15-(2), paragraph 1;

(4) In those cases which come under Article 11, paragraph 2, item (9), the stock which has been acquired by the foreign investor through conversion of the convertible debentures or convertible stock legally owned by the said foreign investor, provided that the payment to a foreign country of the fruit or principal withdrawn is deemed to have been authorized in accordance with the provisions of Article 15 or Article 15-(2), paragraph 1;

(5) In those cases which come under Article 11, paragraph 2, item (10), the stock which has been restored by the foreign investor, provided that the payment was made with those means which are mentioned in Article 8, paragraph 2, item (4), sub-items a. through f. as a return for the restored stock or as its equivalent (the provisions of the latter part of item (1) above shall apply mutatis mutandis to these cases);

(6) The stock or proprietary interest which have been acquired by the foreign investor in those cases which come under Article 11, paragraph 2, item (11), and other stock, etc. as provided for by Cabinet order.

(Confirmation of Inheritance of Compensation for Technological Assistance)

Article 13-(3). In the event that a foreign investor has acquired from another foreign investor through inheritance, bequest or merger the compensation for technological assistance, fruit, principal withdrawn or surplus assets distributed of stock, proprietary interest, beneficiary certificate, debentures or claimable assets arising from loans (here-after referred to as "compensation, etc." in this Article) and that the payment to a foreign country of the said compensation, etc. or the principal withdrawn of the stock or the proprietary interest from which the said surplus assets distributed arose is deemed to have been authorized for the said another foreign investor, the foreign investor desirous of receiving payment of the said compensation, etc. by way of payment to a foreign country may obtain confirmation by the Minister of Finance through filing an application therefore in accordance with the Ministry of Finance ordinance within three months from the day of acquisition (in the case where the acquisition concerned was made through inheritance or bequest, from the day when the foreign investor came to know the commencement of the inheritance or bequest concerned) by the foreign investor concerned of the said compensation, etc., exclusive of those cases to which the provisions of the preceding Article apply.

(Conditions Attached to Validation, Designation or Confirmation)

Article 14. The competent Minister or the Minister of Finance may, while making decisions on validation, designation or confirmation pursuant to the provisions of this Law, stipulate additional conditions as deemed necessary.

2   In the event that a foreign investor who was granted validation, designation or confirmation as prescribed in this Law has filed an

application with the competent Minister or the Minister of Finance in accordance with the ordinance of the competent Ministry or the Ministry of Finance ordinance for alteration of the conditions as mentioned in the preceding paragraph, the competent Minister or the Minister of Finance may alter those conditions only if the competent Minister or the Minister of Finance finds compelling the reasons stated in the said application.

CHAPTER III. REMITTANCES ARISING FROM FOREIGN INVESTMENT

(Guarantee of Remittance of Compensation for Technological Assistance, Fruit or Principal Withdrawn of Debentures or Claimable Assets Arising from Loans)

Article 15. In the event that a foreign investor's desire to receive compensation for technological assistance, fruit or principal withdrawn of debentures or claimable assets arising from loans by way of payment to a foreign country is expressly stated in accordance with the provisions of Article 9 and validation thereof is granted by the competent Minister pursuant to the provisions of this Law, or in the event that a foreign investor desires to receive fruit or principal withdrawn of debentures or claimable assets arising from loans by way of payment to a foreign country and designation of the said debentures or claimable assets arising from loans is made by the Minister of Finance in accordance with the provisions of Article 13-(2), the payment of the said compensation (providing that the day of payment is not earlier than the day of validation if the validation concerned is granted on alteration of articles of the technological assistance contracts such as renewal of the contract), fruit or principal withdrawn (providing that the day of payment is not earlier than the day of acquisition by the foreign investor of the debentures or claimable assets, and that, if the acquisition was made through inheritance or bequest, the day of payment is not earlier than the day when the foreign investor came to know the commencement of the inheritance or bequest concerned) by way of payment to a foreign country shall be deemed to have been authorized to the foreign investor who has had the said validation granted or designation made pursuant to the provisions of Article 27 of the Foreign Exchange and Foreign Trade Control Law, subject to the conditions, if any, stipulated by the competent Minister or the Minister of Finance in accordance with the provisions of the preceding Article.

(Guarantee of Remittance of Fruit or Principal Withdrawn of
Stock, Proprietary Interest or Beneficiary Certificate)

Article 15-(2). In the event that the desire to receive fruit or principal
withdrawn of stock, proprietary interest or beneficiary certificate by
way of payment to a foreign country is expressly stated in accordance
with the provisions of Article 9 and validation thereof is granted by
the competent Minister pursuant to the provisions of this Law, or in
the event that a foreign investor desires to receive fruit or principal
withdrawn of stock, proprietary interest or beneficiary certificate by
way of payment to a foreign country and designation of the said stock,
proprietary interest or beneficiary certificate is made by the Minister
of Finance in accordance with the provisions of Article 13-(2), the
payment of those which are provided for in the below-mentioned items
(providing that the day of payment is not earlier than the day of
acquisition and that, in the case where the acquisition was made through
inheritance or bequest, the day of payment is not earlier than the day
when the foreign investor came to know the commencement of the
inheritance or bequest) shall be deemed to have been authorized to
the foreign investor who has had the said validation granted or designation made pursuant to the provisions of Article 27 of the Foreign Exchange and Foreign Trade Control Law, subject to the conditions, if
any, stipulated by the competent Minister or the Minister of Finance
in accordance with the provisions of Article 14:

(1) Fruit of the stock, proprietary interest or beneficiary certificate
concerned;

(2) Money delivered to the stockholder through redemption by profits of the stock concerned (inclusive only of the redeemable stock);

(3) Proceeds arising from such sale of the stock or proprietary
interest as was made after two years from the day of acquisition (in
the case where the said stock or proprietary interest was acquired
by the foreign investor through inheritance, bequest or merger, from
the day as provided for by Cabinet order) by the foreign investor of
the said stock or proprietary interest (in the case where the acquisition
concerned was of the stock or proprietary interest of a juridical person continuously existing after the merger or newly established through
the merger as provided for by Article 11, paragraph 2, item (4), the
stock or proprietary interest of the juridical person dissolved through
the merger, and in the case where the acquisition was of the stock
issued through split, consolidation or conversion of the outstanding
stock, the said outstanding stock before the split, consolidation or
conversion), including only those which have been deposited in the

Foreign Investors Deposit Account as provided for in Article 9-(2), paragraph 1 continuously from any day within three months after the day of the sale concerned providing that the said payment to a foreign country is to be made after three months from the day of the sale concerned;

(4) Principal withdrawn of the beneficiary certificate, inclusive of only those which have been deposited in the Foreign Investors Deposit Account as provided for in Article 9-(2), paragraph 1 continuously from any day within three months after the day of payment of the principal withdrawn concerned, in the case where the said payment to a foreign country is to be made after three months from the said day of payment of the principal withdrawn concerned.

2   The payment to a foreign country of those which are provided for in the below-mentioned items shall be deemed to have been authorized to the foreign investor as specified in each item pursuant to the provisions of Article 27 of the Foreign Exchange and Foreign Trade Control Law, subject to the conditions, if any, stipulated by the competent Minister or the Minister of Finance in accordance with the provisions of Article 14:

(1) Surplus assets distributed to a foreign investor on the strength of his ownership of stock or proprietary interest, provided that the payment to a foreign country of the principal withdrawn of the said stock or proprietary interest is deemed to have been authorized and that two years or more have passed since the day of acquisition by the foreign investor concerned of the said stock or proprietary interest, including only those which have been deposited in the Foreign Investors Deposit Account as provided for in Article 9-(2), paragraph 1 continuously from any day within three months after the day of payment of the said surplus assets distributed;

(2) Interest arising from the Foreign Investors Deposit Account which is held by a foreign investor as provided for in Article 9-(2), paragraph 1.

(Limitation on the Amount of Remittance of Principal Withdrawn of Remittance-Guaranteed Stock, Proprietary Interest or Beneficiary Certificate)

Article 15-(3). In the event that a foreign investor makes such payment to a foreign country of proceeds arising from sale of stock or proprietary interest as is deemed to have been authorized pursuant to the provisions of the preceding Article, paragraph 1 and that the total amount of the said proceeds exceeds, in each year starting from the day which comes two years after the acquisition by the foreign investor of the said stock or proprietary interest, 20 percent of the total number of shares or of total value of investment of the said stock or proprietary interest as of two years after the acquisition thereof by the foreign investor concerned, the provisions of the preceding Article, paragraph 1 shall not apply.

2 In the event that the amount of the principal withdrawn of the beneficiary certificate (providing that the payment to a foreign country of such principal withdrawn is deemed to have been authorized to a foreign investor pursuant to the provisions of the preceding Article, paragraph 1) paid to the foreign country exceeds, in each year starting from the day of payment of the said principal withdrawn, 20 percent of the total value of the said principal withdrawn, the provisions of the preceding Article, paragraph 1 shall not apply.

3 In the event that the amount of the surplus assets distributed arising from stock or proprietary interest acquired by a foreign investor (providing that the payment to a foreign country of such surplus assets distributed is deemed to have been authorized pursuant to the provisions of the preceding Article, paragraph 2) exceeds, in each year starting from the day which comes two years after the acquisition by the foreign investor concerned of the said surplus assets distributed, 20 percent of the total value of the said surplus assets distributed, the provisions of the preceding Article, paragraph 1 shall not apply.

4 The provisions of paragraph 1 shall apply separately to each group of proceeds arising from the sale of the stock issued by the same juridical person or the proprietary interest of members of the same juridical person; the provisions of the preceding paragraph shall apply separately to each group of surplus assets distributed of the stock issued by the same juridical person or the proprietary interest of members of the same juridical person.

(Guarantee of Remittance of Compensation for Confirmed Technological Assistance)

Article 16. In the event that a foreign investor has obtained a confirmation concerning compensation or claimable assets as provided for in Article 13-(3), the payment to a foreign country of the said compensation, compensation arising from the said claimable assets or interest arising from the said compensation deposited in the Foreign Investors Deposit Account as provided for in Article 9-(2) shall be deemed to have been authorized pursuant to the provisions of Article 27 of the

Foreign Exchange and Foreign Trade Control Law, subject to conditions, if any, stipulated by the Minister of Finance in accordance with the provisions of Article 14.

CHAPTER IV. PROTECTION OF FOREIGN CAPITAL

(Protection of Foreign Capital)

Article 17. In the event that the Government, local public offices or other duly authorized persons expropriate, pursuant to the procedures prescribed in a law other than the Foreign Exchange and Foreign Trade Control Law, the whole or a part of the property legally owned in Japan by a foreign investor, it shall be deemed that the payment to a foreign country of the amount corresponding to the compensation for the said expropriation receivable by the said foreign investor (such amount as is prescribed by Cabinet order in the event that the said foreign investor is other than those mentioned in Article 3, paragraph 1, items a. through c.) is approved in accordance with the provisions of Article 27 of the Foreign Exchange and Foreign Trade Control Law, subject to the condition that the said payment to the foreign country is effected within one year from the day of receiving the compensation concerned.

2   In the event that the whole or a part of the assets of a juridical person which has been de facto controlled by a foreign investor through his ownership of stock or proprietary interest is expropriated as prescribed in the preceding paragraph, treatment similar to those prescribed in the preceding paragraph shall be extended to the stock or proprietary interest concerned pursuant to the provisions of a separate law.

Article 17-(2). A foreign investor (excluding residents) may transfer to another person the preemptive right to new stocks which was given to the foreign investor on the basis of the stocks in his possession.

2   The transfer of the preemptive right to new stocks as provided for in the preceding paragraph shall not be valid with respect to third parties unless the preemptive right certificates or a written consent to the same effect have been issued by the company concerned.

CHAPTER V. ADJUSTMENT OF INVESTMENTS AND BUSINESS ACTIVITIES BY FOREIGN INVESTORS

(Reference to Cabinet)

Article 18. In requesting a Cabinet decision upon important matters concerning investments or business activities by foreign investors, the government agencies other than the Fair Trade Commission as defined in Article 3, paragraph 2 and Article 24 of the National Government Organization Law (Law No. 120, 1948) shall ask for the opinion of the Foreign Investment Council via the office of the Minister of Finance.

2   In those cases which are provided for in the preceding paragraph the Minister of Finance shall transmit the opinion of the Foreign Investment Council on the said matters to the Cabinet.

(Opinion of the Foreign Investment Council)

Article 18-(2). In granting the validation, designation or confirmation pursuant to the provisions of this Law, the Minister of Finance shall ask for the opinion of the Foreign Investment Council in advance, except for matters of minor importance.

2   In granting the validation pursuant to the provisions of this Law, the competent Minister shall respect the opinion of the Foreign Investment Council as prescribed in the preceding paragraph.

Article 18-(3). In licensing the payment to a foreign country of profits arising from legitimate business activities in Japan of the residents in accordance with other laws and orders, the Minister of Finance shall ask for the opinion of the Foreign Investment Council in advance, except for cases of minor importance.

Article 19. Excluding those cases which are provided for in the preceding paragraph, the government agencies shall ask in advance for the opinion of the Foreign Investment Council via the office of the Minister of Finance in proposing to license, validate, approve or take other administrative actions with respect to investments or business activities of foreign investors in accordance with the provisions of other laws and orders, except for minor cases.

2   Government agencies, in taking administrative actions as mentioned in the preceding paragraph, shall respect the opinion of the Foreign Investment Council.

CHAPTER V-II. THE FOREIGN
INVESTMENT COUNCIL

(Establishment)

Article 19-(2). For the purpose of research and deliberation on the important matters concerning foreign investments in Japan, the Foreign Investment Council shall be established as an organization attached to the Ministry of Finance.

(Organization and Operation)

Article 19-(3). The Foreign Investment Council shall consist of the Minister of Finance and nine or less other members.

2   The Minister of Finance shall direct the business of the Foreign Investment Council as chairman of the Council.

3   Members of the Foreign Investment Council shall be appointed by the Minister of Finance from among officials of the relevant administrative agencies of the Government or men of knowledge and experience.

4   The term of service of a member shall be two years; the term of service of a member who fills the vacancy shall be the unserved portion of the term left by the former member.

5   A member of the Foreign Investment Council may be re-elected.

6   Members of the Foreign Investment Council shall serve on a part-time basis.

7   Necessary matters concerning the organization and operation of the Foreign Investment Council other than those which are provided for in the preceding six paragraphs shall be provided for by Cabinet order.

CHAPTER VI. MISCELLANEOUS
PROVISIONS

(Hearing in the Procedure of Motion for Complaint)

Article 20. The competent Minister or the Minister of Finance shall, upon receiving an objection with respect to measures taken under the provisions of this Law, afford the person raising the objection an opportunity for hearing after a reasonable advance notice.

2   The notice mentioned in the preceding paragraph shall state time, place and issues involved.

3   At the hearing, opportunity shall be afforded the person raising the objection and all other interested persons to present evidence and argument concerning the issues involved.

4   In addition to those which are provided for in the preceding three paragraphs, the necessary matters concerning the procedure for hearing under paragraph 1 shall be prescribed by the Cabinet order.

(Relation betweeen Motion for Complaint and Lawsuit)

Article 21. The lawsuit for cancellation of the measures mentioned in paragraph 1 of the preceding Article shall not be initiated until after the decision concerning the said objection has been reached.

Article 22 and Article 23. (Deleted)

(Reports)

Article 24. A foreign investor or the other contracting party shall report to the competent Minister or the Minister of Finance in accordance with ordinance of the competent Ministry or the Ministry of Finance ordinance when, after having obtained validation as prescribed in the provisions of this Law, a technological assistance contract has been concluded, or alteration of the articles of the said contract has been made, or stock, proprietary interest, beneficiary certificate, debentures or claimable assets arising from loans have been acquired.

2   The competent Minister or the Minister of Finance may collect reports concerning the below-mentioned items whenever such collection is deemed necessary for ensuring the enforcement of this Law:

(1) Technological assistance contracts or alterations of the articles of such contracts which have been validated under the provisions of this Law;

(2) Stock, proprietary interest, beneficiary certificate, debentures or claimable assets arising from loans which have been acquired on the basis of validation under the provisions of this Law;

(3) (Deleted);

(4) Stock, proprietary interest, beneficiary certificate, debentures or claimable assets arising from loans which have been designated under the provisions of this Law;

(5) Those compensations and claimable assets which are mentioned in Article 13-(3) and which have been confirmed under the provisions of this Law;

(6) Fulfilment of conditions stipulated pursuant to the provisions of this Law;

(7) Foreign Investors Deposit Account established under the provisions of this Law.

(Power of the Fair Trade Commission)

Article 25. The provisions of this Law or the powers of the competent Minister or the Minister of Finance pursuant to the provisions of this Law shall not be construed to modify the provisions of the Law concerning Prohibition of Private Monopoly and Methods of Preserving Fair Trade (Law No. 54, 1947) or the powers of the Fair Trade Commission.

(Partial Entrusting of Business)

Article 25-(2). The competent Minister or the Minister of Finance may, as provided for by Cabinet order, entrust the Bank of Japan or authorized foreign exchange banks to carry out a part of business concerning the enforcement of this Law.

2   In the event that the Bank of Japan carries out a part of business in accordance with the provisions of the preceding paragraph, the expenses necessary for the task shall be borne by the Bank of Japan.

3   The members of the Bank of Japan and authorized foreign exchange banks who carry out a part of business as provided for in paragraph 1 shall be regarded as officials engaged in public service insofar as the application of the Penal Code (Law No. 45, 1907) and penal provisions of other laws is concerned.

(Competent Minister and Ordinance of the Competent Ministry)

Article 25-(3). The competent Minister and ordinance of the competent Ministry as stipulated in this Law shall be provided for by Cabinet order.

Article 26. Any person who comes under any one of the following items shall be liable to penal servitude not exceeding three years or to a fine not exceeding 300,000 yen, or to both:

(1) Any person who has violated the provisions of Article 9-(2), paragraph 3;

(2) Any person who has violated the provisions of Article 10;

(3) Any person who has violated the provisions of Article 11;

(4) Any person who has violated the provisions of Article 12, paragraph 1;

(5) Any person who has violated the provisions of Article 13, paragraph 1.

Article 27. Any person who has filed a false report in those cases which are provided for by Article 13-(3) shall be liable to penal servitude not exceeding one year or to a fine not exceeding 100,000 yen, or to both.

Article 28. Any person who has failed to make a report or has made a false report in those cases which are provided for by Article 24, paragraph 1 or paragraph 2 shall be liable to penal servitude not exceeding six months or to a fine not exceeding 50,000 yen.

Article 29. When a representative of a juridical person (including those organizations which are defined in Article 3, paragraph 1, item (1), and similarly in the rest of this paragraph), an agent, employee or any other worker engaged by a juridical person or a natural person has committed acts of contravening the preceding three Articles in regard to the business or property of the said juridical person or natural person, such juridical person or natural person shall be liable to a fine specified in each Article in addition to the punishment of the direct offender except for those cases in which it is proved that sufficient care and supervision had been exercised over the said business or property in order to prevent the said contraventions.

2   In the event that a juridical person as specified in Article 3 is to be punished, its representative or supervisor shall represent the said juridical person in the court actions concerned, and the provisions of the laws concerning criminal prosecution of an accused or suspected juridical person shall apply mutatis mutandis.

SUPPLEMENTARY
PROVISIONS

1   The effective date of this Law shall be prescribed by Cabinet order, provided that such date shall not be later than 30 days from the date of promulgation.

[Other provisions have been omitted.]

THE MASTER PLAN FOR LIBERALIZATION OF FOREIGN TRADE AND EXCHANGE*

I   Our Basic Policy Position

The fundamental objective of liberalization of foreign trade and exchange, as is manifested by the charters of GATT as well as IMF, is to achieve an expansion of the world economy through a closer economic intercourse among individual nations. The liberalization has become a mainstream in the present-day world, and our country faces an urgent task of positively participating in this global movement.

The high population density and paucity of natural resources in our country make it imperative that Japan maintain a close economic relationship with the rest of the world. Promotion of liberalization is therefore vital not only as a matter of necessity dictated by the contemporary global trend but also from the standpoint of our own survival and well-being.

After the war we have practiced trade and exchange control in order to carry out the task of reconstruction and recovery from the war and cope with persisting balance-of-payments difficulties. With a favorable turn of external balance in recent years the control has been gradually relaxed. The Japanese economy has demonstrated an

---

*The original text is <u>Boeki Kawase Jiyuka Keikaku Taiko</u>. The Plan was approved by the Cabinet Conference for Promotion of Liberalization of Foreign Trade and Exchange on June 24, 1960.

extraordinarily high rate of growth with domestic price stability, and the trend of rapid growth shows little sign of tapering off. It is our judgment that we are capable of undertaking a further liberalization of trade and exchange.

Relaxation and removal of the trade and exchange restrictions are bound to bring about fruitful results as business firms are persuaded to rely more on the principle of economic rationality and cultivate a deeper sense of creativity and self-responsibility. The liberalization eliminates inefficiency and irrationality associated with the control system, enables firms to import raw materials at lower costs which in turn leads to a reduction in the overall cost of industrial production, and requires Japanese enterprises to strive constantly toward productivity gains. In short, the liberalization will contribute to a rise in the standard of living of our citizens and promote the economic welfare of the nation through a more efficient utilization of resources.

Before actually commencing the liberalization, however, our first task is to make a careful study of the probable effects of liberalization upon the Japanese economy during the period of transition after so many years of operating under a closed system. Furthermore, it is necessary for us to pay due attention to those problems which are unique to Japan: namely, prevalence of miniature units of production in agriculture and fishery together with numerous small firms throughout other sectors of the economy; the weaknesses on the part of many Japanese enterprises in management and technology; the absence of a major, stable regional market (such as the European Common Market) of which Japan is an integral part; and the continuing use of discriminatory import restrictions by many other countries against Japanese products.

We deem it advisable to implement the liberalization methodically and in steps while taking adequate measures relative to the particular problems that exist in the Japanese context. The liberalization is a significant approach to the building of a foundation upon which a further development and growth of the Japanese economy is to take place in the future. With a full awareness of the merits of a freer and more open economy we are resolved to move forward vigorously in pursuing the liberalization policy.

II   Direction of Economic Policies Accompanying the Liberalization

The central objective of economic policy has been to promote a sustained and stable economic growth by solving structural problems and improving the properties of the Japanese economy. The objective is only to be reemphasized in the coming age of liberalization. As regards policy actions more directly related with the liberalization there is a need for tariff reforms and proper measures to prevent market disruptions induced by the trade liberalization. Besides a series of measures for the immediate future, we must also formulate long-run economic policies that will affect the future growth and structural changes of the Japanese economy. Presented below are our guidelines for establishing those long-run policies.

(1) We must achieve a sustained, rapid economic growth, together with economic stability.

The liberalization of trade and exchange raises the degree of inter-relatedness between the Japanese economy and the rest of the world. Changes in domestic prices and internal conditions of supply and demand will quickly induce reflecting changes in Japanese exports and imports. Government policy will be required to focus more than in the past on maintaining the external and internal equilibria of the Japanese economy. Strengthening of both monetary and fiscal measures are essential for the purpose of defending the value of yen and achieving domestic economic stability. At the same time, remembering that expansion of the employment opportunities and national income through a sustained economic growth is our fundamental policy goal, we must continue to carry out a series of measures directed toward increase in exports and investment in plant and equipment.

(2) We must strive to expand employment and increase labor mobility.

The problem of employment is expected to be dissolved over the long run by continual economic growth itself. However, the extensive layers of underemployment still persist in Japan, and we need to pay particular attention to frictional unemployment brought about by the liberalization during the period of transition. In addition to our endeavor to sustain the accelerated economic growth, it is advisable for us to intensify our efforts in the problem areas to increase labor mobility, improve vocational retraining and make available maximum information on new employment opportunities.

(3) We must expand exports and promote international economic cooperation.

Japanese imports are anticipated to increase noticeably as an initial consequence of the liberalization. However, a rise in the

overall productivity of Japanese industry following the removal of
trade and exchange restrictions is expected to induce an even greater
increase in Japanese exports. In light of the international economic
circumstances surrounding our country, we must proceed with caution
to achieve an orderly expansion of our exports by critically analyzing
the problems of overseas markets and promoting economic cooperation
with other nations while not neglecting to urge removal of discriminatory import restrictions practiced by many countries against Japanese
goods. The liberalization will affect many Japanese industries that
are to varying degrees dependent upon trade with developing countries.
It is necessary for us to examine with care the prospects of increasing
our imports of products of those developing countries since such
imports will have an important bearing upon our own future exports
to those countries. From the standpoint of achieving a more effective
use of our resources through closer economic intercourse with the
developing countries, we should intensify our efforts to render more
technical assistance and other forms of economic cooperation which
will contribute to industrial development of those countries.

(4)   We must promote the advancement of Japanese industry by
      taking advantage of the positive aspects of the liberalization.

Development of heavy and chemical industries has long been
recognized as an important path to the long-range expansion of the
Japanese economy. The development of these industries in Japan
has already gone far, and it is unlikely that the trend will be altered
by the impact of liberalization. Nevertheless, we need to pay attention
to the fact that many areas within these industries still show backwardness relative to standards in the Western countries in terms of technology, market development, and the capacity for mass production.

Our future policy concerning heavy and chemical industries
must be directed toward adjusting the structures of these industries
for an increasingly multilateral pattern of international specialization
and future shifts in the commodity composition of world trade. Effective policy measures should be adopted for those sectors whose advancement is believed essential to the future growth of the Japanese
economy.

In connection with the development of heavy and chemical industries, we must likewise strive to achieve a more efficient allocation
and use of resources for these industries. This involves a liberalization plan which encourages more active imports of raw materials
than in the past and which attempts to expand, if and where it is
deemed rational, the indigenous supply of raw materials through

modernization of production facilities and the management system on the part of the domestic suppliers.

The need for continual development and improvement of industrial technology for a further advancement of Japanese industry at large is self-evident. We must take sufficient policy measures to encourage an active induction of superior foreign technology and to promote our own research and development programs that emphasize an effective and fruitful application of the results of research in pure science and technology.

(5)   We must improve the properties of agriculture and forestry, and modernize small businesses.

With respect to agriculture, fishery, forestry, and small businesses which represent major structural problems of the Japanese economy, we should continue to pursue the same policy as in the past while attempting to alleviate adverse effects of the liberalization upon these sectors.

Relative to the international standards, many elements of backwardness are still found in Japanese agriculture, fishery, and forestry: e.g., the unit of production is typically very small; productivity is low; and the low level of income is combined with an overcrowded labor market. Consequently, these sectors are not as yet ready for a full-scale liberalization—particularly with respect to important agricultural commodities and the products of the coastal fishing industry. It goes without saying that advancement of these sectors must be accelerated in response to the rising expectation of the global trend of liberalization. All necessary and available policy measures ought to be undertaken in order to promote research in experimental science in agriculture and fishery, increase productivity through expansion of the scale of production, encourage more livestock and fruits production, develop advanced processing industries associated with these sectors, improve the mechanism of distribution and marketing, and promote activities of producer cooperatives.

Inasmuch as the characteristics and industry-affiliations of small businesses are diverse, the consequences of liberalization upon small businesses are also expected to differ considerably among different industries. We should intensify our efforts to improve the competitive position and export capacity of small businesses, especially those among the liberalized industries, through new equipment investment, technological development, modernization of the management system, and a better finance catering to small-size enterprises.

(6) We must adjust the business environment to improve the performance of enterprises.

The liberalization exposes Japanese firms to a keener degree of competition on an international scale. Increase in the owned-capital ratio and other improvements are necessary to strengthen the foundation upon which Japanese managements can operate. Side by side with endeavors on the part of business firms themselves to establish a more rational management system and restructure their capital composition, we should adopt a new corporation tax system to raise the weight of owned capital in Japanese corporations along with an appropriate system of depreciation allowances in accord with the structural shifts of Japanese industry as a means of stimulating technological innovations and augmenting internal corporate funds.

We should take effective policy actions to assume a steady supply of capital fulfilling the rising demand for industrial funds in Japan in conjunction with the expected inflow of foreign capital following the future relaxation of restrictions over capital transactions. As regards interest rates we should strive to revive their original function, i.e., serving as a medium of balancing supply of and demand for investment funds in the nation's money market. The inflow of foreign capital in the future is expected to help lower the general level of interest rates which has been considerably higher in Japan than those in the Western countries. It is hoped that financial institutions will make their own efforts to lower the rates through increasing efficiency of their operation and allocating funds in a more rational scheme. This will contribute to the reduction of the interest-cost burden on Japanese corporations. At the same time it is desirable for Japanese firms to become less dependent upon the method of external financing than has been the common practice in the past.

(7) We must adjust and maintain industrial order.

Free competition among firms is to be intensified as a result of the liberalization. In view of the present position of many Japanese firms relative to world enterprises, it is necessary for us to take sufficient safeguard measures to avoid the adverse effects of the liberalization. In order to prevent a spread of disruptively excessive competition and assure an orderly adjustment of Japanese industry to the impact of the liberalization, we must strive to promote cooperative endeavors among Japanese enterprises, establish more specialized lines of production together with enlargement of the scales of operation, prevent overinvestments in plant and equipment, and encourage more rational acquisition of foreign or domestic supplies of industrial raw materials.

(8)   We must reform our tariff system.

With relaxation of direct, quantitative control over imports, the relative importance of tariffs as an instrument of industrial policy increases. The present tariff system is not only inconsistent with the structure of Japanese industry today but also inadequate from the standpoint of an effective implementation of the liberalization policy.

Tariff rates on many individual commodities are in need of change and adjustment before liberalization of their imports takes effect. In addition to the general overhaul and restructuring of the rates, we must promptly provide for adequate measures to protect Japanese firms from the shock of wild price fluctuations or a sudden, major influx of foreign goods that may occur after the liberalization.

III   The Liberalization Plan by Commodities

1   Policy Direction

(1) In implementing the commodity-wide liberalization we shall divide commodities into the following four groups. The plan must be carried out with flexibility in response to the changing circumstances, both domestic and international.

(a) Those commodities whose imports should be liberalized as soon as possible.

(b) Those commodities whose imports should be liberalized in the near future, i.e., within the time limit of approximately three years.

(c) Those commodities whose imports should not be liberalized in the near future but whose liberalization should be effected as soon as feasible after approximately three years from now.

(d) Those commodities whose imports should not be liberalized for a long time.

(2) In deciding the order and methods of implementing the commodity-wide liberalization plan, the following points should be carefully taken into consideration.

(a) First priority should be given to liberalization of imports of raw materials inasmuch as one of the prime aims of the liberalization is to reduce the overall cost of industrial production through free imports of resources at the lowest possible prices.

(b) We should liberalize those commodities whose substitutability by imports is nil or very weak and those which can effectively compete against imports. Next in line are those goods whose imports will materially add to the welfare of consumers or whose supply at present is significantly short of demand.

(c) With respect to those industries which are currently in the process of rationalization or catching up in technology, the time table of liberalization should be adjusted to the extent of progress made by those industries.

(d) With respect to those commodities whose liberalization in the foreseeable future is deemed difficult, we should adopt the gradual, case-by-case approach, separately examining conditions affecting each individual commodity.

(3) As of April 1960 the liberalization ratio (i.e., the ratio of nonrestricted imports to total imports, according to customs records, excluding government imports) was 40 percent. We plan to raise the said ratio to 80 percent by the end of a three-year period from now, and to 90 percent by the time imports of coal and petroleum have become liberalized.

2   Outline of the Plan

(1)   The Energy Sector

Reduction in cost of power supply will be one of the major advantages of the liberalization to the Japanese economy. The liberalization of petroleum may become feasible in the not distant future with an adequate industrial reorganization. On the other hand, the rationalization plan for the coal industry is in progress at present, and the problem of employment in the coal industry can be solved only gradually. Given a high degree of substitution between coal and petroleum, the liberalization time table for these two industries ought to be designed with extreme caution. Particular attention must be paid to the policy objective of achieving stable prices of energy resources—especially the price of coal at the projected, optimal level of domestic production relative to the price of petroleum prevailing after completion of the present rationalization plan for the coal industry.

(2) Metallic Industry

(a) Iron and Steel

Iron and steel occupy a position of central importance in heavy industry. A stable and sufficient supply of iron and steel at the lowest possible prices is one of the preconditions for commencing a full-scale liberalization. Assuming that the present modernization of plant and equipment in the steel industry will continue along with a stability or even reduction of raw material prices, we should be able to liberalize imports of pig iron and ordinary steel material immediately, and of special steel and ferro-alloy in the near future. Provided that the raw material prices will continue to decrease, galvanized iron plate and other iron and steel products should also be liberalized in the near future.

(b) Aluminum and magnesium should be liberalized in the near future. On the other hand, liberalization of copper, lead, and nickel should be postponed until the overall preparedness of these industries becomes greater than at present through modernization of mining and refining techniques and development of overseas resources.

Most of the nonferrous metallic ores, including copper ore and nickel ore, have already been liberalized. We should be able to remove import restrictions on zinc ore at an early date. The same cannot be expected, however, of sulphur and manganese ore in the foreseeable future.

(3) Machinery Industry

We should strive to achieve a fuller import liberalization as soon as possible with respect to the following industries: optical instruments, textile machinery, wood-working machinery, agricultural machinery, electric instruments for private uses, ships, and rolling stock.

The supply of common, transferable parts constitutes an important element in the foundation of the entire machinery industry. Except for the special problem areas, the parts sector ought to be liberalized at an early date.

Of manufacturing machines, metal processing machines, and tools, the import liberalization should be postponed for those sectors in which further internal technological development is necessary; the import restrictions should be removed from all other sectors as soon as feasible.

The category of industrial machinery includes those items which are of strategic importance for the future growth of the Japanese economy and in which Japan lags considerably behind the Western countries in terms of technology and mass production techniques. Cases in point are: chemical machines and equipment, regular and small passenger cars, heavy electrical instruments, and industrial electronic instruments. The timing of import liberalization with respect to these sectors must be adjusted to the extent to which modernization and rationalization of the mode of production in the individual sectors have been accomplished.

(4) Chemical Industry

The chemical industry has its unsolved problems: namely, there is much room for a further technological development; in many areas the firm size tends to be less than optimal; and there are dif- ficulties associated with the supply of raw materials. The basic chemicals such as benzol, toluol, and xylol should be liberalized as soon as possible. We should be able to remove restrictions on carbolic acid, acetone, and butanol in the near future. Soda ash, caustic soda, and many other soda products should be ready for liberalization in several years.

Some of the oil and fat products can be liberalized immediately, and the remainder in the near future. Painting materials can also be liberalized in the near future, depending upon the extent of liber- alization of related raw materials and modernization of plant and equipment in the sector.

Among chemical fertilizers, calcium cyanamide, potassic salt, and sodium nitrate should be liberalized soon. So that the current rationalization plan be sufficiently carried out, however, a delay is necessary with respect to urea and ammonium sulfate.

Liberalization of medical drugs—excluding prohibited items such as narcotic drugs and awakening drugs plus certain antibiotics and vitamins—should be undertaken soon. This should be followed by the liberalization of vitamins in general.

(5) Textile Industry

(a) Textiles

Japanese textiles are still discriminated against by many countries in the world. There are problems, both external and internal, associated with the textile industry. The import liberalization with respect to textiles should be undertaken in the near future in conjunction with the implementation of effective policy measures to solve those remaining problems of the industry.

Import restriction of raw cotton and raw wool will take effect, as has been planned, in April, 1961.

Depending upon the consequences of liberalization of raw cotton and raw wool, we should first liberalize cotton products, then wool products in the near future.

Silk products should be liberalized as soon as possible whereas removal of restrictions on rayon and rayon staple products should be postponed until after the liberalization of pulp. A majority of synthetic textile products can be liberalized before long. A gradual and cautious approach, however, is necessary for jute products.

(b) Pulp, paper, and paper products

Pulp used in production of chemical textiles should be liberalized shortly after liberalization of raw cotton and raw wool. Import liberalization of pulp used in production of paper should be carried out at a later date. A similar, gradual approach ought to be applied to paper and paper products.

(6) Products of Light Industry

Glass plate should be liberalized in the near future, to be followed by fire-resistance materials.

Of rubber products, bicycle tire, tube and rubber hose should be liberalized as soon as possible.

Continued protection is needed for leather goods whose imports should be expanded beyond the present level before the liberalization takes effect.

With respect to sundry others, imports of those items which have not been liberalized should be sizably increased before implementing a full-fledged liberalization in this area.

With respect to alcoholic beverages, beer may be liberalized as soon as possible whereas liberalization of wine and whisky should be more gradual.

(7) Agriculture and Fishery

Conspicuously low productivity and massive underemployment characterize Japanese agriculture and fishery. Consequently, a major liberalization cannot be expected in this area for a long time. We should continue to strive for productivity gains in those sectors whose growth adds to an improvement of the employment structure of agriculture and fishery. Needless to say, our ultimate goal is to achieve, over the long run, a full liberalization of these industries.

For the immediate future we should start liberalizing, case by case, with those items whose production cost is already sufficiently low relative to the international standards, those which are under sufficient tariff protection and those for which there are adequate domestic price-stabilizing measures in force (e.g., soya beans).

(a) Agricultural Products

Most important agricultural products such as rice, wheat, and corn starch cannot be liberalized in the foreseeable future. However, we should be able to liberalize cereals soon.

Fresh and processed vegetables—excluding tomato products— should be liberalized in the near future. In view of the existing plans for promotion of the domestic fruits industry, the import restrictions should continue with respect to bananas, canned pineapple, fruit juice, and most of citrus fruits.

Liberalization of sugar cannot be expected soon inasmuch as domestic production of sugar beet is being encouraged now, and related items such as glucose and corn starch continue to be in need of protection.

Soya beans will be liberalized according to the previously set time table. Miscellaneous beans cannot soon be liberalized since their domestic production costs remain conspicuously high. Similarly, an early liberalization of black tea and rape-seed is difficult because domestic producers are currently undergoing a series of transformations in planting and cultivating methods. On the other hand, we should be able to liberalize raw silk and cocoons at an early date.

(b) Livestock

The livestock industry is one of the important domestic industries in need of protection for growth. Therefore, an early liberalization of dairy products, fresh and processed meats is not anticipated. However, refined lard and some categories of domestic animals and livestock products can be liberalized in the near future.

(c) Fishery Products

Products of the coastal fishing industry such as seaweed, sardine, horse-mackerel, mackerel, and herring cannot be liberalized in the near future; but canned tuna and salmon should be liberalized in the immediate future.

(d) Forestry Products

Logs have already been liberalized. Most of the processed lumber products should be liberalized soon. Special products of forestry such as chestnut, walnut, and mushroom should be liberalized gradually in accord with the pace of productivity gains in these sectors.

e. Oil, Fat, Foodstuff

We need to protect rape-seed, the major source of domestic supply of edible oil. Consequently, we should not liberalize, for some time, rape-seed oil and other edible oils that are close substitutes for rape-seed oil. Industrial oil and those edible oils which do not substitute for rape-seed oil should be liberalized in the near future. Industrial oil lees and edible oil lees (excluding lees of oils that substitute for rape-seed oil) should be liberalized in the not distant future.

High prices of sugar, wheat, and dairy products in Japan make it difficult to liberalize confectionery at an early date. As a preliminary measure the volume of confectionery imports should be increased.

IV   The Foreign Exchange Liberalization Plan

1   Policy Direction

For the purpose of liberalizing foreign exchange transactions we make a distinction between current transactions and capital transactions. We plan to complete liberalizing current transactions within two years. However, it is difficult to make precise predictions as to when we shall be in a ready position to liberalize capital transactions. We plan to proceed gradually, depending upon the domestic economic conditions and the consequences of removal of restrictions over current transactions.

2   Outline of the Plan

(1) Liberalization of Current Transactions

(a) The following measures will be taken within this year.

(a-1) Starting from July 1st the nonresident free yen account will be established; and yen exchange will be introduced.

(a-2) By the end of September this year the Foreign Currency Fund Special Allotment System will be abolished. Before the above action is taken, regulations pertaining to acquisition of foreign exchange for foreign travel and transfer of funds to overseas offices of Japanese trading companies under the above System will be terminated. Application rules concerning foreign travel will be relaxed and simplified. Freedom will be given as a rule to the opening of overseas offices of Japanese trading companies and other firms while the rules concerning transfer of funds to those offices will be relaxed.

(a-3) Rules and regulations concerning foreign exchange transactions of foreign exchange banks and trading companies in Japan as well as abroad will be relaxed.

(a-4) Transactions concerning chartering of foreign ships (excluding tankers) by Japanese shipping companies for a period not exceeding six months will be liberalized.

(a-5) With respect to exchange transactions in connection with foreign films shown in Japan, we shall attempt to dissolve accumulated yen balances by raising the approved monthly rate of exchange transfer.

(a-6) We shall relax regulations concerning transfer of funds by foreign trading companies after establishing the new accounting standards. We shall be examining the possibility of easing restrictions over transfer of profits of foreign trading companies in connection with the schedule of liberalization of capital transactions.

(a-7) Relaxation of regulations over transfer of expense funds related to foreign trade will be undertaken.

(b) All the rest of the foreign exchange restrictions over current transactions will be removed within next year.

(2) Liberalization of Capital Transactions

(a) Liberalization of Foreign Investments in Japan

Restrictions in this area will be removed gradually in order to prevent adverse effects on Japanese firms—particularly small businesses. In carrying out the liberalization priority will be given to technical assistance contracts, foreign loans to Japanese firms, and transactions in stocks and bonds through the market.

Rules and regulations concerning redemption of principals by foreign investors, the profit-retaining period, and the like will be gradually relaxed. Redemption of original investments by foreigners in Japanese stock and real estate before the war will be approved.

(b) Liberalization of Japanese Overseas Investments

The standards and restrictions concerning Japanese overseas investments in the form of establishing legal persons or branches to engage in commercial activities will soon be eased. Regulations over other forms of Japanese investments abroad will gradually be relaxed in the not distant future.

OPINION ON THE LIBERALIZATION*

There is no doubt about the urgent need to remove the strict control over foreign trade and exchange which has remained in force since World War II if we are determined to sustain a rapid growth of our economy and continue to expand our exports in a new environment of the world economy wherein all other advanced countries have steadily been removing their trade and exchange restrictions.

The past trade and exchange control system has provided Japanese industry with a thick and elaborate wall of protection, and has served its purpose as a means of assuring recovery of the Japanese economy from the war. At the same time the control system has caused an attitude and propensity of laxity and complacency on the part of private business and industry which have leaned toward an easy way of taking advantage of protection rather than striving toward rational management and vigorous entrepreneurship. We must realize that the latter effect of protectionism has increasingly become a constraint upon the further expansion of our economy. In this sense we believe that an implementation of the liberalization will stimulate autonomous activities of Japanese firms, encourage more rational undertakings, and help enhance the properties of Japanese enterprises.

With a gathering of attention to the problem of liberalization, the subject has increasingly become a political issue. Many have argued that the liberalization represents a threat to the domestic employment market. While we do not deny that the liberalization can generate adverse effects in agriculture and small businesses, the sort of liberalization we are concerned with is in the nature of being a means of promoting our own trade primarily with other advanced countries. Namely, we uphold the view that, given Japan's international obligations as a country heavily dependent upon foreign trade, we can no longer justify our continuation of the control system for one-sided reasons and objectives. It is not wise and appropriate to make a political issue out of the liberalization because whatever unemployment that may occur in some sectors due to the liberalization—as the critics point out—will be more than offset by gains in employment through trade expansion and further economic growth resulting from promotion of the liberalization.

---

*The original text is Jiyuka ni taisuru Ken, issue by Keizai Dantai Rengo Kai (commonly known as Keidanren), April 19, 1960.

On the basis of the foregoing suppositions we have gathered and appraised opinions of a wide range of business and industry groups that will be directly affected by the liberalization. After a careful study of their views we have concluded that the following policy directions concerning the liberalization should be followed.

First, in implementing the liberalization policy we must take special care to see that the liberalization measures with respect to foreign trade and exchange transactions will be consistent with one another.

Second, we must immediately start taking policy actions to improve the properties of Japanese enterprises. The time schedule of liberalization must be coordinated with the results of the preparatory measures for those industries which will be affected by the liberalization.

With respect to those industries which are already exposed to intense international competition and are in danger of being adversely affected by the liberalization (e.g., marine transportation), the existing policy measures should be thoroughly reexamined to promote an effective preparation of these industries.

Within the framework set by the above guidelines we present the following policy recommendations. It is hoped that joint efforts of and a close cooperation between the government and private businesses will bring about a fruitful result of the liberalization.

1   Improvement of the Properties of Japanese Enterprises

(1)   Promotion of Capital Accumulation and Tax Reforms

(a)   Japanese corporations in general are in need of substantially increasing their owned-capital. To promote internal capital accumulation, the government should reexamine and improve the present corporation tax system, and the firms should also make their own efforts through such means as market-value sales of their stocks. The accelerated depreciation and special depreciation systems should be preserved and improved so as to encourage rationalization and modernization of Japanese firms. For the purpose of promoting growth of new industries we should preserve and expand the present important commodity tax exemption system.

(b)   To mitigate the impact of market fluctuations that may occur after the liberalization, we should strengthen and expand the reserve for the price fluctuation system as well as the reserve for the default system.

(2) Improvements in Finance

We should continue the present preferential systems pertaining to trade finance. Total efforts, including a more active induction of import usance and impact loans, are required to increase the supply of capital and lower the rates of interest in the nation's money market.

(3) New Investment in Plant and Equipment

The government should adopt special measures to encourage investment in new plant and equipment, and to accelerate replacement investment under the scrap-and-build method in those industries in which sufficient innovations have not been taking place (e.g., machinery industry).

2   Promotion of Science and Technology

Multi-directional endeavors are necessary to raise the overall level of science and technology in our country if Japan is to survive in the world market in face of a global trend of technological innovations. Expansion of the Agency of Science and Technology in terms of its budget and legal-administrative power is recommended. There should be adopted a series of policy measures to encourage research in basic and applied science in private industries, and to promote education in science and technology particularly at the university level.

3   Preservation of Industrial Order

(1) Appropriate reforms of the present Anti-Monopoly Act seem necessary to enable Japanese enterprises to make an autonomous effort in preserving an orderly market condition in industry and trade after the liberalization, and to allow for mergers and regroupings of Japanese firms as a means of effectively competing against world enterprises.

The reform plan, which the government prepared several years ago, should serve as a basis for deciding the specific nature and contents of the reforms of the Anti-Monopoly Act which we are proposing.

(2) Separate Acts to Preserve Industrial Order

The nature of the reforms should be such that industrial order be preserved autonomously through self-adjustment and endeavor on the part of private business and industry. If and where such autonomous attempts fail to preserve an industrial order, separate Acts (such as the Textile Equipment Extraordinary Measures Act) should be legislated.

(3)   Reforms of the Export-Import Transactions Act

To promote orderly trade transactions, the reforms of the Export-Import Transactions Act which the Ministry of International Trade and Industry is currently preparing should be implemented at an early date. There is much room for improving the existing rules and regulations pertaining to the Exporters' Association, the import agreements affecting Japanese importers and the internal transactions agreements affecting Japanese firms producing those goods which compete with imports.

(4)   Legislation of the Trading Business Act

To promote and preserve orderly export-import transactions, there should be legislated a new, effective Trading Business Act which, inter alia, institutes a comprehensive system of registration of all trading businesses.

4   Policy Measures for Raw Materials and Semi-Finished Goods

With respect to those important raw materials which are indigenously produced and whose prices are high relative to the international market prices (e.g., coal, pulp, and special metallic materials), we must establish and implement the rationalization plans to reduce their domestic prices through productivity gains. Particularly important is increasing the output of the domestic pulp industry through an improved and effective use of the nationally owned forest.

5   Improvement of Foreign Investment Policy

We should liberalize, to the fullest extent possible, foreign capital transactions as long as they do not create adverse effects upon Japanese industries. As a preliminary step in progressively reducing government intervention in this area we should grant automatic approval of joint ventures involving foreign enterprises provided that the foreign-investment ratio in such ventures does not exceed 50 percent.

6   Tariff Reforms

(1)   The presently employed methods of classification and assessment are in need of major changes. The tariff rates should be

readjusted in accordance with the Brussels System, and the principal
assessment criterion should be shifted from the present ad valorem
approach to the specific tariff system. Individual rates ought to be
determined in light of varying degrees of protection required for
domestic industries in the absence of nontariff (quantitative) import
restrictions.

(2) Reforms in Tariff Administration

Domestic industrial policy has much bearing upon the determination of tariff rates, and developments in the area of foreign economic
relations necessitate, from time to time, discretionary changes in
the rates. We therefore deem it desirable to transfer the tariff administration to the Ministry of International Trade and Industry, to change
the tariff law so that each tariff reform need not be approved by the
Diet, and to provide an emergency clause in the tariff system in order
to cope with unexpected circumstances.

7   Export Promotion and International Economic Cooperation

(1) Removal of Discriminatory Import Restrictions Against Japanese Goods

Through diplomatic channels we must urge other countries to
repeal their discriminatory import restrictions (e.g., invocation of
Article 35 of GATT) against Japanese goods as soon as possible.

(2) Promotion of Exports to Underdeveloped Countries

There is a possibility that after the liberalization trade between
Japan and some underdeveloped countries will decline. If the deterioration is anticipated to be serious, sufficient corrective actions should
be taken promptly. Particular measures are necessary to promote
exports to underdeveloped countries in general after the liberalization.

(3) Economic Cooperation with Underdeveloped Countries.

We should strive for advancement of economic cooperation
with underdeveloped countries in order to contribute to the cause of
their economic growth and, at the same time, to develop new markets
for our own industrial goods as a part of our post-liberalization
industrial policy.

(4)   Improvement and Extention of the Export Income Exemption
System

In order to assure export expansion and the balance-of-payments
equilibrium after the liberalization, we should improve and extend
the Export Income Exemption System.

(5)   Improvement of Port Administration and Simplification of
Export-Import Procedures

There is an urgent need to radically improve and simplify the
present, overly complicated rules and regulations in connection with
port administration and export-import procedures.

8   Consumer Education

Both the government and private business should strive to
eradicate the irrational propensity of Japanese consumers to prefer
foreign (Western) goods irrespective of the true quality of domestically
produced counterparts.

RECOMMENDATIONS CONCERNING LIBERALIZATION
OF FOREIGN TRADE AND EXCHANGE*

The global movement to liberalize foreign trade and exchange
has entered the final stage of completion with restoration of currency
convertibility in Western Europe last year. The tempo of the movement has been faster than anticipated. Western Germany recently
declared its compliance with Article 8 of the IMF Charter; Great
Britain and Italy are soon to follow suit. Any major country today
can no longer justify its continuation of trade and exchange restrictions, and there is little likelihood of the trend of liberalization being
reversed in the near future.

---

*The original text is Boeki Kawase Jiyuka ni taisuru Teigen,
issued by Keizai Doyu Kai, October 16, 1960.

When we look at Japan—a country which foreign observers as well as we ourselves acknowledge as a major industrial country—we realize that our country is far behind West European countries in the liberalization movement. For example, our present import liberalization ratio is only 31 percent in contrast to 90 percent within Western Europe and 80 percent for Western Europe vis-à-vis the dollar area. The importance and necessity of liberalization, however, have long been recognized in Japan. As far as attention goes, we have been concerned with the problem since before the restoration of currency convertibility in Western Europe.

Our concern notwithstanding, the actual progress we have made thus far has been little and slow. Since the beginning of this year only a few minor steps have been taken such as an increase in the number of appointed currencies for official conversion, changes in the standard settlement rules and liberalization of the dollar exchange. Little to speak of has been accomplished with respect to more substantive issues such as introduction of yen exchange or expansion of the automatic approval system.

Why has so little progress been made in the liberalization of trade and exchange? In our view the answer is found in the Government's conservatism and stubborn resistance to taking any drastic policy action that may upset the norm of the establishment.

We all realize that the liberalization is easier said than done. However, it is our belief that the basic assumption of the liberalization (namely, the long-run benefits of liberalization far exceed the short-run costs in friction and market disturbance) is applicable to Japan despite her being a relatively less advanced industrial country than the United States and West European countries.

There are two main factors that constrain the liberalization movement: apprehension about the balance-of-payments disequilibrium; and the need for protection of domestic industries.

As for external balance, at present, Japan's reserve of gold and foreign exchange equals approximately 40 percent of the value of her annual imports. This ratio is less than those of Western Germany and Switzerland, about the same as that of Holland, and higher than those of Great Britain, France, and Scandinavian countries. Of course, a nation's optimal foreign exchange reserve cannot be judged by this simple ratio alone. Inasmuch as Japanese imports have a notable tendency to fluctuate widly and her secondary reserve (e.g., borrowing from IMF and credit from various international

financial institutions) is small relative to those of West European
countries, one may argue that the present reserve can hardly be
viewed as sufficient. Thanks to her semi-advanced status, however,
Japan has greater access than West European countries to grants
and credit from the international development funds such as the World
Bank. Furthermore, import fluctuations may be substantially mitigated
by the Government's effective policy measures. Consequently, we
believe that the present reserve is sufficient from the standpoint of
implementing the liberalization. We do not see any reasons why we
cannot proceed to relax the existing regulations concerning the amount
of foreign exchange which Japanese trading companies are allowed to
hold, to widen the range within which the exchange rate is permitted
to fluctuate, to introduce yen exchange, and to repeal the area-wide
import restrictions. The bilateral agreements, purporting to establish country-by-country trade balance, and discriminatory exchange
restrictions to prevent dollar drains violate the principles of IMF
and GATT. The bilateral trade agreement necessitates imports for
the sake of exports; it is questionable that this approach will enhance
the future prospect of Japan's plant export to underdeveloped countries.
As has been illustrated by the West German example, the success in
exporting capital goods is more crucially determined by long-term
credit, terms of payment, technology, and after-service. We should
also note that the discriminatory restrictions practiced by the dollar
area have already lost much of their meaning thanks to the restoration
of currency convertibility in Western Europe.

What can be said about the second constraint—the need to protect domestic industries? We do not deny that the problem here is
complex and difficult to solve. Japan's import control system is not
only (1) to protect domestic, import-substituting industries and (2)
prevent excessive competition or overinvestments among domestic
producers but also to (3) protect the operations of small businesses.
To compound the problem, goods and industries involved in each of
these functions are hardly mutually exclusive from one another.

The postwar recovery period in the proper sense of the term
is over, and continuation of direct import control for reasons other
than balance-of-payments considerations is clearly a violation of
the principles of GATT. Of the above three objectives of the import
control system, (1) should be served by appropriate tariff policy
whereas (2) and (3) should be pursued through internal economic
policies—i.e., flexible monetary policy and small business policy,
together with autonomous adjustments on the part of small business.
From now on, direct import control should be applied only to those
goods for which tariff as a protective device is ineffective or to

those in which Japan is already highly self-sufficient. We firmly
believe that the Japanese economy, which has demonstrated a magni-
ficant growth record after the war, is viable enough to withstand the
temporary strains resulting from policy changes.

In concluding we restate our position that we have passed the
stage where one should be discussing the necessity of the liberalization
or pros and cons of some minute aspects of it. The present boom in
the world economy at large and our favorable external balance make
this a truly opportune time to commence a major liberalization. If
we miss the present opportunity, the combination of internal and
external economic conditions during future years will more likely
than not make the task of liberalization harder to accomplish than at
present, and Japan will entertain a dubious reputation in the world
as the only industrial country that continues to indulge in direct
trade and exchange control. Our inaction will cause a perpetuation
of internal structural disequilibrium and hamper the prospect of
long-run growth of our economy.

The fifteenth general meeting of GATT will soon be held in
Tokyo. We urge the Government to seize the opportunity to appraise
our recommendations as well as views of other representative groups,
and build a momentum to start taking concrete policy actions to
implement the liberalization of foreign trade and exchange.

OUR ATTITUDE TOWARD THE LIBERALIZATION
POLICY*

Preface

On March 8th we issued a policy statement bearing the same
title as the present one. Much debate has been heard since the end
of last year concerning the Government's pronounced policy on liberalization of foreign trade and exchange. Within the capitalists' camp
there were expressed numerous divergent opinions, but their views
all had a common, unifying theme, i.e., their aggressive intent

---

*The original text is Jiyuka Seisaku ni taisuru Wareware no
Taido, issued by Sohyo Choki Seisaku Iinkai, July 4, 1960.

vis-à-vis the working class. The discussions on the liberalization
have exerted strong political, social and ideological pressure against
the working class, creating a climate of fear and apprehension within
the labor unions. Our previous policy statement was issued to express
our interpretation of and attitude toward the liberalization policy, and
to declare the fundamental position of the trade unions concerning
numerous problems associated with the liberalization.

The document in question later served a useful function as a
guideline for many labor unions in discussing and formulating policy
strategies toward the liberalization. During the past four months—
since the publication of our previous document—the Government has
already taken many preparatory steps for the liberalization. In order
to update our previous statement and incorporate results of studies
and discussions that have been conducted by the Long-Range Policy
Committee of the General Council, we are hereby issuing our new
policy statement which, it is hoped, will explain our position in greater
detail and clarity.

1   How to Cope with the Liberalization Policy

The liberalization policy with respect to trade, exchange and
foreign investment, now propagated by the Government and monopoly
capital, is singularly aimed at one target for attack—which is the
working class. What the policy is to bring about is an intensification
of price competition in the domestic and international markets and
a growth of control power on the part of those big businesses which
win the competition. However, in substance the competition among
big businesses is tantamount to competition to exploit workers. The
liberalization policy is only to aggravate the exploitative competition
and add a new chapter to the capitalists' offensive against labor which
has persisted throughout the postwar period under the banner of
rationalization. The monopolists are now preparing to launch a new,
major offensive in order to cope with the liberalization or (more
aptly) in the name of liberalization. The present turmoil at the Miike
mines where 100,000 coal miners are being threatened with lay-offs
as a means of reducing the coal price is symbolic of not only the
attitude of the mining interest but also the mentality of all monopoly
capitalists as they implement their so-called rationalization plans
at the expense of workers' welfare. The recent management-labor
cease fire agreement at Kokusaku Pulp, the firing of sick-leave
workers and tightening of work rules in connection with the steel
price reduction plan at Yawata Steel, a 7000 yen wage cut among
subcontractors for Minsei Diesel, allegedly necessitated by the
liberalization, are but other examples of the management's naked

offensive related to the liberalization policy. If we tolerate these offensives, the world-famous low-wage structure in Japan will become more rigid, the rate of exploitation of workers will reach a new peak, the employment market will witness a further worsening of its conditions, and the labor organizations will be forced to experience a tragic disintegration.

The oft-heard argument that "we must bear the burden in order to improve our international competitive position" itself is an ideological attack against the working class with a hidden intent to blind the workers to the class bias of the liberalization policy and to discourage workers from resisting the capitalists' offensive. Many corporations have already been conducting propaganda campaigns emphasizing labor-management cooperation and restraint on the part of unions.

We shall confront the liberalization policy by exposing its audacious class motives, by making demands of our own representing the entire working class, and by establishing a united battle front under the leadership of the progressive party.

Our opposition to the currently propagated liberalization hardly implies our support of the government's trade and exchange control after the war. Both the past trade and exchange control and the present liberalization policy are trade policy of and for the monopolists, and there are little substantive differences between the two. We must understand that monopoly capitalists are using liberalization as a leverage to intensify their rationalization offensive against workers. It is with that understanding that we should confront the liberalization policy and continue to destroy and reform the remaining mechanism of trade and exchange control that is designed to protect profits of the monopolists.

Our opposition is directed toward control and exploitation by capitalists through the liberalization, and should not be confused with some capitalists' own opposition to the liberalization policy based upon a narrow, selfish objective to protect their profits. It is easy for us to take advantage of the anti-liberalization position of small and weak industries or conditionally support their position. To do so, however, will mean our yielding to the trap of the so-called management-labor cooperation principle which is devoid of true representation of our own class interest.

Our struggle against the liberalization policy consists of our political fight in demanding a radical transformation of trade policy and of our resistance to a further rationalization and concentration of capital to be brought about by the liberalization.

(1) We oppose the kind of liberalization of trade, exchange and foreign investments which benefits only a handful of monopoly capitalists. We demand that the government make fundamental changes in the present trade and industrial policies.

(a) Foreign trade is not to benefit monopoly capitalists in making profits and controlling markets; it is to promote social progress and raise standards of living of workers and the people at large. We object to the present system of trade and exchange control which is mainly serving the interest of monopolists. We demand that the government let the people's will be reflected in the determination of trade policy.

(b) We must trade on equal terms with all countries irrespective of their political systems, adhering to the principle of peaceful coexistence. We must reopen or expand trade relations with socialist countries as well as underdeveloped countries.

(c) With the unity of all workers in the world we shall continue our struggle to establish world peace through promotion of international economic cooperation and trade among socialist countries as well as industrial and underdeveloped countries.

(d) Our fight to transform the trade policy ought to be grasped as an integral part of our overall struggle to transform the Government's fiscal, monetary and industrial policies affecting all aspects of the Japanese economy.

(2) In line with the above basic objectives we shall fight for our following demands in the immediate future.

(a) We demand continual wage increase and promulgation of a genuine Minimum Wage Law (including a domestic workers law). We are strongly opposed to the kind of liberalization policy which further aggravates the low wage structure in Japan. We emphasize that it is the low wages in Japan that have been the secret of rapid capital accumulation, a cause of discriminatory import restrictions abroad against Japanese goods and a hindrance in the way of export expansion.

(b) We demand that the government achieve a true full employment eliminating extensive layers of unemployment as well as underemployment in the country, and abolish the kind of employment policy which perpetuates undemocratic institutions such as the system of temporary workers in Japanese factories. We are opposed to the liberalization policy which will worsen the condition of the employment market.

(c)   We oppose any so-called rationalization measures during the period of liberalization which will add strain to workers. We demand a complete cessation of lay-offs and a reduction in work hours. We shall defend the democratic rights of workers.

(d)   We reject the attempts of management to popularize and impose upon us the idea of company unions and loosen solidarity of the labor organizations. We shall endeavor to realize a massive united labor front by organizing all labor groups representing permanent as well as temporary workers, employees in big and small businesses, the employed as well as unemployed. Given the international character of the liberalization policy, we deem it exceedingly important to achieve a closer bondage with workers of other countries and promote international mutual assistance in the common struggle against exploitation and control by international monopoly capitalists.

(e)   We object to the capitalists' attempts to repeal or reform the Anti-Monopoly Act and the Export-Import Transactions Act for the purpose of promoting cartels and other forms of monopolization.

(f)   We oppose the reforms of the Foreign Investment Act which will induce a greater inflow of foreign capital (mainly from the United States), exposing the working class to ever increasing exploitative forces of foreign monopolists. We demand the government to rescind the present U.S.-Japan Treaty on Commerce and Navigation.

(g)   We demand that the government abolish the U.S.-Japan Mutual Security Agreements as well as the COCOM regulations that are severely restricting our trade with the socialist countries. We further demand that trade between Japan and Red China be reopened immediately.

(h)   Inasmuch as Japanese agriculture and small businesses will be subjected to adverse effects of the liberalization, we shall strive to form a labor coalition that includes farmers and workers in small businesses.

(i)   We demand that the government abrogate the New Mutual Security Pact with the United States which signifies an avowed revival of Japanese militarism.

2   International Background of Liberalization

(1) The liberalization policy with respect to foreign trade, exhange and investment, currently pursued by the government and monopoly

capital in Japan, has as its background the global stream of liberalization among capitalist nations which began to gather momentum with
restoration of currency convertibility among fifteen nations of Western
Europe at the end of 1958.

The liberalization of trade and exchange typically manifests
itself as a demand of powerful, advanced capitalist countries to have
access to domestic markets of other countries. The United States,
which came to assume a position of leadership in the capitalist bloc
of nations after the war, has persistently tried to acquire greater
access to West European markets. For some years after the war,
however, the technological gap was so great that the countries of
Western Europe were unable to liberalize trade and exchange in
response to the U.S. demand.

The U.S. economic aid to Western Europe began for the purpose
of accelerating economic recovery of Europe. The economic recovery
was necessary to realize an opening of European markets to American
firms, and the aid was also a price the United States had to pay for
the anti-communist military alliance in Western Europe. Thus the
Marshall Plan came into being.

(2) Thanks to the U.S. government's enormous military expenditures
for national defense as well as for anti-communist military alliances
abroad, capital accumulation was deterred while inflation continued
in the United States. Consequently, the international competitive
position of the United States began to deteriorate. The U.S. export
surplus continued to diminish. The chronic deficit in the overall
balance of payments was but a reflection of the steady drain of dollar
and gold from the United States. The tremendous recovery and growth
of West European economies brought a halt to the postwar dollar
shortage. Unbalanced economic growth within the capitalist bloc of
nations over the past decade or so have brought about a relative
closing of the technological gaps among those nations.

(3) Faced with the balance-of-payments deterioration, the United
States began to press harder for removal of import restrictions in
Western Europe. It was no longer a matter of demand for liberalization as part of the dollar offensive of the kind witnessed in the early
postwar years but was a matter of defending the quickly weakening
dollar. Given the relative equalization of economic power between
the United States and Western Europe (together with the world boom
and concomitant trade expansion that enabled West European countries
to accumulate sizable dollar reserves), the countries of Western
Europe could move to restore convertibility of their currencies

vis-à-vis the dollar, and to liberalize dollar imports and inflow of American capital. It was not a case of Europe's passively yielding to the U.S. demand; rather on the basis of newly gained economic strength West European countries began to challenge the U.S. domination of the world market, using the liberalization as a means of enlarging the markets for new competition against the United States.

(4)   As part of the dollar-defense policy the U.S. government has adopted a tight fiscal policy and attempted to reduce its foreign economic aid. Pressure exerted on West European countries and Japan to share the burden of aid to the underdeveloped countries is another sign of difficulty of the U.S. government. With respect to military aid the U.S. government has been experiencing a dilemma in that an increased share of the burden of military expenditures on the part of recipient countries, as imposed by the U.S. government, has meant a lossening of strings attached to the military assistance to those countries. The United States' struggle for defense of the dollar is also manifest in the New U.S.-Japan Mutual Security Pact in which Japan promises to increase her own defense spending.

(5)   As the above observations illustrate, the liberalization of trade, exchange and investment is a form of fierce struggle of capitalist countries for acquisition of new markets after completion of economic recovery and relative equalization of industrial strength among the imperialist nations.

In contrast to the 1920's, another period of balance of power among the imperialist nations, return to the gold standard is not conceivable today; the liberalization is therefore being carried out within the framework of the international managed currency system.

In the 1930's compartmentalization of the world economy occurred as a result of the Great Depression and the disintegration of the gold standard. The world then witnessed the never-ending competitive depreciation of currencies and the use of armed forces by major imperialist powers as a way of gaining new markets.

During the postwar period there has been a concomitant development of the Common Market with France and Western Germany as its core and the Free Trade Area centering around Great Britain. The fact that the liberalization has been accompanied by a split of the European market into two blocs illustrates the instability of the ground upon which the liberalization has been proceeding. It is indicative of the inherent contradictions of world capitalism that may cause a setback or even a total disintegration of the liberalization movement in the not too distant future.

3   The Liberalization Policy and Its Consequences

(1)   Pressure from Without and the Capitalists' Response

In recent years the tide of the global liberalization movement
has been steadily rising before the Japanese shores, forcing Japanese
monopoly capitalists to take preparatory actions. It was strong pressure from the United States, however, that motivated the Japanese
government to take hasty and abrupt steps toward the liberalization
since the end of last year   Beyond reasonable doubt the government
was concerned with the adverse, retaliatory responses, which Japan's
indecision would have invited, from other advanced countries—particularly from the United States—in connection with trade and tariff negotiations as well as the prospects of reforms of the Mutual Security
Pact.

Inasmuch as the government's policy statement on the liberalization carried a strong overtone of being a piece of composition for a
foreign audience, the statement was met with opposition by some
monopoly capitalists within Japan. This initial reaction does not
signify that Japan is as yet totally unprepared for liberalization or
that the Japanese capitalists at large are basically opposed to the
liberalization. The initial opposition reflected a mixture of disturbed
elements in the country such as: (i) objection voiced by vulnerable
industries and small, weak capitalists; (ii) reluctance on the part of
many capitalists to lose numerous special privileges and benefits
hitherto assured of them by the trade and exchange control; and (iii)
demand by many monopolists for compensatory provisions in tariffs
or legalization of cartels, together with the terms and timing of liberalization to their advantages. It is only natural that the monopoly
capitalists voice opposition of the sort when a major policy change
with far-reaching consequences is about to occur—especially when
that change is induced by the pressure from without.

(2)   Monopoly Capitalists' Objective in Connection with the
      Liberalization Policy

Needless to say, the monopoly capitalists' interest and will
were behind the government's decision to move toward liberalization.
The pressure from without acted, one might say, merely as a catalyst
for the policy change.

After fifteen years of growth and accumulation of power the
monopoly capitalists are now attempting to take advantage of the
liberalization in order to achieve a greater concentration of capital,
a more extensive control of the domestic market, and a more active

participation in international cartels as a means of expanding their share of the world market. The main objectives which monopoly capital is pursuing through the liberalization movement are as follows.

(a)   The Foreign Currency Allotment System, which helped monopolization after the war, has at the same time resulted in inflation of raw material prices, overprotection (and inefficiency) of small businesses, and reluctance on the part of the firms to invest in new plant and equipment. Monopoly capital is interested in control of domestic markets by dissolving the inefficiency brought about by the trade and exchange control system through the liberalization while continuing to exploit the relatively weak position of small businesses.

(b)   Using the liberalization as a leverage, monopoly capital is interested in conducting a vigorous rationalization drive as a major offensive against the working class. For this purpose monopoly capital is hurriedly seeking closer ties with foreign capital while openly demanding from the government a series of protective measures to strengthen the basis of state monopoly capitalism in Japan.

(c)   Monopoly capital is attempting a so-called modernization of Japan's industrial structure without dissolution of the dual economy as monopolistic firms seek continual capital accumulation of their own while readily abandoning or disassociating with weaker firms which are considered a hindrance in the way of the monopolists' gaining greater market shares. In order to exploit low wages and low raw materials costs, monopoly capital is interested in developing large-scale agriculture with no regard for its consequences upon Japanese farmers who operate on small-unit lands.

(d)   Monopoly capital is attempting to gain a larger share of the world market by using the liberalization as a weapon to let the United States and West European countries remove their discriminatory import restrictions against Japanese goods. Monopoly capital is interested in induction of more foreign capital as well as increase in Japanese capital exports as a means of acquiring more raw materials from abroad.

(3)   Revision of the Mutual Security Pact and the Liberalization
        Policy

The liberalization is to begin about the same time as signing of the New Mutual Security Pact. While the liberalization policy is an economic means of strengthening the control by monopoly capital, the Mutual Security Pact is a political and military attempt to solidify the system of exploitation by monopoly capital. In this sense the liberalization policy may be interpreted as an economic version of the Mutual Security Pact. The fact that the Mutual Security Pact forces Japan to maintain a close military alliance with the United States is not only intensifying the cold war vis-à-vis Red China and the Soviet Union but also creating new tension in international political relations which in turn adds difficulties to the liberalization.

Contradictions of capitalism manifest themselves in the economic as well as political domains. Monopolists' attempt to raise their productivity and efficiency through exploitation of workers only intensifies the class war, and political "stability" in the nation is thus threatened no matter how earnestly monopolists may desire such stability. Expansion of military power aimed at a firmer political and military control of the economy leads to inflation through unending growth of defense expenditures, and the inflation weakens Japan's competitive position in the world market. Monopoly capital then seeks to dissolve this contradiction at the expense of the working class.

(4) Weakness of Japanese Capitalism and the Characteristics of the Liberalization

Japanese capitalism contains some unique elements of weakness that are not present in European imperialism, and those elements constitute a background for Japan's lag behind Western Europe in liberalizing trade and exchange and for the sort of vulnerability and unpreparedness Japan has been revealing in the face of the strong pressure exerted by the United States.

The weaknesses of the Japanese economy in connection with the liberalization are as follows.

(a) There are many sectors in which the scale of production is small and the level of technology low relative to those in the Western countries.

(b) Costs of raw materials tend to be high because many of them must be imported from distant places.

(c) Despite the recent expansion the volume of Japanese exports is still not sufficiently large to assure an adequate reserve of foreign exchange.

(The above (b) and (c) have much to do with the absence of trade with Red China.)

(d)   Shortage of investible funds is causing high interest rates and a vulnerability in the capital structure of Japanese corporations.

(e)   The so-called dual economy is aggravating the employment problem.

(f)   The political and military subservience to the United States is causing Japan's dependence upon the United States in trade and finance as well.

(g)   There exist no major capitalist countries around Japan with which Japan can form a common regional market.

(h)   The volume of trade with underdeveloped countries is likely to contract as a result of the liberalization.

The liberalization has both offensive and defensive aspects. On the offensive side it is an attempt to gain a larger share of the world market by winning in international competition. On the defensive side it is a way of avoiding isolation in the world economy and the resulting deterioration in the country's terms of trade. The aforesaid elements of weakness are adding defensive characteristics to the liberalization policy as conceived by the Japanese Government. It is doubtful that the liberalization will bring about export expansion and other beneficial results as propagated by the Government and monopoly capital. The liberalization policy says little about trade with Red China. Many aspects of the policy point to a distinct possibility that Japan's trade with underdeveloped countries will decrease. There is no assurance whatsoever that the United States and West European countries will remove their discriminatory import restrictions against Japanese goods inasmuch as those restrictions are induced by Japanese low wages. Monopoly capital is doing its best to disguise these problematical aspects of the liberalization. It has been promoting rapid technological innovations with accelerated investment in new plant and equipment while continuing to exploit the low wages in the country. It has advanced ideas about the Southeast Asia Economic Development Fund and the Pacific Common Market—though these ideas have not been materialized on account of opposition from the United States. The graver the difficulties and contradictions of the liberalization become, the more aggressive monopoly capital becomes in imputing its burden to workers, farmers and small businesses. More aptly, monopoly capital regards the liberalization merely as a tool of solving its own problems.

The specific manners in which the liberalization will be carried out depend upon political and economic conditions in the world, the degree of preparedness with respect to tariff, cartel and finance as well as the nature of struggle among monopoly capitalists. The liberalization will not necessarily proceed linearly and smoothly as planned by the government. There will likely be setbacks and alterations while monopoly capitalists will attempt industrial reorganizations to suit their own needs.

If the world economy experiences a major recession in the near future, the difficulties inherent in the liberalization will be compounded to such an extent that the whole scheme may probably fall into total disintegration. The intensification of price competition and drive for more profits lead to a tendency for firms to overinvest, which in turn raises the probability of a major panic.

(5) Consequences of the Liberalization

The liberalization will bring about uneven and disproportionate consequences upon various industries, depending upon whether or not a given industry is to be liberalized as well as the degree of preparedness and the international competitive position of an industry in question. In general, it is believed that agriculture, mining, construction and industrial machinery and pulp will be most adversely affected whereas the impact will be relatively weak upon cotton spinning, chemical textiles, iron and steel, ship-building, camera, sewing machine and electrical machinery.

The liberalization will strengthen the position of big businesses closely allied with large banks, state capital and/or foreign capital, and promote expansion of heavy and chemical industries in the country. It will increase the importance of low wages as a factor in Japanese exports, and perpetuate the presence of small businesses. The problem of a dual economy will be more likely aggravated than solved.

Both exports and imports of Japan heavily depend upon the United States. The liberalization of trade, exchange, and investment will help establish a closer tie between American and Japanese monopolists. Such an alliance will expose Japanese workers to a menace of joint aggression by the international monopoly capitalists. As the struggle between American and Japanese monopolists becomes fierce and violent, dissolution of the friction will be sought at the expense of the welfare of the workers and the general public. A rise in Japan's dependence upon the U.S. market means an increasing volatility on the part of Japan to the changing political and economic conditions in the United States. Instability of the Japanese economy will give capitalists one more opportunity to launch an offensive against the working class.

The government and monopoly capital are misleading the people with a false claim that the liberalization will reduce prices of goods, enhancing consumer welfare. Even if it is true that the liberalization is in principle geared toward reduction of prices, there is no reason to believe that the prices will necessarily fall inasmuch as there are numerous other factors in price changes which have little to do with the liberalization per se. If prices of some specific goods fall, monopolists will likely use the occasion as an excuse for a further rationalization and wage cuts. Large corporations will try their best to raise monopoly prices. As long as the market remains controlled by monopoly capital, every fall in price will be taken as a convenient justification of cost-reducing measures. Wage cuts will remove from workers and farmers more purchasing power than that which was gained through falling prices. Decrease in prices of some consumer goods will be more than offset by rise in monopoly prices. It is to be remembered that there is no consumer welfare as such apart from the welfare of workers, farmers and the general public.

In those sectors which are adversely affected by the liberalization management will readily exploit, suppress and sacrifice workers in order to gain a more powerful monopolistic control of the market. The kind of rationalization offensive to be launched by management will differ from sector to sector. But the substance of such an offensive is always the same—it is directed toward a naked exploitation of the working class. It is extremely important for us to establish a clear vision of the class struggle and understand the true nature of the liberalization policy. We must not let the uneven and disproportionate impact of the liberalization upon different industries help disunite us and cause frictions and conflicts of short-run interests among us. Of decisive import is that we build a unified anti-monopoly front in confronting the liberalization policy.

**DOCUMENTS
CONCERNING
LIBERALIZATION
OF
CAPITAL TRANSACTIONS**

THE REPORT OF THE FOREIGN
INVESTMENT COUNCIL*

Preface

   (The Basic Way of Thinking About the Liberalization of
   Capital Movements)

   Our country has been striving to establish closer ties with the
international economic community by way of liberalizing foreign
trade and exchange, and participating in the Kennedy Round of tariff
negotiations. We are now ready to take further steps in liberalizing
capital transactions.

   We joined the OECD in 1964 because we believed that closer
international economic cooperation would contribute to the expansion
and prosperity of individual national economies as well as the world
economy at large, and because we judged then that the liberalization
of capital and other nontrade transactions would be in our own interest from the long-run perspective of the growth of our economy.

---

   *The original text is Gaishi Shingi Kai Toshin, a report prepared
by the Foreign Investment Council and submitted to the Minister of
Finance on June 2, 1967, in response to the Minister's request, dated
February 24, 1967, to the Foreign Investment Council to investigate
and make policy recommendations concerning the liberalization of
foreign investments in Japan. The council normally consists of

Now that three years have passed since our joining the OECD, our economy, on the basis of its growth already achieved, is expected to make further progress in the new context of an open economy as stipulated in the recently announced Economic and Social Development Plan.

Meanwhile, technological development has been very rapid in the Western countries, and an increasing number of Western firms have been gaining the status of world enterprises while taking full advantage of the liberalization movements. At the same time, industrialization in many developing countries has made much progress. Some of the developing countries today have become formidable rivals to Japan in the area of labor-intensive goods.

These changing circumstances surrounding Japan illustrate that our country is now at the crossroads where we must mobilize our energy and wisdom to achieve a further expansion and flourishing of our economy. It is our view that we must face the problem of liberalization of capital movements—especially of foreign direct investments—with a firm and positive attitude and as a challenge to the prospects of the long-run growth of the Japanese economy.

Foreign direct investment is a matter of immediate concern to this Council. It is to be noted, however, that the liberalization of capital movements includes many other aspects such as overseas investments by Japanese firms. We are in a position to comment in this report mainly about foreign direct investments and foreign portfolio investments in Japan. Besides these two areas, we believe that Japan should proceed as fast as possible to relax or remove the presently held reservations as our economy moves onto an advanced stage of development.

---

selected officials from various Ministries and is chaired by the Minister of Finance. In preparing this particular report the membership of the Council was reorganized to include individuals from various segments of the private sector in order to assess and incorporate diverse views. Ataru Kobayashi was appointed by the Minister of Finance to act as chief representative and eight other members served on the Council. A specially appointed committee of seven experts, chaired by Takeo Suzuki, collaborated with the Council. Some parts of the report, which are irrelevant to our purpose or whose contents reappear in Cabinet Decision (Source IV-B) or elsewhere in the book, have been omitted.

(How to Proceed with the Liberalization of Foreign Direct
Investments)

Of the various aspects of the liberalization of capital transactions,
what concerns us most is the entry of foreign enterprises into the
Japanese market, i.e., the liberalization of foreign direct investments
in our country.

After the war we promulgated the Foreign Investment Law which
encourages induction of sound foreign capital into Japan under the
approval system and guarantees rights of the approved foreign enterprises to transfer their funds. The regulations enforced by the Law
have been gradually relaxed over the years along with the recovery
and subsequent expansion of the economy. Concerning foreign direct
investments in particular, after 1964—the year of our joining the
OECD—the previous rule of not approving as a matter of general
principle the foreign-capital ratio exceeding 49 percent in manufacturing combines was removed, and application for a foreign-capital ratio
of 50 percent became acceptable. Simpler and faster screening procedures have also been put into effect.

In view of the changing conditions, both domestic and international, it is our judgment that we should move toward a further
liberalization, beginning with a wider application of the automatic
approval system. For the immediate future we should start liberalizing those industries which are already sufficiently prepared to face
the inflow of foreign capital, and strive to have achieved, in the
absence of radical changes in the internal and external circumstances,
a comprehensive and substantial liberalization by the end of fiscal
1971 in line with the projection of the Economic and Social Development Plan.

An ideal situation as we envision it is one in which the entering
foreign enterprises compete fairly and effectively with Japanese firms
on equal terms, thus jointly contributing to the increase in the nation's
economic welfare. From now on it is the responsibility of all of us—
the general public, business, industry and the government—to bring our
economy to an advanced stage where such an ideal circumstance may
prevail.

As we appraise the present economic reality, however, we observe
the persisting gaps between Japanese and Western enterprises in terms
of not only price and cost factors but also capital accumulation and the
capacity to develop new technology and markets. Consequently, it is
premature to expect a large number of industries to be placed

immediately under the 100 percent automatic approval system. It is
also apt for us to remember that in those industries for which up to
50 percent of the foreign-capital ratio is automatically approved there
may be found many individual Japanese firms which cannot as yet withstand the impact of the liberalization.

We should therefore set our target for the period through the end
of fiscal 1971 to maximize the number of industries to be placed under
the 50 percent automatic approval category while striving to increase
the number of industries under the 100 percent approval category. In
the present context we believe this to be the most realistic and forward-
looking policy direction.

The degree of international competition among world enterprises
has been steadily rising. Total efforts are required to those who
manage Japanese business and industry to improve their competitive
position vis-à-vis foreign enterprises through development of new
technology, acquisition of high-grade capital and labor, efficient use
of resources, and productive management.

In order to guide and complement private endeavors the government is also required to make the utmost efforts in promoting research in science and technology, building industrial and financial
environments suited to an effective implementation of the liberalization, and minimizing its own administrative costs. Such joint endeavors
of both the government and private businesses will establish a foundation upon which Japanese firms can effectively cope with the incoming
foreign enterprises. The liberalization process should proceed subject to a periodic review every two years or so, depending upon the
results of private efforts and government policy measures for preparing the Japanese economy for the inflow of foreign investments.

I   The Basic Attitude Toward Liberalization of Foreign Direct Investments in Japan

1   Policy toward Liberalization

(Impact of the Liberalization upon Our Economy)

We may conceive of the following benefits to our economy to be
derived from the liberalization.

(i) Advanced foreign technology becomes available, and the induction of foreign technology will act as catalyst for the advancement
of our own science and technology.

(ii) The stimulus given by the intensified competition will help increase the overall efficiency of our economy.

(iii) Modernization of Japanese firms will be promoted by advanced management methods and market development techniques of the incoming foreign enterprises.

(iv) Consumer welfare will be enhanced through qualitative improvement of products, and Japanese exports will expand through a newly opened international network of sales channels.

On the other hand, the liberalization may bring about the following difficulties to Japan, the severity of which will depend upon our preparedness and policy actions.

(i) Thanks to technology gaps and capital deficiency, Japanese firms or industries may fall under control of powerful world enterprises.

(ii) Development of advanced technology may take place in an exclusive manner in countries where foreign enterprises operating in Japan originate, so that autonomous development of new technology within Japanese industry will actually be hindered.

(iii) Foreign enterprises in Japan may generate excessive competition among Japanese businesses, causing social and economic frictions especially in those sectors dominated by small businesses.

(iv) Foreign enterprises in Japan may not cooperate with the Japanese government so that the government will face difficulties in carrying out long-run structural policies as well as short-run counter-cyclical policies.

We must examine those problems with care and take all necessary, precautionary measures to minimize the negative consequences of the liberalization. Decisions concerning specific contents of the implementation policy ought to be made after carefully assessing all the implications of the liberalization in connection with private and governmental measures that are available.

2   Policy Measures to Implement the Liberalization

(Basic Direction of the Policy Measures)

The ability to compete with foreign firms in terms of price is usually a sufficient condition to be met before a country may liberalize its trade without danger of internal disruptions. In the case of trade liberalization, tariff, transportation cost and the labor supply in the home market work in favor of domestic, as against foreign, firms. When capital movements are liberalized, however, the test of competition becomes severer inasmuch as the incoming foreign enterprises now have equal access to whatever favorable internal factors were hitherto available only to domestic enterprises. So that Japanese firms become able to compete effectively with foreign enterprises on equal terms, it is necessary for Japanese business and industry to accelerate their qualitative improvements in management, organization and production, development of an autonomous capacity to innovate together with a major adjustment in financial organizations toward reduction of long-term interest rates in Japan. It is also necessary to build sufficient safeguard measures to prevent foreign firms from causing undue disruptions in the domestic market and moving into unliberalized sectors through evasive tatics. The international competitive strength of Japanese firms as well as avoidance of disturbances in the home market caused by the entering foreign capital are essential not only for the implementation of the liberalization but also for our country to derive benefits from the conditions of an open economy.

(Private Efforts and Actions)

Individual firms are expected to strive toward an increase in their overall productivity and efficiency by attacking problems and making improvements in all areas—management, technology, capital, labor, and finance. On the basis of such autonomous efforts at the level of individual firms, each industry must design a long-range plan to carry out a steady and orderly liberalization. For this objective closer cooperation among business and industry groups is necessary. No less essential is the deepening of understanding between labor and management concerning the common problem they face and the joint strategy for the liberalization. Japanese business and industry should be able to inform the incoming foreign interests of their plans and intentions, and to persuade them with firmness to respect and adhere to the rules of conducting business in Japan.

The financial institutions are expected to cooperate with business and industry by making their own efforts to make available greater investible funds at lower costs. The implication of their actions for the economic welfare of the entire nation cannot be overemphasized.

(Government's Policy Actions)

There are three main objectives of government policy.

(i) To prevent disruptions caused by the influx of foreign capital.

(ii) To build a foundation upon which Japanese firms can compete with foreign enterprises on equal terms.

(iii) To help enhance through all available means the preparedness on the part of Japanese business and industry.

It is necessary for the government to take sufficient measures to minimize confusion and disruptions within our economy caused by the entry of foreign enterprises equipped with superior technology, a more advanced know-how on market development, and greater financial resources. Over the long run, reforms of the existing laws and legislation of new regulations will be needed to prevent foreign enterprises in Japan from abusing their superior corporate power in taking over Japanese firms or aggressively forcing a transfer of control rights from Japanese enterprises against the will of the Japanese management.

No less important than these direct, preventive measures are the government's policy actions to guide and supplement endeavors of private business and industry in developing technology, augmenting owned-capital and increasing a supply of funds (especially for long-term investments) at low interest rates. In the United States and Western Europe the governments have been instrumental to technological development; and this fact is largely responsible for Japan's present technological lag behind the West. There is a pressing need for the Japanese government to launch a series of forceful, long-run plans to promote research in science and technology.

Japanese firms rely heavily upon the method of external finance. This fact, together with the high interest rates in Japan relative to those in the Western countries, places Japanese firms in a position of disadvantage. Every effort is expected of the government to assist financial institutions in raising efficiency of their operations. What is vital is to develop a stable capital market capable of supplying large, long-term investment funds to the Japanese firms. Appropriate policy measures should not be ignored concerning installment sales of consumer durables whose popularity is anticipated to increase in the future along with the liberalization.

In order to improve the overall competitive position of Japanese firms there is a need to undertake a far-reaching structural reform in the organization of Japanese industry. Such reform is expected to be initiated and carried out autonomously by private industry. However, there is much assistance that the government can render by way

of fiscal and monetary measures and rearranging the present legal
system pertaining to industrial organization.

A strong impact of liberalization will likely be felt by small
businesses operating throughout many sectors of the Japanese economy
Effective fiscal and monetary measures and administrative guidance
of the government are needed to prepare them for the changing circumstances. In the light of experiences of West European countries particular attention should be directed to medium-size enterprises which
seem especially vulnerable to, and likely to become preferred targets
for, the aggressive take-over attempts of foreign enterprises.

The liberalization policy toward those industries which require
supplies of raw materials from the primary industries (agriculture,
fishing, and forestry) should emphasize, as a policy objective, a substantial gain in productivity of the primary industry through structural
reforms and other means.

Distribution represents a most backward sector in the Japanese
economy and lacks the capacity to resist the adverse effects of the
incoming foreign capital. Disruptions occurring in the sector are
bound to spread to the related production sectors. The liberalization
policy in this area must attempt to modernize the existing mechanism
of marketing and raise efficiency of the distributing firms.

The Small Business Modernization Promotion Act, the Machinery
Industry Expansion Extraordinary Measures Act and other related
laws ought to be thoroughly reexamined to better prepare small businesses for the age of liberalization. Depending upon future circumstances, tightening of legal means of protection and rescheduling of
the time table of liberalization with respect to small business may be
advisable.

As regards the employment market the policy should focus on
improvement of labor productivity and transferability of Japanese
workers.

Our central objective is to gain maximum benefits from the
liberalization while minimizing harm to our economy resulting from
uncontrolled influx of foreign capital. Such objective will be fulfilled
when massive efforts for self-improvement on the part of the industrial and financial sectors are combined with effective policy actions
of the government in support of the private endeavors.

3 What We Expect of Foreign Investors

In return for our own efforts to prepare the nation's economy for liberalization we expect the entering foreign firms—be it independent entries into the Japanese market or joint ventures with Japanese firms—to respect the laws, customs, and conventions in Japan and refrain from activities that will grossly upset the orderly working of the Japanese economy. We present the following list of suggested guidelines for foreign enterprises so as to assure benefits to us from new competition and cooperation between Japanese and foreign firms in the liberalized industries.

(i) For an interim period foreign direct investments in Japan should assume the form of joint ventures with Japanese firms on an equal basis and adhere to the principle of coexistence and co-prosperity.

(ii) A simultaneous, concentrated entry of foreign capital into a single sector should be avoided.

(iii) Foreign enterprises entering into those sectors where production is carried out mainly by small businesses should refrain from causing undue strain among those small businesses.

(iv) Foreign management is expected to understand and cooperate with autonomous efforts of those in Japanese business and industry for preservation of an orderly market.

(v) Foreign enterprises in Japan should refrain from signing unduly restrictive and exclusive agreements with parent companies abroad vis-à-vis Japanese firms and from practicing improper control of business transactions or engaging in unfair competition.

(vi) Foreign concerns in Japan should try to help and contribute to the development and promotion of industrial technology in Japan.

(vii) Foreign enterprises are expected to cooperate with Japan's effort to improve her balance of payments through such means as promotion of exports.

(viii) Foreign firms should employ as many Japanese officials as possible and hold open sales of their stocks.

(ix) Foreign firms should refrain from such disrupting acts as sudden plant closures or mass lay-offs and from disregarding Japanese conventions pertaining to employment and wages.

(x) Foreign firms are expected to cooperate with the economic policy of the Japanese government.

4   What We Expect of Japanese Firms

As the liberalization proceeds the number of contracts on technology and sales or of joint ventures between foreign and Japanese enterprises will inevitably increase. There is a need for Japanese management to rectify its conceptions of business contracts. While Japanese management tends to rely upon verbal agreements and inter-personal connections, a stricter adherence to details of a contract is taken for granted by the Western counterparts. There have already been several cases whereby Japanese firms were unable to protect their interests because of the inadequate phrasing of the existing con-tracts. When a Japanese firm enters into a contract with a foreign partner, it is essential for the management of the Japanese firm to understand fully all the meaning and implication of the contract and see to it that the intended objective of the contract is duly achieved.

Before a Japanese firm decides to participate in a joint venture with a foreign enterprise, it is useful for the Japanese firm to con-duct a careful study of the record of similar ventures, if any, of that foreign enterprise in other countries as well as the character, intent, philosophy, and methods of the foreign management in question. The decision to form a joint venture must be preceded by due considera-tion of the impact of such an attempt upon related industries in the country. Any move that is likely to cause market disturbances should be avoided.

After a joint venture is established the Japanese management should diligently learn as much as possible from the foreign partner about technology and management techniques; at the same time it should not hesitate to express its own views on the contracts and make demands to the foreign partner concerning language, customs, and other problems of management in the Japanese context.

II   The Liberalization Measures for the Immediate Future

Direction of the Liberalization Policy for the Immediate Future

(The Basic Orientation)

The following is our recommendation concerning the liberaliza-tion measures for the immediate future. We believe that these measures are consistent with the long-run objective of deriving maximum benefits to Japan from the general and complete liberalization.

(Classification of Industries)

The degree of preparedness differs from industry to industry. Therefore, an approach to liberalize simultaneously a group of industries under the same formula will likely cause difficulties. With respect to direct investments in subsidiaries and joint ventures the best approach, in our view, is to adopt a separate liberalization measure for each industry as deemed most appropriate.

(Distinction between Foreign Investments in New as against Existing Companies)

The impact of foreign investment in an already existing firm is believed stronger in general than that in a newly established enterprise. There is also a widespread concern in Japan about take-over of the existing Japanese firms by foreign enterprises because capital endowments of Japanese firms are generally small relative to those of world enterprises and shares of their stocks are often thinly distributed. Taking this concern under serious consideration would have led us to draft too restrictive a liberalization plan to be justifiable. The interim measures we recommend deal mainly with foreign investments in new enterprises. Nonetheless, we propose a liberalization of foreign investments in old enterprises up to 7 percent per single foreign investor and 20 percent for the total foreign capital invested in a Japanese company (15 percent for Japanese companies under the limited category).

2   The Liberalization Measures concerning Foreign Direct Investments in Subsidiaries or Joint Ventures in Japan

(1) The Framework of Liberalization Measures

(Classification by Industry, by Old-New Criteria)

There are several alternative approaches to partial liberalization—by industry, by capital endowments, by region, etc. As stated earlier, we believe that the best approach is to liberalize by industry, starting with those industries which are judged to involve the least potential difficulties. As to the measure for the immediate future we make a distinction between foreign investments in the newly established enterprises—be it formation of a new subsidiary or a new joint venture—and those purporting to participate in management of the already existing firms.

(Classification by the Stock Ratio)

Japan is not yet ready for a general and complete liberalization of capital transactions. However, there may be exceptional cases of industries already well advanced in preparation for the liberalization. We allow for these individual cases by incorporating into the general format a criterion of adjustable ratio of foreign-owned stocks of Japanese firms.

(Specific Measures)

The following measures are designed to specify the framework of liberalization and clarify the distinction between automatic approval and case-by-case examination.

(i) New enterprises are classified into two categories: the liberalized industries and the nonliberalized industries.

(ii) The liberalized industries are subdivided into Category I and Category II. Category I includes those industries for which up to 50 percent of the foreign-owned stock ratio is to be automatically approved. Category II consists of those industries to which automatic approval of up to 100 percent of the said ratio is applied.

(iii) As regards the nonliberalized industries automatic approval may be granted for those portfolio investments within the limits entrusted by the Bank of Japan.

(iv) Names of liberalized industries in Categories I and II shall be announced.

(v) Application of a foreign investor for acquisition of shares of stock of a newly established enterprise under Category I or Category II may be automatically approved subject to conditions set forth below.

(vi) Application of a foreign investor for acquisition of shares of stock of a newly established enterprise under the category of nonliberalized industries and application for acquisition of shares of stock of an already existing enterprise in the amount beyond the limit entrusted by the Bank of Japan shall be subject to case-by-case examination.

(2) Conditions for Automatic Approval

(The Relationship with the OECD Code of Liberalization)

The OECD Code of Liberalization allows for the following measures for those industries to which the rule of automatic approval applies.

(i) To examine whether the statements in the application are true or false.

(ii) To prevent evasion or violation of the existing laws and ordinances.

(iii) To impose regulations if and when there exists an exceptionally serious threat to the national interest.

(Separate Examination under the Automatic Approval System)

As regards the liberalization measures for the immediate future we make an important distinction between new as against old enterprises, and presuppose that Japanese management can function on equal terms vis-à-vis foreign enterprises. We therefore deem it proper to allow for case-by-case examination of those applications which fall technically under the automatic approval category if:

(i) Foreign investments are in those Japanese firms which are formally new but in actuality little different from old ones;

(ii) The Japanese-owned stock ratio is larger than 50 percent but the foreign investor is capable of gaining a managerial control of the firm; and

(iii) Foreign investments in question are likely to cause exceptionally severe harm to the national interest.

(Determination and Announcement of Conditions for Automatic Approval)

The objective criteria for determining whether or not an application refers to one or more of the above conditions for automatic approval should be established and announced to the general public.

(Qualifications Accompanying Automatic Approval)

In the following cases automatic approval shall be accompanied by a qualification that a separate permit from the competent Minister be obtained to comply with Article 14 of the Foreign Investment Law.

(i) When automatic approval is given to a firm wherein the foreign-owned stock ratio is more than one-third, and the same firm later decides to move into another industry different from the one mentioned in the initial application.

(ii) When a newly established firm later attempts to transfer the rights of management control from another, already existing firm.

(3) Selection of Liberalized Industries

(Liberalized Industries: Category I)

Category I consists of those industries which are already well advanced in terms of some separate criteria such as technology, capital, plant and equipment, resources, etc. but whose overall strength is not yet comparable to that of world enterprises. Automatic approval and the foreign-owned stock ratio of up to 50 percent are applied to this Category to assure promotion of competition on equal grounds.

(Liberalized Industries: Category II)

Category II consists of those industries which are already well advanced in terms of separate criteria such as technology, capital, plant and equipment, resources, etc. as well as in terms of the over-all competitive strength vis-à-vis world enterprises. Automatic approval and the foreign-owned stock ratio of up to 100 percent may be applied to this Category.

(Direction of Our Future Efforts)

Along with a further advancement of Japanese industries we must naturally continue our efforts to widen areas to which the automatic approval system is applied. In view of the present conditions, however, it seems realistic to direct our endeavors toward a gradual increase in the number of liberalized industries under Category I for some years to come.

(4) Procedures of Automatic Approval

(Agencies to Administer Automatic Approval)

While implementing the liberalization it is essential that approval be granted as soon as possible after the authorities decide that the application qualifies for the automatic approval system. There are conflicting views as to which agency or agencies of the government should administer issuance of the approval. Our plan for the immediate future assigns the task to the Minister of Finance and other competent Ministers in charge of liberalized industries in accordance with the Foreign Investment Law. However, we regard it proper that the Bank of Japan will eventually assume the sole administrative responsibility.

(Distinction from Case-by-Case Examination)

Competent Ministers should make clear a distinction between automatically approved cases and those which are referred to the system of case-by-case examinations. For this purpose a major simplification and clarification of the screening procedures is needed.

III Other Problems Related to the Liberalization of Foreign Direct Investments in Japan

1 The Liberalization Measures concerning Foreign Portfolio Investments

(Present Regulations)

At present the Bank of Japan automatically approves foreign portfolio investments in Japanese stocks provided that, of those cases whereby the ratio of stock owned by a single foreign investor does not exceed 5 percent, the total foreign-owned stock ratio is less than 15 percent under the nonrestricted category. The intent of the present rule is to give as full a liberalization as possible as long as foreign investors are not interested in participating in the management of Japanese corporations.

(Relaxing the Present Restrictions)

This Council recommends that the maximum ratio of stock of a Japanese firm owned by a single foreign investor, total foreign-owned stock ratio, ratio under the nonrestricted category, and the said ratio under the restricted category be raised to 7 percent, 20 percent and 15 percent, respectively. The consideration behind our recommendation is as follows:

(i) According to the Japanese Commercial Code a shareholder whose ownership is 25 percent or more of total shares can claim a right to be elected to a post of directorship;

(ii) After the war the stock ownership has been extensively decentralized and diversified. The average ratio of stock owned by leading shareholders with respect to stocks registered at the Tokyo Stock Exchange has been 8 to 9 percent.

2 Liberalization of Foreign Direct Investments through Branches of Foreign Enterprises in Japan

(Present Regulations)

Establishment and maintenance of branches by foreign enterprises in Japan may be interpreted as a form of direct investment. Under the present rules, however, establishment of a new branch requires only a registration, and there is little restriction over transfer of money through branches except for manufacturing.

(Policy for the Immediate Future)

Given the substantial freedom that is already given to capital movements via branches of foreign enterprises, we see little need for a further relaxation of the present rules at this moment. But we recommend that the restriction over transfer of funds via branches engaged in manufacturing be removed whenever results of case-by-case examinations indicate little possibility of market disruptions. In order to prevent a branch from penetrating the nonliberalized industries, however, the authorization of transfer of funds should be accompanied with a qualification that funds be used only for those purposes which are stated in the initial application.

3 Liberalization of the Inflow of Over-Five-Year Loans from Foreign Creditors

Over-five-year loans to Japanese firms from those foreign creditors who are interested in influencing and establishing a lasting economic relationship with the management of the borrowing firms are technically classified as direct investments. Inasmuch as it is extremely difficult in practice to appraise such motives objectively, adoption of the automatic approval system seems inappropriate in liberalizing the inflow of loans from foreign investors.

4 Relationship with Technical Assistance Contracts

Liberalization of foreign direct investments involves the problem of how to coordinate it with the existing regulations concerning technical assistance contracts. However, we have not dealt with the problem since liberalization of rules concerning technical assistance involves many aspects that are outside the domain of interest of this report, and in the near future the OECD is expected to investigate Japan's reservations concerning the "technical assistance" section of the OECD Code of Liberalization of Current Nontrade Transactions.

5 Simplification and Expedition of the Screening Procedures

We have often been criticized by foreign observers on the grounds that our rules, criteria, and procedures concerning foreign investments in Japan are overly complicated and difficult to understand. It goes without saying that the administrative agencies of the Japanese government must constantly strive to simplify the procedures to the fullest extent possible. There were some major efforts in the past to raise administrative efficiency such as a series of measures adopted by the government in August, 1966. Further efforts on the part of the Government are necessary to simplify procedures of the automatic approval system as well as case-by-case examinations. The following guidelines are suggested for carrying out the task.

i. The foreign investor's request for pre-investment consultation should be met by a considerate response. However, such consultation ought to be clearly distinguished from a more substantive examination of the application that is to be administered later.

ii. A formal application should, as a working rule, be processed within one month after it is submitted to a proper agency.

iii. The screening criteria must be stated as clearly as possible.

iv. Requirements concerning documents to be submitted as part of application should be as simple as possible.

IV Conclusion

We believe that the recommendations contained in this report provide a significant and useful frame of reference for implementing the liberalization. We urge the government to study this report with care and promptly proceed to take actions in determining and announcing the industries to be liberalized under Categories I and II, and expressing its policy position and expectations to foreign investors and Japanese businesses.

In the absence of unexpected, abnormal developments—domestic or overseas—the liberalization should be carried out in steps, each step lasting for one to two years, while the whole nation continues to strive toward achieving a greater advancement of the economy.

We hope that the government, private business and industry, and the general public will all deepen their understanding of the problem and make a joint effort in accomplishing a successful implementation of our liberalization plan.

CABINET DECISION CONCERNING THE LIBERALIZATION OF FOREIGN INVESTMENTS IN JAPAN*

I   The Liberalization Measures for the Immediate Future Concerning Foreign Direct Investments in Japan

(A) A competent Minister shall automatically approve application for acquisition of shares of stock by a foreign investor submitted in accordance with Article 11 of the Foreign Investment Law if it fulfills any of the following conditions.

1   Liberalized Industries

a Application is for acquisition of shares of stock of a newly established company that belongs to Category I of liberalized industries

---

*The original text is Tainai Chokusetsu Toshi nado no Jiyuka no Kakugi Kettei, June 6, 1967. This Cabinet Decision which took effect on July 1, 1967 is heavily based upon the Report of the Foreign Investment Council of June 2, 1967 (Source IV-A). What is reproduced here in translation is an abridged version of the original text as I have deleted large portions of the Report which are repeated almost verbatim et litteratim in the Cabinet Decision.

(see page 242); the foreign investment ratio (i.e., the ratio of foreign-owned shares of stock) does not exceed 50 percent; and all of the following sub-conditions are met.

(1) Such foreign investment shall not cause exceptional damage to the national interest of Japan.

(2) Physical assets used as a means of investment by Japanese shareholders (i.e., shareholders other than foreign investors in question) and physical assets which the newly established company is to acquire from an already existing company as a means of investment may be real estate other than factories, stores and warehouses.

(3) The newly established company shall not intend, shortly after its incorporation, to transfer management or rental rights as well as the right to continue to use physical assets (excluding factories, stores and warehouses) of an already existing company, or to merge with an already existing company.

(4) The Japanese owners of shares of stock of the newly established company, who also operate other similar businesses in the same industry, may own more than 50 percent of total shares of stock of the newly established company; and at least one of the above Japanese shareholders may own more than one-third of the total shares of stock of the said company.

(5) The ratio of Japanese directors and supervisors of the newly established company, elected by Japanese shareholders, shall be higher than that of total Japanese-owned shares of stock of the said company.

(6) The decision-making method employed by the newly established company shall be consistent with the Japanese Commercial Code; and execution of important matters within the company shall not presuppose consensus of a particular official or all shareholders.

b Application is for acquisition of shares of stock of a newly established company that belongs to Category II of liberalized industries (see page 244); and the above sub-conditions (1), (2) and (3) are met.

2 Nonliberalized Industries

Application for acquisition of shares of stock of a newly established company which does not belong to Category I or Category II of

Liberalized Industries: Category I

Ministry in Charge	Type of Business	Remark
Ministry of Welfare	Western-style restaurants	Capital stock of more than 50 million yen only
	Commercial laundry	Linen supply only
	Medical drugs	
Ministry of Agriculture and Forestry	Canned fishery products	Includes jars and pots
	Soup Manufacturing	
	Veterinary drugs	
	Agricultural chemicals	
Ministry of International Trade and Industry	Electrical machines and tools	Private uses only
	Radio and television	Excludes color television
	Tape recorder	
	Record player	
	Telephone receiver and telephone exchange equipment	
	Vacuum tubes	
	Camera and parts	Excludes lens and exposure meter
	Watch and parts	
	Ammoniacal fertilizers	
	Caustic soda	
	Printing ink	
	Plate glass	
	Fire-resistance bricks	
	Worsted spinning	
	Acetate	
	Synthetic textiles	
	Records	
	Titanium refining	
	Cobalt refining	
	Rolling of titanium and titanium alloy	
Ministry of Transportation	Extra-large ships	Those built in docks with capacity of more than 200,000 tons
	Engines for ships	
	Rolling stock	
	Warehousing	
Ministry of Construction	Building consultant	
	Architectural design control	

liberalized industries is subject to the same conditions as are set
forth in the section, "Foreign Investments in Japan," below.

3   Application for acquisition of shares of stock of an already existing company is subject to the same conditions as set forth in Section
II below.

(B)   If the foreign investment ratio exceeds one-third while automatic approval is granted in the manner indicated in (A) above, the
following qualifications shall be attached to the approval in accordance
with Article 14 of the Foreign Investment Law.

1   A separate approval of a competent Minister must be obtained
if the newly established company later decides to conduct business in
an area different from one indicated in the initial application.

2   A separate approval of a competent Minister must be obtained
if the newly established company later decides to merge with an
already existing company, or to acquire management rights and/or
properties (excluding factories, stores, and warehouses) from another
company for the purpose of conducting business of the newly established company provided that such a decision requires an affirmative
vote at the general meeting of shareholders.

C)   Government ordinances concerning implementation of the
Foreign Investment Law shall be reformed so that foreign investors
may not evade the rules and regulations under the said Law by acquiring in yen shares of Japanese stock for the purpose of gaining managerial control. A special permit shall be required of a foreign investor
who wishes to acquire in yen shares of stock of a Japanese company
which conducts business under the nonrestricted category for a purpose
other than an ordinary transfer of portfolio.

II   Foreign Portfolio Investments in Japan

The Bank of Japan shall grant automatic approval of foreign
portfolio investments (i.e., acquisition of shares of Japanese stock
with no interest in participating in the management of Japanese company) provided that the ratio of shares of a company stock acquired
by a single foreign investor does not exceed 7 percent and the ratio
of shares owned by all foreign investors per company does not exceed
20 percent and 15 percent under the nonrestricted and restricted
categories of industries, respectively, in accordance with the Bank
of Japan's classifications.

Liberalized Industries: Category II

Ministry in Charge	Type of Business	Remark
Ministry of Finance	Beer	
Ministry of Agriculture and Forestry	Glutamic soda	
	Commercial ice	
	Reeling	
Ministry of International Trade and Industry	Ordinary steel	
	Motorcycle and scooter	
	Carbide	
	Cement	
	Cotton and rayon staple spinning	
	Synthetic textiles	Restricted to those which employ the cotton or rayon staple spinning method
	Rayon	
	Piano	
	Organ	
Ministry of Transportation	Ship building	Excludes extra-large ship
	Travel service	
	Tourist hotels	

THE ATTITUDE OF THE JAPAN ASSOCIATION
OF TEXTILE MANUFACTURERS TOWARD
LIBERALIZATION OF CAPITAL
TRANSACTIONS*

Since last year the demand of the United States and West European countries for Japan's liberalization of capital transactions has been rising conspicuously. At the same time, the negotiations for all-around tariff reductions have been in progress. As a member of the OECD, Japan today faces an urgent obligation to remove her restrictions on movements of foreign capital.

The free, international movement of capital leads to a better allocation of resources and a greater division of labor in the world economy. It is also an effective means of solving problems of the underdeveloped countries. To promote economic development and dissolve poverty among the less developed countries through a greater flow of capital signifies a contribution to world peace.

At present there exists a pessimistic argument in our country that Japanese industry is not yet strong enough to withstand the test of an open economy. Side by side with this pessimism is the view that the free entry of American capital into Japan will place Japanese monopoly capital in a role subservient to the American interests, thus making the country a de facto colony of the United States; not unlikely is the possibility that a greater militarization of our economy will occur as Japan is forced to share more of the American involvement in Vietnam.

However, the weakness of Japan industry is a reflection of the structural faults of the Japanese economy, and it is the internal faults of our economy that cause difficulties associated with the liberalization. The right course of action for Japan to take is not to continue a closed-door policy—thus perpetuating the structural defects of the economy—but rather to take advantage of the global trend toward liberalization by encouraging technological progress and other aspects of modernization in order to remove the internal defects of our economy. Blinding ourselves to our problems and indulging in a political ideology as a basis for opposing the liberalization policy will not only

---

*The orignial text is Shihon Torihiki no Jiyu-ka ni taisuru Zensen Domei no Taido, March 3, 1967.

fail to serve a useful purpose but also ultimately lead to Japan's assuming a subservient role vis-à-vis the United States.

The Japanese textile industry as a whole—except for the chemical textiles—does not anticipate serious difficulties in the free entry of foreign capital. The main reason for this outlook is that the textiles as a declining industry are believed to represent a less than attractive investment opportunity for foreign interests. It is possible, however, that foreign firms will come to dominate the manufacturing sector first, and then proceed to control some of the raw materials and spinning sectors. Textile manufacturing in the United States and Western Europe is strong enough to be able to pose a threat to Japan. The possibility that the textile marketing and textile machines sectors will be subjected to the influence of foreign capital is also recognized.

It is of the utmost importance to formulate a positive policy toward the liberalization—a policy which takes into account advantages as well as disadvantages of the entry of foreign capital and which does not underestimate the potential impact of foreign capital upon the Japanese textile industry.

We do not, of course, welcome foreign capital open-handedly and without reservations. We deem it urgent to reform the Foreign Investment Law and the Foreign Exchange Control Law, as well as to promulgate various measures directed toward improving efficiency and productivity of our industry. Particularly necessary for the textile industry is to eliminate parochial conservatism present in some segments and to vigorously promote its modernization. We strongly oppose, however, any policy which, in the name of open economy, favors big businesses. Mergers, combines, and other forms of industrial reorganization should not be allowed if they contribute to a further oligopolization of the kind that benefits big business at the expense of consumer welfare. Unjust firing of textile workers under the banner of rationalization should also not be permitted.

It is not realistic to expect only advantages out of the liberalization. If we take sufficient measures to cope with the disadvantages, the liberalization will result in a further growth and a greater prosperity of the textile industry in Japan.

We believe that there ought to be: 1. establishment of a new industrial order, measures to improve the production and distribution sectors, and elimination of excessive competition; 2. avoidance of undue social conflicts and disruptions in the employment market due to the liberalization; 3. reforms of the Foreign Investment Law and

the Foreign Exchange Control Law so that the managerial rights of
Japanese firms and the control system vis-à-vis foreign capital in
Japan be well established; 4. measures to encourage technological
development in Japan along with the improved standards for induction
of foreign technology; 5. prevention of dumping of foreign goods in
Japan and removal of discriminatory import restrictions abroad
against Japanese goods; and 6. consumer education directed toward
cultivation of deeper interest in Japanese goods.

On the eve of liberalization, we believe in promotion of these
measures as we move forward to pursue a greater economic welfare
of our country.

OPINION CONCERNING LIBERALIZATION
OF CAPITAL TRANSACTIONS*

Now that the full-fledged liberalization of capital transactions
is around the corner, our economy finds itself in a transitional period
of historic importance. Hoping that the Japanese economy will continue its sustained growth in the context of an open economy and that
our economy will entertain a rising prestige in the international community, we hereby present the following policy recommendations to
those concerned with the liberalization.

1   We should maintain a forward-looking posture toward the
liberalization of capital movements; but the steps we take should be
cautious and gradual so as to avoid adverse effects on our economy.

The liberalization of capital transactions is a mainstream in the
world economy today. As we move toward the status of an advanced
country, it is imperative that we maintain a positive attitude toward
the global trend. However, compared with the Western countries,
our economy still contains elements of vulnerability: the scale of
management is typically small by Western standards; there are
numerous small businesses; and our industries continue to depend
heavily upon borrowed technology. An abrupt influx of foreign capital

---

*The original text is <u>Shihon Torihiki ni Kansuru Iken</u>, March,
1967.

is likely to cause frictions in the society and disrupt the course of stable growth of our economy.

What is necessary for us is to follow a gradual path of liberalization, paying due attention to all the problems, foreseen and unforeseen, that are bound to arise, and to develop promptly a unified and comprehensive set of policy measures dealing with modernization of industry and legal aspects of the liberalization.

2   We should take the following steps.

(1)   Taking the cumulative voting rights into consideration, we propose that the present 15 percent limit on the foreign-owned shares of stock of businesses in the general category to be raised to about 20 percent.

(2)   The liberalization should begin with those industries whose capital and technological conditions are advanced by international standards. Much caution is needed, however, with respect to small businesses and those industries which rely heavily upon numerous small-scale sub-contracting firms.

(3)   The approval conditions in terms of contents of business and scales of operation of entering foreign firms, irrespective of whether they are independent or joint-ventures with Japanese firms, must be carefully examined. If the foreign firms later attempt to move into new sectors or to change contents of business, such attempt should be subject to a reexamination and a new approval.

3   We recommend the following policy actions.

(1)   Efforts should be concentrated on those sectors of Japanese industry which have thus far remained relatively backward so that the overall efficiency and productivity of Japanese industry will be enhanced significantly. Urgently needed is a new, comprehensive vision for modernization of the Japanese economy, which will guide a formulation of the long-range policies to modernize the low-productivity sectors, to develop new technology within Japan, and to improve the general business environment. The Government should widen and intensify its dialogue with private business and industry; it should clarity its role and position in the making of a new environment so that an effective government-business partnership and cooperation may be expected.

(2) A vigorous implementation of all available policy measures to improve Japan's capacity to develop her own technology and catch up with Western countries is necessary.

(a) There should be a more effective division of labor than in the past between the government and the private sector in the field of technology development; the government should be more responsible for basic research.

(b) The government should sizably increase its funds for research in science and engineering, and should take tax (and other) measures to promote technological development in the private sector.

(c) No less urgently needed is an effective policy for the development of human resources, such as training of engineers and technicians.

(3) With respect to small businesses, particular care is essential during the initial period of liberalization. Selective, concentrated efforts to remedy the chronic problems of small businesses are also necessary.

(a) Until the situation improves sufficiently, liberalization should be deferred with respect to those categories of firms which come under the Small Businesses Modernization Promotion Act, the Machine Industry Expansion Extraordinary Measures Act, the Electronics Industry Expansion Extraordinary Measures Act, and the Small Business Organizations Act. Careful, case-by-case examination is essential as regards those small businesses which are not covered by these Acts.

(b) We should develop a "Long-Range Plan for Modernization of Small Businesses" and, along with the Plan, a set of monetary and fiscal policies designed to accelerate the transition of the small business sector to one more in accord with an advanced economy. Particular measures for encouraging technological development and mitigating labor problems in the small business sector are recommended.

(c) Measures should be taken which will help small businesses to achieve optimal scales of operation through mergers and combines. There should be a new tax policy to encourage small businesses to increase their owned-capital ratio. There should be more financial organizations to channel greater investment funds to the small business sector.

(d) Backwardness as characterized by the dense distribution of extremely small firms is notable in the commercial sector. Vigorous, selective policy actions are needed to accelerate the modernization of this sector through mergers, improvement of financial facilities betterment of the distribution system and the like. We propose a "Five-Year Plan for Modernization of the Commercial Sector."

(e) The present system of laws and ordinances concerning the liberalization of capital transactions need be reexamined and reformed. The Anti-Monopoly Act should be applied flexibly in guiding the industrial reorganization. The Act should be implemented in order to avoid excessive concentration of capital, unfair trade practices, and improper market controls with respect to not only Japanese firms but also foreign firms entering the Japanese market. Reforms are needed of the existing patent laws and the installment sales laws so as to eliminate monopoly over technology and excessive competition; however, the reforms should not be carried to such an extreme as to hamper freedom of activity on the part of business enterprises.

RECOMMENDATIONS CONCERNING LIBERALIZATION OF CAPITAL TRANSACTIONS*

Having joined the OECD, our country is required to liberalize capital transactions at an early date. In preparation for this requirement big businesses have steadily been modernizing plants and equipment, and expanding scales of operation.

On the other hand, small businesses have thus far been too busy coping with day-to-day problems of labor shortage, excessive competition, and advance of large corporations into the small business sector to make adequate preparation for the liberalization of foreign capital movements. The small businesses would be adversely affected if the liberalization took place now and in full force.

---

*The original text is Shihon Torihiki Jiyu-ka ni Kansuru Yobo Iken, issued by kenkoku Chusho Kigyo Dantai; Chuokai, May1, 1967.

We duly recognize advantages of the liberalization. It will help expand our foreign trade and overseas investments. The conditions pertaining to sales as well as acquisition of raw materials for small businesses are expected to improve. We also acknowledge that from the viewpoint of international politics it is unwise and problematical to postpone the liberalization indefinitely. However, the present condition of small businesses points to the lack of sufficient preparation for a sudden, major influx of foreign capital. Consequently, we present the following recommendations based upon our belief that the approach toward liberalization should be gradual and start with those areas where the least adverse effects are anticipated.

1 The area where the entry of foreign capital is most probable and influence of foreign investment is likely to be felt strongly is one in which large, Japanese firms have been attempting to develop markets in recent years. The area refers to food processing, services, commerce, and distribution. The labor-intensive business in these sectors has traditionally been carried out by small firms. Thanks to recent innovations and the growth of demand, the capital-intensive mode of operation in these sectors has become feasible, and the entries of large firms into these sectors have already been causing multitudes of difficulties on the part of small businesses. Given this situation, the liberalization with regard to these sectors, which is more than lilely to further aggravate the situation, should not be approved for a while. Capital accumulation among and modernization of small businesses should proceed during the period of reservations.

2 Foreign firms specializing in those categories of advanced machinery about which small firms in Japan lack knowledge and experiences are likely to cause disruptions. Induction of foreign capital linked with those categories of machinery should be carefully controlled until the Japanese small firms become sufficiently capable of competing with the foreign firms in the use and production of those categories of machinery.

3 With respect to those goods whose imports have been restricted as part of the nation's protectionist policy, such as products of the food processing industry using sugar and dairy products as raw materials, the foreign firms from the countries that supply those raw materials are bound to obtain the materials on more advantageous terms than Japanese firms. Also, many of the Western firms operating in Southeast Asia as a supply source as well as a market for their products will likely strengthen their strategic position by moving into Japan. In this area, a thorough liberalization of imports of the raw

materials and a major reduction of tariff rates on them are recommended. The entry of foreign capital into this area should be restricted until the Japanese small firms concerned have cultivated a sufficient, competitive strength vis-à-vis the foreign companies.

4   Excessive competition among small businesses not only destabilizes management on the part of many firms but also has adverse effects on exports. The Small Business Organizations Act is designed to regulate business activities as a means of mitigating the excess of competition. The movement of foreign capital into the area covered by the Act should be regulated with care so that it will not further worsen the situation.

5   At present various measures are being taken, under the Small Businesses Modernization Promotion Act, to improve the competitive position of specified businesses. The central objective of these measures is to help small businesses adapt themselves to the changing structure of the Japanese economy and prepare for the impact of the liberalization. However, many businesses have come under the jurisdiction of the Act only recently while others often have had difficulty in understanding the implications and technicalities of the Act. Approval of the entry of foreign capital into this area must be preceded by a careful examination of the applications so that the intent of the Act will not be jeopardized.

6   It is difficult to predict precisely which of the small business sectors will attract foreign capital and what the ultimate effects will be. Therefore, applications by foreign firms should carefully be examined case-by-case. Before reaching a decision, the authorities should duly consult representatives of the sectors that are likely to be affected.

7   From the standpoint of promoting capital accumulation among small businesses, we believe that the expansion of public as well as private financial intermediaries supplying investible funds to small businesses is preferable to soliciting direct investments of large foreign firms capable of disrupting the market.

8   In some fields our small businesses are capable of competing with foreign firms even if they entered those fields today. However, the same Japanese firms will not be able to withstand the impact of massive and intensive dumping and advertising campaigns which the foreign firms may conduct deliberately for the purpose of establishing monopoly over the market. In order to avoid such adversity a more forceful and effective implementation of the Anti-Monopoly Act and the Small Business Organizations Act is recommended.

9   Many Western firms, endowed with voluminous research funds, are able to win over the Japanese firms with new products and innovations. The paucity of research and development funds is an outstanding feature of small businesses in Japan. Those Japanese firms which are at present highly competitive may find their market position quickly weakened as the new products developed by the foreign companies begin to march in. We recommend establishment and expansion of research facilities purported to stimulate product development in the small business sector.

10   Our small businesses are subjected to both direct and indirect impacts of the liberalization. Big corporations have been imposing increasingly unfavorable terms of business upon smaller sub-contracting firms, all for the alleged purpose of improving the international competitive position of big firms. The foreign firms' recruiting of workers will add to the labor shortage among Japanese small businesses.

Of central importance is to develop and implement a comprehensive set of policies to improve the labor and sub-contracting conditions and raise the overall productivity of small-size enterprises.

RECOMMENDATIONS CONCERNING
LIBERALIZATION OF CAPITAL
TRANSACTIONS AND THE
PROBLEM OF
INDUSTRIAL CAPITAL*

I Introduction

The decade 1945-1955 was the period of recovery from the war, and the following decade 1955-1965 signified the period of rapid economic growth. The next decade which the Japanese economy has just entered is demanding a new way of industrial capital formation. The demand is dictated by the following changing circumstances.

------

*The original text is Teigen: Shihon Torihiki Jiyuka to Sangyo Shihon no Arikata, issued by Sogo Seisaku Kenkyu Kai, May 25, 1967. The text is signed by Hiromi Arisawa, Saburo Okita, Kamekichi Takahashi, Yoshitaro Wakimura, Hidezo Inaba, Shigeji Kawano, Kiyoshi Tsuchiya, Jiro Enjoji, Masao Mukaisaka and Toshiyuki Fukuyoshi.

1   External as well as internal conditions of Japanese corporations
are deteriorating. Rapid economic growth was possible on account of
the abundant supply of labor; however, the labor shortage has become
increasingly conspicuous, and there will certainly be a wage-cost
inflation in the years to come. As a result of voluminous investments
in plant and equipment, the owned-capital ratio in general has fallen,
lessening the capacity to resist recessions and causing financial
instability of the firms. The overall efficiency of capital has declined,
and there has been a trend of decreasing profit rates. The insufficiency
of social overheads such as highways and port facilities, together with
the rising public nuisances of water and air pollution, have been inflat-
ing costs to the firms. The number of small businesses unable to
stride with the tide of accelerated growth has increased, and their
difficulty has been constraining growth of large corporations as well.

2   International competition has been intensified; our firms are
expected to have confrontations with world enterprises. Waves of
technological innovations continue in the world. Large-scale investments induced by new technology and production methods have been
expanding rapidly in other countries. In the past Japanese industry
has managed to modernize itself through borrowing technology from
the West, but it is highly dubious that our industry can proceed in
the same manner for too long. Voluminous investments are necessary
to preserve our competitive position in the world market. If we
attempt a vigorous investment drive without appropriate adjustive
measures, there is danger that Japanese industry will suffer a further
decline in the efficiency of capital resulting from the condition of
overinvestments. Besides increasing the size of the firm, Japanese
industry is confronted with an urgent task of making significant improvement in the areas of capital accumulation, finance, marketing
and technological development.

3   A characteristic of the present decade is that Japanese firms
must compete with foreign enterprises abroad as well as in the home
market. Tariff reductions make it easier for foreign firms to penetrate the Japanese market, but of greater significance today is the
liberalization of capital transactions. From an entirely new angle
liberalization imposes a strong demand that Japanese firms meet the
requirement of international competition. The United States, which
agreed to give Japan some tariff concessions, is not expected to
assume a posture of leniency concerning the liberalization of capital
movements. Prompt but cautious formulation of policies to face the
U.S. demand by both Japanese industry and government is therefore
essential.

Given these changing circumstances, we face the problem of clarifying and establishing a new way of accumulating and structuring our industrial capital so that the Japanese firms in this decade of liberalization will become capable of effectively competing with world enterprises. From this perspective we make the following recommendations.

II   How to Proceed with the Liberalization of Capital Transactions

(1) The Basic Attitude

1   Japan has thus far liberalized capital movements far less than the OECD countries. While pressure from the OECD and the U.S.-Japan Joint Economic Committee on Japan has been mounting, pessimism about the prospects of liberalization has been rising in our country. The pessimism has some justification, but it is fitting to recall that Japan's joining the OECD was motivated by our judgment that the country had reached the stage where liberalization would represent an advantage to Japan as well as to the rest of the international community. Some reservations were taken for granted, but at the time of Japan's acquiring membership in the OECD no one seriously expected those reservations to last indefinitely. Liberalization is the direction Japan herself chose. Undesirable is the attitude that Japan undertake liberalization only as a hesitant response to mounting pressure from without.

2   In lieu of a posture of passivity, it is more sensible to develop a forward-looking view that Japan liberalizes capital transactions because she derives benefits from it. Trade liberalization and attempts to bring down tariff barriers constitute a global trend. The importance of not breaking away from the tide of international cooperation for a country such as Japan whose economic life crucially depends upon foreign trade cannot be overemphasized. A positive attitude toward liberalization will help persuade other countries to terminate their discrimination against Japanese products. On the other hand, we should not underestimate the adverse reactions of other countries if we stubbornly persist in refusing to undertake the liberalization.

3   The liberalization provides a superb opportunity to implement structural improvements throughout Japanese industry and help develop internationally competitive enterprises in our country. Japanese corporations have been conscious of the necessity of building their competitive strength in the world market, but modernization and rationalization of industry have tended to be neglected through

the complacency of easy life in a closed, protected environment. Liberalization as it becomes a reality will give a powerful stimulus to incentives on the part of Japanese firms. The government will also be forced to take positive actions. The alertness of both industry and the government, induced by the liberalization, will contribute to the rapid progress and transformation of Japanese industry. We have much to learn from Great Britain's decision to join the EEC as a "shock" treatment to cure her problem of internal stagnation.

4   The liberalization of capital movements has its own unique advantages. With the inflow of foreign capital, the induction of foreign technology becomes easier. The shortage of capital in the home market will be lessened with the lowering of interests rates. New employment opportunities will expand, and a trend toward higher wages, together with efficient management, will be established.

5   Fundamentally, the liberalization brings benefits to Japan. However, we are aware of its negative implications. While an irrational phobia of liberalization on account of those negative implications is to be avoided, we ought not to neglect taking sufficient precautionary measures against them.

There is one aspect of the liberalization of capital transactions which distinguishes itself from the liberalization of imports. In the case of trade liberalization, foreign goods entering the Japanese market are still subjected to the tariff barrier and the disadvantages of transportation cost. The Japanese firms can take advantage of low, domestic wages to which the foreign firms have no direct access. When capital transactions are liberalized, however, foreign enterprises become able to make direct investments in Japan, combining their enormous capital, advanced technology, and managerial skills with relatively cheap Japanese labor. Those foreign enterprises may deeply penetrate the Japanese market causing a series of disruptions.

6   The liberalization of capital transactions cannot be separated from the problem of economic nationalism. West European countries, alarmed by the vigorous advance of American enterprises in response to the initial liberalization policy, have of late been showing a new attitude of caution mixed with a revival of nationalistic sentiment concerning the influx of foreign capital. This European trend has added to the anti-liberalization feeling in our country as well. Granted, each nation seeks its own national interests; and economic nationalism, if it stands for pursuit and protection of national interests through reasonable economic means, is understandable. What is to be protected, however, is not the profits of individual corporations but

rather the welfare of people. The defense industry and the strategic and newly organized industries need protection. Nonetheless, it is a gross misunderstanding of the fundamental purpose of the liberalization to try to prevent every single advance of foreign enterprises that may cause shifts and reorganization of the domestic market in the name of economic nationalism.

7   The effects of liberalization upon numerous small businesses scattered throughout the production and distribution sectors need particular attention. Inasmuch as these small businesses are endowed only with insufficient capital, technology, and managerial skills, the sudden influx of foreign capital is bound to cause them difficulties. While their condition calls for the government's protective measures, the policy must aim at accelerating their modernization rather than merely perpetuating their present relative backwardness.

8   The liberalization may cause an added difficulty in implementation of the nation's internal economic policies.

(a) Foreign firms in Japan may behave counter to the intent of government policy and may not necessarily follow the government's administrative guidance or moral suasion.

(b) Counter-cyclical policy may fail to yield its effect on foreign firms in Japan whose financial resources are supplied from outside Japan. Conversely, a policy change (e.g., the dollar defense) initiated in another country may bring about adverse effects on foreign firms in Japan, thus spreading disruptions in the Japanese market.

(c) There is a danger that foreign firms in Japan, backed by enormous capital funds, may ignore the indigenous economic order and pursue their own way not in harmony with the established mode of business transactions in this land. In the past economic policy as well as the manner of its implementation have been far from ideal. It is well for us to remember that the liberalization will make the policy application more difficult and complicated than ever before.

9   It is our view that, despite the above negative implications, we should positively proceed with the liberalization. Our view rests upon the belief that liberalization is basically good for the Japanese economy and that most, if not all, of the problems associated with liberalization can be solved through effective planning and policy measures. What is of prime importance to us today is to develop an integrated system of plan and policy toward a successful implementation of the liberalization.

10   Since we accept the liberalization, notwithstanding its inherent difficulties, it is legitimate for us to expect foreign concerns to understand the Japanese situation and adhere to reasonable standards of conduct so that their operations in Japan will contribute to further growth of the Japanese economy. Following the example of the Canadian government, the Japanese government should declare the general principles applicable to foreign investments in Japan by issuing "Recommendations to Foreign Enterprises Contemplating Investments in Japan."

(2) The Implementation Plan for the Liberalization
    of Capital Transactions

1   The liberalization is to take effect in gradual steps in light of the existing market conditions in Japan pertaining to capital, technology, managerial skills, and plant capacity.

The First Stage—through June 1967

(a) In the case of direct investments, foreign firms are allowed to purchase up to 20 percent of old shares of stock of a Japanese firm in the general category, and up to 15 percent of stock of a Japanese firm in the limited category. A foreign individual may purchase up to 10 percent. The list of industries included in the limited category will be adjusted as needs arise.

(b) In the case of direct investments for the purpose of establishing a new legal person in Japan, the foreign-owned stock ratio may automatically be 100 percent for category A, and 50 percent for category B whereas the ratio under category C will be individually examined before approval. Category A should include approximately fifteen industries that are already highly developed such as steel, cement, ship-building, cotton textile, and beer. B includes most of those industries that are not in A or C, and our liberalization plan is concerned primarily with these industries. C should include about thirty industries as exemplified below plus those dominated by small businesses.

(i) Those in which technological progress is rapid and Japanese technology lags behind that of Western countries (e.g., electronic computers);

(ii) Those which have a great growth potential and are expected to become strategic industries but as yet have not developed sufficient competitive strength vis-à-vis Western countries (e.g., automobiles and petrochemicals);

(iii) Those which are of public interest (e.g., air transportation); and,

(iv) Those which are important from the standpoint of national security (e.g., atomic energy, nuclear fuel).

(c) Though automatic approval applies to categories A and B, foreign firms under these categories are expected to practice "voluntary restraint" in Japan. The foreign firm's moving into a new sector different from that for which initial application was made is conditional upon the competent Minister's authorization. With respect to category B the principle of mutual co-prosperity and equal competitive strength will be emphasized.

(d) Of the eighteen reservations Japan made against the OECD Code of Liberalization, the number of reservations should be reduced to about ten after a comprehensive examination—particularly of the nondirect investment items.

The Second State—through March 1972

Substantial steps of liberalization are to be taken in this period. The following policy and legal measures should be adopted.

(a) The foreign ownership of old shares of Japanese stock will be allowed up to 33 percent under the general category, and 25 percent under the limited category.

(b) With respect to foreign investments in new legal persons in Japan, as many industries as possible will be shifted from B to A and from C to B. C will include only about fifteen industries plus those heavily dependent upon small businesses.

(c) With respect to nondirect investments, only about five partial reservations will remain outstanding.

The Third Stage—after April 1972

Japan will move as far as West European countries have in the liberalization of capital transactions. The deadline for completion of a full liberalization will be determined at the beginning of this period in the light of the then prevailing international situation.

2   As we implement the liberalization, we should demand that other countries remove their discriminatory import restrictions against Japanese goods. This demand is legitimate and necessary

for consistency of liberalization policies in Japan as well as from the standpoint of deriving mutual benefits for all concerned from the liberalization movement.

(3) Policy to Prepare for the Liberalization

1   The policy to prepare for the liberalization, in lieu of being merely a defensive attempt to preserve the status quo, should have a positive and creative intent. The policy objectives are as follows:

(a) To build Japanese firms capable of operating in an open economy;

(b) To restructure the Japanese economy so as to raise its overall productivity;

(c) To alleviate social and economic frictions;

(d) To protect public welfare.

2   To achieve these objectives we must develop a system of policies consistent with the liberalization plan. The present Plan for Economic and Social Development must be carried out effectively. We recommend the drafting of a New Plan, a successor to the present Plan, which will incorporate policy requirements for the Second Stage of liberalization.

3   It is the government's task to formulate and implement policies. However, the task will not meet with success in the absence of hard and creative work on the part of business firms. Private enterprises ought to rid themselves of the attitude of dependence toward the government. It is regrettable that the Japanese business community lacks the spirit of independent action-taking and a sense of responsibility in confronting foreign enterprises. Deplorable is the mood of passivity prevalent today among businesses in contrast to the positive response which the Japanese business leaders had shown toward the trade liberalization and the determination of the single exchange rate at the beginning of the recovery period.

National policies should be broad and dynamic rather than overly particular and meticulously concerned with minute detail. There will necessarily be new problems and difficulties initially unpredicted. But these can be met later with additional measures to be adopted in accordance with the changing circumstances.

4   The liberalization of capital transactions brings to the participants the benefits of free competition on an international scale. It is
therefore problematical that the highly restrictive, protective laws
such as the Department Stores Act and the Banking Act remain in
force. The legality and rationale of these Acts must be reexamined
from the standpoint of liberalization. The spirit of the Anti-Monopoly
Act, insofar as it attempts to promote free competition, must be respected. In some ways, however, the Act is too idealistic to meet the
needs of changing reality. Some provisions in the Japanese Anti-
Monopoly Act (e.g., total ban on holding companies) seem too extreme
in comparison with similar Acts in Western countries. We should not
hesitate to revise those sections of the Anti-Monopoly Act which have
become obsolete and are deemed too unrealistic in the present context
as long as the central intent of the Act is not violated.

Aspects of Policy

(A) Technological Development

1   Japanese technology still lags considerably behind that of the
Western countries. Over the past decade Japan has made impressive
progress in absorbing Western technology. However, there is a limit
beyond which an advancing economy cannot effectively rely upon
borrowed technology. What is needed for Japan is a more autonomous
development of technology. If nothing drastic is done in this area,
Japan's future hardly looks promising, particularly with respect to
such new industries as electronics, atomic energy, and space science.
The superiority of American technology has been one of the main
sources of difficulty which European countries have been facing in
connection with the liberalization. The technological gap between
Japan and the United States is ever greater. Massive efforts must
be taken by both the government and private business in order to close
the gap as quickly as possible.

2   The proportion of Japanese national income spent on research
and development in 1963 was 1.8 percent. The proportions in the same
year were: 3.7 percent in the United States; 2.7 percent in the U.S.S.R.;
2.4 percent in Western Germany; and 2.3 percent in France. The share
of government expenditures in total research and development cost is
characteristically small in Japan; it is about 30 percent in Japan in
contrast to the average of 70 percent in Western Europe. The small
share of the Japanese government is partly due to the smallness of
the government's defense-oriented research expenditures. It does
not stand to reason, however, that since Japanese military spending

is small the government's spending on research and development in general should also be small. Research funds of the kind which other countries today allocate for their defense objectives should be made available by the Japanese government for peaceful uses in order to enhance the long-range prospects of the country's economic growth through technological development. There are also numerous wasteful subsidies in force at present that can be terminated so that the funds can be reallocated for research in science and technology.

3   With respect to the latest, most advanced technology whose development is costly but of strategic importance to the nation's economy, the government should provide substantial research funds to supplement private endeavors. Production of advanced jet engines and of ammoniac materials through the latest techniques are cases in point. The government should concentrate allocation of funds on a limited number of key projects at a time, rather than thinly spreading funds over numerous research programs as has been the tendency in the past. The various research institutions in the country ought to be reorganized and restructured so that they attain a greater flexibility and adaptability in responding to changing needs of the economy.

4   In areas other than those in which the government assumes a major responsibility, autonomous and independent research activities of private enterprises play a central role in the nation's technological development. So that private research and development become an important contributory source to the nation's economic progress, we recommend an incentive system consisting of tax write-offs, reserve for research and development, selective subsidies, long-term-low-cost finance from the Japanese Development Bank, and the like. Special consideration must be given to the prevention of brain drain and the shortage of competent research scientists. To raise the productivity of research, joint research projects, pooling of patents, and systematic exchange of technical information are desirable. A logical extention of this perspective is that industrial reorganization, discussed below, will have an important bearing upon technological development in Japan.

(B) Industrial Reorganization

1   Industrial reorganization is necessary to cope with the liberalization; at the same time liberalization provides an impetus to industrial reorganization. Now is the opportune time for initiating the industrial reorganization which has been intensely debated in recent years. There are few historic turning points such as at present where the national economy is in an ideal condition to accelerate

improvement of corporate structures vis-à-vis competing foreign enterprises.

2   The direction of industrial reorganization depends upon particular industries.

(a) With respect to the large-scale, heavy, capital-intensive industries (e.g., iron and steel, petro-chemicals, chemical fertilizers, and petroleum refinery), reorganization must be examined from the standpoint of avoiding over-investments relative to demand. Joint administration, mutual investment adjustments, and joint investment projects are the major aims of the reorganization. It seems inevitable that the reorganization in this area will resolve itself into mergers and holding-company arrangements so that the Japanese firms will become large and strong enough to engage in effective competition with foreign enterprises in the world economy.

(b) Concerning those industries in which success depends crucially upon the firm's ability to keep up with the rapid pace of technological innovations (e.g., petrochemicals and electronics), we recommend mergers and establishment of holding companies aimed at mobilization of resources for research and development.

(c) As regards those consumer goods industries characterized by mass production and product-diversification (e.g., automobiles, electrical appliances, and processed foods), the desirability of joint ventures and mergers should be studied from the viewpoint of obtaining greater economies of scale, not merely through output expansion but also by a more systematic research and product development, a greater specialization of each firm in terms of product lines, standardization of parts, and development of common export channels.

(d) With respect to those highly specialized and/or labor-intensive industries (e.g., manufacturing machinery, industrial machinery, textile manufacturing), merger and other similar concentration measures are not necessarily effective. A higher degree of specialization and grouping of output categories among firms seem a more sensible approach.

3   While the necessity of industrial reorganization has long been talked about, little has actually been put into practice thus far. The inaction is due to the complacent attitude of Japanese businesses protected by the tariff wall and restrictions over the inflow of foreign capital, as well as to the lack of positive initiatives on the part of the government. Japanese corporate executives often hesitate to make

decisions of critical importance even when their collective security
and growth potentials are at stake. Similarly, the government has
tended to seek an easy way out by partial, ad hoc measures such as
authorization of temporary cartels in recession, while financial institutions have continued to indulge in an overly protective credit
policy. Added to these, industrial reorganization has not been implemented very far because of the opposition from labor unions as
well as some segments of financial circles and of the involved inter-
personal relationships among corporate executives that often act as
a barrier against making rational personnel decisions.

4   The government should take full advantage of the liberalization
movement in establishing a new, straightforward policy direction concerning industrial reorganization and adopting appropriate fiscal and
monetary measures. In order to help materialize the structural
reform plan and the industrial reorganization plan of business and
industry, the government is expected to cooperate with private financial
institutions in making available sufficient, long-term-low-cost funds.
There should be special tax measures to promote mergers and joint
investments. For the efficient use of private funds for the purpose
of industrial reorganization, the government should study the feasibility
of authorizing a system of joint corporation bonds of the kind that has
been operating in France.

5   It is essential that each firm act on the principle of self-care
and self-responsibility. This does not mean, however, that industry-
wide cooperation is unnecessary. Each firm is expected to refrain
from those moves and maneuvers which may be beneficial to the firm
in the short run but have adverse effects on the industry as a whole.

         There may arise occasions that call for government interven-
tion. But as a future trend we expect it to become increasingly
difficult for the government to impose upon private firms the rules
of voluntary restraints and other forms of administrative guidance.
Instead of extra-legal means, reforms of the Anti-Monopoly Act to
legalize certain cartels for adjusting investments, clarification of
legal bases for the government-business cooperation schemes, and
promulgation of separate Acts to cope with particular problems of
particular industries under extraordinary circumstances are recommended.

6   As another means of dissolving difficulties induced by the
liberalization, we should study the possibility of re-legalizing holding
companies whose prime function is to consolidate funds for new investments and technological development. These holding companies

must be sharply distinguished from those which aim at managerial control as were closely associated with Zaibatsu in the past. The new holding companies should be recognized as an exception to the jurisdiction of the present Anti-Monopoly Act. Joint sales corporations and other forms of holding companies ought to be studied in the light of the needs of various industries.

7   The roles to be played by financial intermediaries and trading companies in the process of liberalization should not be underestimated. Finally, we recommend organizing committees consisting of able and highly respected, private individuals whose third-person views and counsel are to assist firms and industries as they cope with the problems of liberalization.

(C) Adjustments in the Financial System

1   The financial system in Japan has the following weaknesses from the standpoint of preparing for the liberalization: (a) relative to the demand for large-scale investment funds, the supply capacity tends to be deficient; (b) interest rates in Japan are considerably higher than those in the Western countries; and (c) as a result of prolonged indulgence in the system of finance based upon hierarchical grouping of firms, Japanese financial institutions tend to supply funds to firms for historical ties and connections rather than the productivity of proposed investments, and this practice has been hampering the efficient allocation of funds.

The monetary panic of 1927 occurred mainly because of the lack of preparedness on the part of Japanese financial institutions in response to the tremendous expansion of the Japanese economy after World War I. Without prompt and major reforms it is no exaggeration to hold that the financial system will again become a bottleneck in the further growth of the Japanese economy.

2   One of the major defects in the present system of finance in Japan is that the system fails to mobilize and channel sufficient investment funds to city banks and the Long-Term Credit Bank where demand for large-size funds is concentrated. Furthermore, units of financial institutions tend to be too small and numerous, causing inadequate supply capacity as well as excessive competition among themselves. If the present system continues, Japanese industrial capital will not unlikely be dominated by foreign capital, thanks to the inadequacy of the Japanese financial system in absorbing the impact of the liberalization.

3   In line with the above observations we make the following recommendations concerning financial reorganization.

(a) Simplification, rationalization, and greater specialization are essential for the financial system. To achieve these objectives, careful studies ought to be made of the present functions and structures of ordinary banks, public financial agencies, Long-Term Credit Bank, trust banks, mutual banks, Credit Fund, Agriculture and Forestry Fund, Small Business Fund, etc.

(b) Desirability of mergers of city banks as well as consolidation of other financial institutions ought to be examined.

(c) The rates of interest need to be lowered through rationalization and modernization of the financial institutions. In this connection policies of the Bank of Japan and the Ministry of Finance must be reexamined. The inflow of foreign capital in general has a lowering effect upon interest, but new policy measures ought to be studied so that foreign debentures may be utilized as a means of reducing long-term rates in Japan.

4   Banking belongs to the limited category under the Foreign Investment Law, and incorporation of a new bank is regulated by the separate Banking Act in Japan. Given these legal arrangements, control of Japanese banks by foreign interests may be checked without difficulty. It is possible, however, that through expansion of branch activities foreign banks will exert increasing influence over Japanese firms. If their influence becomes so far-reaching as to threaten Japanese firms' management rights, then some appropriate, preventive measures will have to be provided.

5   In connection with the objective of increasing the owned-capital ratio of Japanese firms, it is important to raise the general standards of conduct, quality, and efficiency of services of brokerage houses and the securities market. In addition to the recently promulgated license system for securities companies, strong regulatory measures are needed. Securities dealers do not belong to the limited category under the Foreign Investment Law. However, the present license system for securities companies is sufficient, in our view, to block the adverse entry of foreign capital in this area.

(D) Prevention of Transfer of Management Rights

1   The entry of foreign capital into Japanese firms is a natural consequence of liberalization. However, we need sufficient preventive

measures to guard against excessive and undue control of foreign interests over the management rights of Japanese firms. This does not mean of course that all cases of foreign control—including those which are with the understanding and consent of Japanese managers and are not in conflict with the national interest—must be banned.

2   With respect to foreign interests' acquisition of old shares of Japanese stock, we have various regulatory measures in force; but it is well to remember that those measures have loopholes such as allowing foreign capital to take over Japanese firms through dummy companies. It is now legal for branches of foreign firms in Japan to purchase Japanese stocks in yen. However, such purchase will be problematical if the real motive is to gain managerial control of the Japanese firm. These observations suggest that the stable stock-ownership pattern and the abundance of capital in Japan constitute the only reliable defense of Japanese corporations.

3   The problem of capital shortage may be solved by more investments and a greater accumulation of owned-capital by Japanese firms. For this objective tax reforms are urgently needed. Firms are understandably interested in maintaining a high level of profitability as a means of keeping their stock prices high while their investments are increased. Given the fact that total dividends paid and total "entertainment" expenditures of Japanese corporations are approximately the same, it does not appear too difficult for Japanese corporations to promote their internal capital accumulation without reducing their earning capacity. This is a matter of the efficacy of managerial control on the part of Japanese corporations. The market-value sale of stocks is another alternative approach to the promotion of internal capital accumulation.

4   For a more stable stock-ownership pattern in the country the existing regulations restricting stock ownership by commercial banks and insurance companies should perhaps be relaxed. However, any move in that direction should be cautious inasmuch as the experiences of Western Europe indicate that the transfer of managerial control rights may actually be accelerated through greater stock transactions by commercial banks. Increase in stock ownership by institutional investors such as pension funds and mutual aid funds is expected in the future. But the clue to the building of a stable distribution of stocks is to increase the number of investors who approach portfolio investments not so much for short-term speculative motives as for accumulating wholesome assets along with long-run growth of the corporations. In this connection the future popularization of joint-ownership plans involving employees' greater acquisition of their company stock is anticipated.

5   The stock market where stock transactions are concentrated makes possible a prompt delivery of information concerning transfer of management rights. The quick information enables us to take appropriate actions where and if necessary. There is an argument that there should be a set of new rules to regulate transfer of management rights at the level of the stock market. While this argument deserves examination, we feel that such rules will probably hamper the very function of the stock market.

6   There should be an Industrial Adjustment Association whose membership primarily comprises the private business groups and whose objective is to take safeguard actions if and when actual transfer of management rights occurs in such a way that the national interest will be seriously hindered. The Association will be funded by specified quota payments from the member business organizations. The initial endowment will tentatively be 50 billion yen, all tax-exempt. There may be a government contribution to the initial endowment.

When the transfer of management rights of a serious nature occurs, the Association will first decide whether it is likely to hamper the national interest. The highest organ of the Association will be the Industrial Adjustment Committee consisting of about five competent individuals from private business and industry. The Association's adjustment actions vis-à-vis the troubled firm consists of a variety of measures such as: purchase of the company stock, issuance of loans, guarantee of debt payments, extention of credit to another Japanese firm which has agreed to take over the firm in trouble, and the like. In case of the stock purchase the above Committee will appoint an executive to assume new management or commission a company to manage the firm in trouble. Frozen shares will be disposed at the market as a rule. In some cases the Association itself may assume ownership of such shares.

7   For the defense of small businesses the present Small Business Investment Promotion Corporation should be expanded together with a greater allocation of long-term-low-cost government funds to the Corporation. Its function should be broadened to include stock purchase, loans, credit extention, guarantee of debt payments and the like vis-à-vis troubled firms. On this occasion the entire small-business policies of the conventional kind ought to be thoroughly reexamined in order to accelerate modernization and rationalization of small businesses in the country.

(E) Preservation of Economic Order and Prevention of
Market Disruptions

1   In order to prevent foreign capital from unduly disturbing the
economic order in Japan, the government and business groups ought
to cooperate with each other in building a network of fair and orderly
business transactions. The foreign interests are naturally expected
to adhere to the rules of transactions in Japan. At present there
exist regulations concerning terms of installment sales involving
foreign interests. It may be desirable to increase the enforcability
of these regulations.

2   Reforms as well as a more flexible application of the present
patent laws may be necessary to prevent foreign firms' monopolistic
control of the market through patent manipulation. If a patent is
utilized to monopolize the market, the government should be able to
enforce splitting or open sales of the patent right.

3   Market disruptions caused by firms, foreign or domestic, are
subject to sanctions in accordance with the Anti-Monopoly Act. However, action to be taken under the Act may conceivably be delayed.
In that event, we may resort to a quicker and more flexible measure
to be adopted by the aforesaid Industrial Adjustment Association.

4   Penalties against those foreign companies which failed to obtain
a proper authorization of the competent Minister for moving into a
new area of business different from one specified in the initial application need to be increased beyond the present practice. Penalties
should include large fines, dismissal of responsible managers and
the closing of the business firm in question. The same ruling applies
to those foreign firms which de facto moved into a new, different sector
and gained managerial control in that sector through substantial
portfolio investments without a proper authorization of the competent
Minister.

5   Foreign capital is likely to give Japanese small businesses the
strongest impact in the area of distribution. A sufficiently long preparatory period for the distribution sector is necessary before completely liberalizing capital transactions in this area.

     The present Department Stores Act should be repealed.
Strengthening of the retailing business must be attempted through

a variety of approaches such as expansion of the voluntary chain-store system, adjustments of super markets and more cooperative endeavors among specializing stores including those that retail regional products.

THE LIBERALIZATION OF CAPITAL TRANSACTIONS AND THE FINANCIAL STRUCTURE*

I   The Industrial Reorganization as a Precondition for the Liberalization

We must support the movement toward the liberalization of capital transactions as the whole community of free nations is to benefit from it. However, given the existing economic conditions in our country, a sudden liberalization will invite various forms of friction and confusion.

It is necessary for us to strive to strengthen our international competitive position, raising the managerial and productive efficiency of our industry, and expanding our overseas investments. In preparing for liberalization the initiative must come from business and industry themselves. Efforts need be directed toward reorganization of industries aimed at deriving benefits of larger scales of production, diversification of products, and production of more advanced goods. As a means of enhancing the financial health of the enterprises, internal corporate savings must be increased. Now is the opportune time for taking action as our economy finds itself amidst a sustained boom.

II   Reforming Financial Structure

1. The Way of Finance

The Japanese financial world is also in need of structural reforms. The liberalization of capital transactions implies advocacy of market principles under which any firm failing to meet the international standards of competition is to be penalized. In Japan, industry

---

*The orignial text is Shihon Jiyuka to Kinyu no Kamae, issued by Keizai Doyu Kai, May 25, 1967.

and finance are integrated to a degree and in a way rather uncommon in other countries. Therefore, failure on the part of a producer is prone to quickly transmit strain to the related financial firm. In this sense the financial organizations are hardly free of the impact of the liberalization as it first affects the manufacturing sector.

As the first corrective measure, financial institutions must radically change their manner of issuing loans. They must restrain from indulging in fierce loan competition among hierarchically divided industrial groups as has been witnessed during the past years. They ought to strive for cultivating a new philosophy of finance, building a more sound system of finance based upon sufficient liquidity and solvency.

2. The Financial Structure

As the Japanese economy was experiencing accelerated growth over the past decade or so, there was a tendency for the financial institutions to supply growth funds in a loose manner. This has led to the rise of a kind of financial structure encompassing both industry and lending institutions which is not compatible with the requirements of an open economy. The kind of financial structure which can survive only under the shadows of a closed economy must be eradicated and transformed into one consistent with the test of an open economy. The emergence of a new sound financial system will be conducive to reforms in industry as well that are called forth by the changing international environment surrounding the Japanese economy. Industry and finance, then, can act as equal partners on the basis of efficiency and effective competition in lieu of clinging to the principle of hierarchical adhesion.

3. Reorganization of the Financial System

In order to cope with the new circumstances brought forth by the liberalization, the financial world must rationalize many aspects of its operations. Cost reductions should be pursued through a greater use of office machines and equipment, restraining excessive competition in building numerous branch offices, and discouraging scrambles for deposit money. A more uninhibited induction of impact loans as a means of encouraging greater uses of low-interest foreign exchange loans may help correct the rates structure in Japan. We must examine the possibility and desirability of authorizing some Japanese banks to issue foreign exchange bonds.

To prepare for the full impact of liberalization, a series of
rationalization measures within the context of the existing structure
of finance is not sufficient. Sustained economic growth has brought
forth changes and new requirements in the functions of financial
institutions, many of which have not been dissolved into a new order,
thus causing considerable waste in the utilization of funds at present.

The financial reorganization must be preceded by a thorough
examination of the demand of the new era for financial services in
all sectors including production, distribution, and consumption.

4. Financial Administration

We believe that it is time for the government's financial policy
and intervention with financial institutions to be reexamined. In our
view the government's protectionism toward banks has been excessive.
While the alleged rationale of the government policy has been to protect depositors and guard the safety of the nation's credit system,
in practice the main beneficiary of protectionism has been banks
rather than depositors. The government has been partly responsible
for the lack of incentives for rationalization on the part of the financial
institutions. The new financial policy must aim at stimulating optimal
competition among banks and other financial intermediaries. Promulgation of a deposit insurance system is urgently needed. Not only
deposits but also the earning capacity of the banks must be criteria
for guiding the government's financial policy.

III   The New Relationship Between Industry and Finance

The new era dictates to us the important task of establishing
a new relationship between industry and finance through autonomous
reforms in the financial structure and a new way of financing in
accord with the principles of an open economy.

Japanese industry has reached a turning point where, in lieu
of single-mindedly pursuing the quantitative expansion of output with
the aid of easy and loose finance, it is required to be more concerned
with qualitative improvement in the choice of investments and products
to be produced. For this task Japanese industry must develop sound
policy with respect to investment funds by depending less upon the
method of external finance and diversifying the sources of funds.

Similarly, financial institutions must improve their own internal
funds position. They assume an extremely important task of supplying
sufficient funds at internationally competitive rates of interest to

finance investments of the nation's strategic industries in the home market as well as overseas investments by Japanese firms.

As a new way of finance, the financial institutions ought to increase their owned-capital ratio, and develop a network of responsible managements as foundation for a sound credit system in the country. We expect the financial institutions to make significant contributions to the building of a new industrial order and to the overseas expansion of Japanese industry.

The industrial and financial reorganizations, initiated and carried out autonomously by each, will establish a new healthy relationship between the two, repalcing the old, problematical system of hierarchical adhesion. The new order than emerges will add to Japan's readiness for liberalization.

Finally, the public financial institutions, supplementing private finance, are also in need of reform and reorganization. Public finance must emphasize investments for social development, and for optimal results refrain from activities that substitute for private finance.

JAPANESE GROSS NATIONAL PRODUCT (Billion yen)		JAPANESE FOREIGN TRADE ($ million)		
Fiscal Year	GNP	Year	Exports	Imports
1952	6,236.8	1946	103.3	305.6
		1947	173.6	526.1
1953	7,343.7	1948	258.3	684.2
		1949	509.7	904.8
1954	7,834.7	1950	820.1	974.4
1955	8,785.0	1951	1,354.5	1,995.0
		1952	1,272.9	2,028.2
1956	9,892.4	1953	1,274.8	2,409.6
		1954	1,629.2	2,399.4
1957	11,206.5	1955	2,010.6	2,471.4
1958	11,518.2	1956	2,500.6	3,229.7
		1957	2,858.0	4,283.6
1959	13,377.2	1958	2,876.6	3,033.1
		1959	3,456.5	3,599.5
1960	16,046.9	1960	4,054.5	4,491.1
1961	19,307.7	1961	4,235.6	5,810.4
		1962	4,916.2	5,636.5
1962	21,189.7	1963	5,452.1	6,736.3
		1964	6,673.2	7,937.5
1963	24,726.2	1965	8,451.7	8,169.0

Fiscal Year	GNP	Year	Exports	Imports
1964	28,585.7	1966	9,776.4	9,522.7
		1967	10,441.6	11,663.1
1965	31,349.2	1968	12,971.7	12,987.2
		1969	15,990.0	15,023.5
1966	36,661.4	1970	19,317.7	18,881.2
1967	43,263.7			
1968	51,431.7			
1969	60,524.8			
1970	72.081.4			

Source: Economic Planning Agency, Economic Statistics Monthly.

Source: Ministry of Finance, Customs Statistics.

INFLOW OF FOREIGN CAPITAL: ACQUISITION OF CORPORATE SHARES

($ thousand)

Fiscal Year	Participation in Management	Through Market	Others
1950	2,572	1,560	578
1951	11,646	2,106	119
1952	7,166	1,205	851
1953	2,687	1,268	1,110
1954	2,467	1,527	235
1955	2,309	3,155	1,265
1956	5,360	3,297	1,005
1957	7,282	5,133	911
1958	3,698	9,550	2,519
1959	14,561	21,960	2,920
1960	31,593	55,848	20,598
1961	40,170	91,850	20,124
1962	22,618	91,185	50,200
1963	42,656	42,635	51,420
1964	30,644	33,347	11,566
1965	44,643	68,901	5,341
1966	39,812	126,981	18,021
1967	29,777	396,165	3,163
1968	41,178	403,287	7,810
1969	51,249	449,163	8,105
1970	60,389		9,233

Sources: Ministry of International Trade and Industry, and Bank of Japan.

INFLOW OF FOREIGN CAPITAL: OTHER THAN CORPORATE SHARES
($ thousand)

Fiscal Year	Corporate Debentures	Beneficiary Certificates	Loans	Foreign-Currency Bonds
1950				
1951	25		4,026	
1952		146	34,457	
1953		562	49,362	
1954	7	58	15,279	
1955	15	52	47,054	
1956		115	93,652	
1957		128	123,979	30,000
1958	28	116	231,473	
1959	30	214	127,615	9,800
1960	20	555	127,132	72,425
1961	77	1,280	387,605	155,000
1962	86	650	358,419	194,050
1963	247	798	503,954	174,500
1964	851	1,828	650,760	62,500
1965	2,726	398	379,551	
1966	261	390	329,711	50,000
1967	123	284	637,544	143,980
1968	31	159	673,648	235,141
1969	501	206	789,621	122,082
1970	99,042	602	845,903	

Sources: Ministry of International Trade and Industry, and Bank of Japan.

TECHNOLOGY IMPORTS		JOINT VENTURES	
Fiscal Year	Number of Type-A Contracts	Fiscal Year	Number of Joint Ventures Formed
1950	27	1950	22
1951	101	1951	23
1952	133	1952	16
1953	103	1953	9
1954	82	1954	6
1955	72	1955	2
1956	144	1956	5
1957	118	1957	7
1958	90	1958	1
1959	153	1959	10
1960	327	1960	12
1961	320	1961	19
1962	328	1962	22
1963	564	1963	53
1964	500	1964	77
1965	472	1965	69
1966	601	1966	78
1967	638	1967	87
1968	782	1968	95
1969	1,099	1969	103
1970	1,218	1970	124

Source: Ministry of International Trade and Industry.

Source: Ministry of International Trade and Industry.

JAPAN'S BALANCE-OF-PAYMENTS POSITIONS, 1960 and 1967
($ million)

	1960	1967
1) Current Transactions Balance	143	-19
2) Trade Balance	271	1,15
3) Capital Transactions Balance	-72	-29
4) Overall Balance	104	-55

Source: International Monetary Fund, Balance of Payments Yearbook, Washington, D.C.

FOREIGN STOCK ACQUISITION AND FOREIGN SHARE HOLDING
RATIO IN JAPAN

Year	Number of Companies	1.00	1.00-0.50	0.50	0.50-0.30	0.30-0.15	Less than 0.15
1950-53	70	4	17	15	8	8	18
1954	6	1		1	2	1	1
1955	2				1		1
1956	5		1		1	2	1
1957	7			1	2	2	2
1958	1					1	
1959	10		1	1	3	3	2
1960	12	1		3	6	2	
1961	19			3	13	3	
1962	22			1	15	3	3
1963	53	2		10	33	7	1
1964	77	8	3	18	39	9	
1965	69	14	3	18	29	3	2
1966	78	12	8	23	28	6	1
1967	93	16	9	23	29	10	6
Total	524	58	42	117	209	60	38

Source: Fuji Bank Bulletin, January, 1969.

BIBLIOGRAPHY

BOOKS

Adams, T. F. M., and Noritake Kobayashi. The World of Japanese Business. Tokyo and Palo Alto: Kodansha International, 1969.

Allen, G. C. Japan's Economic Expansion. London-New York-Toronto: Oxford University Press, 1965.

_____. Japan's Economic Recovery. London-New York-Toronto: Oxford University Press, 1958.

Araki, Nobuyoshi and Fukutaro Watanabe, Nihon no Boeki to Kokusai Shushi [Japanese Foreign Trade and Balance of Payments]. Tokyo: Toyo Keizai, 1967.

Balassa, Bela, ed. Studies in Trade Liberalization, Problems and Prospects for the Industrial Countries. Baltimore: Johns Hopkins Press, 1967.

Broadbridge, Seymour. Industrial Dualism in Japan. Chicago: Aldine Publishing Company, 1966.

Cohen, Jerome B. Japan's Postwar Economy. Bloomington, Indiana: Indiana University Press, 1958.

Dimock, Marshall E. Japanese Technocracy. New York and Tokyo: Walker/Weatherhill, 1968.

Ekonomisuto, ed. Nihon Keizai no Bunseki to Tembo [Japanese Economy: Analysis and Survey]. Tokyo: Mainichi Shimbun Sha, 1965.

Fujii, Shigeru. Boeki Seisaku [Trade Policy]. Tokyo: Chigura Shobo, 1967.

_____

*This bibliography lists (mostly) Japanese sources that deal with the control of imports and foreign capital in postwar Japan, including those that are not cited in the text.

_____. Keizai Hatten to Boeki Seisaku [Economic Growth and Trade Policy]. Tokyo: Kunimoto Shobo, 1964.

Fujita, Keizo and Kiyokura Miyata, eds. Nihon Keizai Seisaku no Tembo [Survey of Japan's Economic Policy]. Tokyo: Kansho In, 1955.

Hayashi, Yujiro. Nihon no Keizai Keikaku [Economic Planning in Japan]. Tokyo: Toyo Keizai Shimpo Sha, 1957.

Hiraoka, Kinnosuke. Boeki Seisaku Ron [Theory of Trade Policy]. Tokyo: Yuhikaku, 1956.

Hirayama, Yuji. Kokkyo no Nai Keizai [The Economy without National Borders]. Tokyo: Diamond Sha, 1967.

Hishinuma, Isamu. Senji Keizai to Boeki Kokusaku [The Wartime Economy and National Trade Policy]. Tokyo: Nogyo Keizai Gakkai, 1941.

Hunsberger, Warren. Japan and the United States in World Trade. New York: Harper and Row, 1964.

Ikeuchi, Nobuyuki, ed. Boeki Jiyuka Ron [Theory of Trade Liberalization]. Kyoto: Horitsu Bunka Sha, 1961.

Inaba, Hidezo et al., eds. Kokusai Keizai to Boeki [International Economy and Trade]. Tokyo: Nihon Hyoron Sha, 1965.

_____. Nihon no Keizai Seisaku to Keizai Keikaku [Economic Policy and Planning in Japan]. Tokyo: Nihon Hyoron Sha, 1965.

Inaba, Hidezo and Tetsuo Sakane, eds. Shihon Jiyuka to Dokusen Kinshi Ho [Capital Liberalization and the Anti-Monopoly Law]. Tokyo: Shiseido, 1967.

Kamino, Masao. Shihon Jiyuka to Kokusai Kyoso Ryoku [Capital Liberalization and International Competitive Strength]. Tokyo: Shiseido, 1968.

Kanamori, Hisao. Chikarazuyoi Taiyo: Nihon Keizai no Ko Seicho Ryoku [The Strong Sun: Growth Capacity of the Japanese Economy]. Tokyo: Diamond Sha, 1968.

_____. Nihon no Boeki [Japanese Foreign Trade]. Tokyo: Shisei Do, 1961.

Kanazawa, Yoshio. Keizai Ho [Economic Laws]. Tokyo: Yuhikaku, 1968.

Kanri Boeki Kenkyu Kai, ed. Sengo Nihon no Boeki Kinyu Kyotei [Financial and Trade Arrangements between Occupied Japan and Other Countries]. Tokyo: Jitsugyo No Nihon Sha, 1949.

Kato, Seiichi and Nobukuni Mitsuma. Jiyuka to Chusho Kigyo [Liberalization and Small Businesses]. Tokyo: Shiseido, 1962.

Koizumi, Akira, and Miyohei Shinohara, eds. Nihon no Boeki. [Japanese Foreign Trade]. Tokyo: Seirin Shoin Shin Sha, 1964.

Kojima, Kiyoshi. Nihon Boeki to Kanzei Hikisage [Japanese Foreign Trade and Tariff Reductions]. Tokyo: Toyo Keizai Shimpo Sha, 1965.

_____. Sekai Keizai to Nihon Boeki [World Economy and Japanese Foreign Trade]. Tokyo: Keiso Shobo, 1962.

Komiya, Ryutaro and Ryuichiro Tachi. Keizai Seisaku no Riron [Theory of Economic Policy]. Tokyo: Keiso Shobo, 1965.

Kubota, Jun. Boeki no Riron to Seisaku [Trade Theory and Policy]. Tokyo: Shin Hyoron, 1966.

Meier, Gerald M. The International Economics of Development. New York: Harper and Row, 1968.

Miyake, Takeo. Nihon Keizai no Kadai [Problems of Japanese Economy]. Tokyo: Diamond Sha, 1965.

Miyazaki, Yoshikazu. Sengo Nihon no Keizai Kiko [Structure of Postwar Japanese Economy]. Tokyo: Shin Hyoron, 1968.

Nakai, Shozo. Boeki to Gaikoku Kawase [Trade and Foreign Exchange]. Tokyo: Kanshoin Shinsha, 1961.

Nakayama, Ichiro. Sengo Keizai no Tembo [Survey of the Postwar Economy]. Tokyo: Hakujitsu Shoin, 1947.

Nihon Kanzei Kyokai, ed. Nihon no Kanzei [Japanese Tariffs], Tokyo, 1959.

Nihon Keiei Gakkai, ed. Boeki Jiyuka to Keieigaku no Sho Mondai [Trade Liberalization and Various Problems in Management Sciences]. Tokyo: Diamond Sha, 1962.

Nihon Keizai Shimbun Sha, ed. Hachijo Koku e no Michi [The Road to Comply with Article 8]. Tokyo, 1963.

_____. Kaiho Keizai Nyumon [Introduction to the Open Economy]. Tokyo, 1964.

_____. Kanzen Jiyuka to Nihon Sangyo [Complete Liberalization and Japanese Industry]. Tokyo, 1963.

_____. Shihon Jiyuka to Nihon Keizai [Capital Liberalization and Japanese Economy]. Tokyo, 1967.

Niida, Hiroshi and Akira Ono, eds. Nihon no Sangyo Soshiki [Industrial Organization in Japan]. Tokyo: Iwanami Shoten, 1969.

Ohkawa, Sentaro, ed. Gaikoku Kawase Gaikoku Boeki Kanri Ho ni yoru Atarashii Yushutsu Hoshiki [New Export Methods under the Foreign Exchange and Foreign Trade Control Law]. Tokyo: Boeki Shiryo Shuppan Sha, Tokyo, 1949.

Oka, Shigeo. Sengo Nihon no Kanzei Seisaku [Tariff Policy in Postwar Japan]. Tokyo: Nihon Hyoron Sha, 1968.

Okuhara, Tokizo. Shihon no Jiyuka [Capital Liberalization]. Tokyo: Nihon Kokusai Mondai Kenkyu Sho, 1967.

Patterson, Gardner. Discrimination in International Trade, the Policy Issues 1945-1965. Princeton, N.J.: Princeton University Press, 1966.

Ryokaku, Yoshihiko. Sangyo Seisaku no Riron [Theory of Industrial Policy]. Tokyo: Nihon Keizai Shimbun Sha, 1966.

Sazanami, Yoko. Keizai Seicho to Kokusai Kyoso Ryoku [Economic Growth and International Competitive Strength]. Tokyo: Toyo Keizai, 1968.

Shimojo, Shin-ichiro, ed. Shihon Jiyuka no Genjo to Tembo [Capital Liberalization: Present Condition and Outlook]. Tokyo: Kinyu Zaisei Jijo Kenkyu Kai, 1967.

Shimomura, Osamu. Nihon Keizai Seicho Ron [Theory of Japanese Economic Growth]. Tokyo: Kinyu Zaisei Jijo Kenkyu Kai, 1962.

Shinohara, Miyohei. Sangyo Kozo Ron [Theory of Industrial Structure].
Tokyo: Chikuma Shobo, 1968.

Shinohara, Miyohei and Tadao Uchida, eds. Nihon Keizai Seisaku no
Kaimei [Exposition of Japanese Economic Policy]. Vol. I.
Tokyo: Toyo Keizai Shimpo Sha, 1964.

Shishido, Toshio. Nihon Keizai no Seicho Ryoku [Growth Capacity of
Japanese Economy]. Tokyo: Diamond Sha, 1965.

Sogo Seisaku Kenkyu Kai, ed. Shihon Jiyuka: Honshitsu to Taisaku
[Capital Liberalization: Substance and Policy]. Tokyo: Shakai
Shiso Sha, 1967.

Sugioka, Tetsuo, ed. Shihon Jiyuka to Sangyo Saihensei [Capital Liberalization and Industrial Reorganization]. Tokyo: Tokuma
Shoten, 1967.

Takagaki, Torajiro, ed. Nihon no Boeki Seisaku [Japan's Trade Policy].
Tokyo: Yuhikaku, 1955.

Takami, Shigeyoshi. Boeki Saiken no Kihon Koso [Basic Approach to
Reconstruction of Our Foreign Trade]. Tokyo: Nihon Keizai
Shimbun Sha, 1950.

Tanaka, Hiroshi, ed. Hachijo Koku Jidai no Nihon Keizai [Japanese
Economy in the Article-8 Era]. Tokyo: Diamond Sha, 1963.

Umezu, Kazuro. Nihon no Boeki Shiso [Japanese Thought on Foreign
Trade]. Tokyo: Mineruva Shobo, 1963.

Watanabe, Makoto, Kawase Kanri Kaiso [Recollections of Exchange
Control]. Tokyo: Gaikoku Kawase Boeki Kenkyu Kai, 1963.

Yamanaka, Tokutaro, ed. Sengo Nihon Keizai Seisaku no Bunseki
[Analysis of Japan's Postwar Economic Policy]. Tokyo: Keiso
Shobo, 1958.

Yeager, Leland B. and David G. Tuerck. Trade Policy and the Price
System. Scranton, Pennsylvania: International Textbook Company, 1966.

Yoshida, Fujio. Shihon Jiyuka to Gaishi Ho [Capital Liberalization
and the Foreign Investment Law]. Tokyo: Zaisei Keizai Koho
Sha, 1967.

Yoshino, Toshihiko. Shihon no Jiyuka to Kinyu [Capital Liberalization and Finance]. Tokyo: Iwanami Shinsho, 1969.

Yumoto, Toyokichi. Boeki to Boeki Seisaku [Trade and Trade Policy]. Tokyo: Kobun Sha, 1965.

ARTICLES

Aiyoshi, Jun. "Jiyuka no Shin Dankai to Jidosha Yushutsu" [New Phase of Liberalization and Auto Exports], Keizai Hyoron (May, 1966).

Akamatsu, Sakae. "Boeki Jiyuka no Genkai" [Limits of Trade Liberalization], Boeki to Kanzei (June, 1956).

Amaya, Naohiro. "Atarashii Sangyo to Sangyo Seisaku" [New Industry and Industrial Policy], Japan Economic Research Center Report (September 1, 1969).

_____. "Jidai wa Wareware ni Nani o Motomete Iruka" [What Does the Present Age Expect of Us?], Anarisuto (April, 1967).

_____. "Jiyu Kyoso e no Kisogatame o" [Building the Foundation for Free Competition], Japan Economic Research Center Report (July 15, 1968).

_____. "Mirai no Sangyo to Sangyo Seisaku" [Future Industry and Industrial Policy], Japan Economic Research Center Report (April 1, 1969).

_____. "Sangyo Seisaku no Hansei to Tenkai no Tameni" [Industrial Policy: Reflections and Thoughts for Its Future Expansion], Tsusan Journal, Vol. 2, No. 5, (1969).

Araki, Yoshinobu. "Hogo Boeki Shugi no Doko to Haikei" [Trend and Background of Trade Protectionism], Sekai Keizai Hyoron (February, 1965).

_____. "Nihon Boeki no Kosei" [Composition of Japanese Trade], Boeki to Kanzei (October, 1966).

Arima, Shunji. "Boeki Jiyuka no Yukue" [Future of Trade Liberalization], Sekai Keizai Hyoron (October, 1959).

Asada, Shiro. "Nihon no Jiyuka Taisaku" [Japan's Liberalization Measures], Keizai Seminar (August, 1968).

Ashiya, Einosuke. "Shihon Torihiki no Jiyuka to Hachijokoku Iko" [Capital Liberalization and Compliance with Article 8], Keizai Hyoron (March, 1963).

Azuma, Yoneo. "Boeki Jiyuka to Nihon Keizai" [Trade Liberalization and Japanese Economy], Seisan Sei (April, 1960).

_____. "Jidosha Sangyo no Jiyuka ni tsuite" [Liberalization of the Automobile Industry], Sekai Keizai Hyoron (November, 1968).

Baba, Keinosuke. "Boeki Jiyuka to Nogyo Seisaku" [Trade Liberalization and Agricultural Policy], Norin Tokei Chosa (May, 1960).

Baba, Masao, et al., "Keizai Seicho to Seifu no Yakuwari" [Economic Growth and the Role of Government], Ekonomisuto (October 20, 1968).

Chuo Koron, a special issue on "Macro-Analysis of Capital Liberalization" (October, 1967).

Demizu, Koichi. "Takamaru Shihon Jiyuka no Atsuryoku" [Rising Pressure on Capital Liberalization], Ekonomisuto (September 14, 1965).

Ebisawa, Michio. "Sekai Keizai no Antei Seicho to Boeki Jiyuka" [Stable Growth of the World Economy and Trade Liberalization], Gaikoku Kawase (January, 1960).

Ehata, Kiyoshi. "Boeki Jiyuka to Rodo Kumiai" [Trade Liberalization and Labor Unions], Rodo Jiho (May, 1960).

Endo, Yoshio. "Waga Kuni Yunyu Kozo no Tokucho to Mondai Ten" [Characteristics and Problems of the Structure of Our Imports], Tsusho Sangyo Kenkyu, No. 154 (1969).

Fujii, Shigeru. "Boeki Seisaku no Basho to Kadai" [Place and Problems of Trade Policy], Kobe Daigaku Keizai Gaku Kenkyu Nempo (August, 1963).

_____. "Boeki Seisaku to Sangyo Seisaku" [Trade Policy and Industrial Policy], Kokumin Keizai Zasshi (October, 1962).

_____. "Nihon Boeki Seisaku no Kicho" [Basic Pattern of Japanese Trade Policy], Kokumin Keizai Zasshi (November, 1958).

_____. "Nihon Keizai no Hatten to Boeki Seisaku" [Expansion of the Japanese Economy and Trade Policy], Kokumin Keizai Zasshi (August, 1964).

_____. "Nihon no Boeki Seisaku" [Japanese Trade Policy], Sekai Keizai Hyoron (April, 1969).

_____. "Sengo Nihon Keizai no Hatten to Boeki Seisaku" [Postwar Growth of the Japanese Economy and Trade Policy], Kokumin Keizai Zasshi (June, 1960).

Fukuyoshi, Toshiyuki, et al. "Boeki no Jiyuka to Rodo Mondai" [Trade Liberalization and Labor Problems], Nihon Rodo Kyokai Zasshi (June, 1960).

Furukawa, Tetsu. "Shihon ni totte Kokuseki towa Nanika [What is the Nationality of Capital?], Keizai Hyoron (January, 1968).

Gomei, Teruo. "Fujubun na Jidosha Sangyo no Jiyuka Yoryoku" [Insufficient Readiness of the Automobile Industry for Liberalization], Boeki to Kanzei (October, 1968).

Hanahara, Niro. "Boeki no Jiyuka to Doru no Kiki" [Trade Liberalization and the Dollar Crisis], Keizai Shirin (January, 1961).

Hara, Takeo. "Saikin no Wagakuni Kawase no Jiyuka no Kadai" [Problems of Recent Liberalization of Foreign Exchange in Japan], Doshisha Shogaku (February, 1961).

Hara, Yasuzaburo. "Jiyuka to Kanzei Mondai" [Liberalization and Tariff Problems], Keidanren Geppo (July, 1960).

Hayakawa, Yoshiaki. "Boeki Jiyuka no Kihon Mondai" [Basic Problems of Trade Liberalization], Zaisei Keizai Koho (June, 1960).

Hayashi, Shintaro. "Jukagaku Kogyo Seisaku to Jiyuka" [Policy toward Heavy and Chemical Industries and Liberalization], Tsusho Sangyo Kenkyu (February, 1960).

_____. "Shihon Jiyuka to Keiki Chosei Saku" [Capital Liberalization and Counter-Cyclical Policy], Boeki to Kanzei (November, 1967).

_____. "Kokusai Bungyo e no Taio" [Adaptation to International Specialization], Chuo Koron (June, 1964).

Hidejima, Shibasaburo, et al. "Seigen Gensoku kara Jiyu Gensoku e" [From the Principle of Restriction to the Principle of Freedom], Keidanren Geppo (July, 1956).

Hirayama, Yuji. "Shihon Jiyuka Mondai no Nihon Teki Seikaku" [Japanese Characteristics in the Problem of Capital Liberalization], Boeki to Kanzei (January, 1967).

Hirota, Hiro-o. "Boeki Kawase Jiyuka e no Teigen" [Recommendations Concerning Trade and Exchange Liberalization], Ekonomisuto (March, 1960).

_____. "Jiyuka to Kokusai Shihon Ido" [Liberalization and International Movements of Capital], Zaisei Keizai Koho (January, 1960).

Hirota, Toshiro. "Boeki Kawase Jiyuka no Zentei" [Presuppositions of Trade and Exchange Liberalization], Sekai Keizai Hyoron (October, 1959).

Horie, Shigeo. "Boeki Kawase no Jiyuka ni tsuite" [Note on Trade and Exchange Liberalization], Keidanren Geppo (March, 1960).

Ihara, Takashi. "Kawase Boeki Jiyuka no Ippan Teki Eikyo to Mondai Ten" [General Effects and Problems of Exchange and Trade Liberalization], Gaikoku Kawase (April, 1960).

Iida, Tsuneo, "Keizai Seisaku ni Okeru Minshushugi no Genkai (Limits of Democracy in Economic Policy)," Chuo Koron, March 1968.

Ikeno, Hiroshi. "Boeki Kawase Jiyuka no Waga Kuni Kinyu ni Oyobosu Eikyo ni tsuite" [On the Effects of Trade and Exchange Liberalization on Japanese Finance], Kinyu (March, 1961).

Ikuno, Minoru. "Boeki Jiyuka to Kagaku Kogyo" [Trade Liberalization and the Chemical Industries], Kagaku Keizai (February, 1960).

Ikuta, T. "Gijutsu Donyu to Royalty Shiharai" [Technology Imports and Royalty Payments], Tsusho Sangyo Kenkyu, No. 98 (1961).

Inagaki, Heitaro. "Kawase Kanri Seido no Kaizen ni tsuite" [Improving the Exchange Control System], Keidanren Geppo (February, 1958).

Ishihara, Takeo, et al. "Tsusho Sangyo Seisaku no Kadai" [Problems of Trade and Industrial Policy], Tsusho Sangyo Kenkyu, No. 100 (1962).

Ishikawa, Niro. "Saikin no Tsusho Kosho no Genjo to Mondai Ten" [Conditions and Problems of Recent Trade Negotiations], Boeki to Kanzei (July, 1965).

Ishimaru, Tadatomi. "Boeki Jiyuka to Kanzei Seisaku" [Trade Liberalization and Tariff Policy], Tsusho Sangyo Kenkyu, No. 84, (1960).

Ishizaka, Taizo, "Shihon Jiyuka to Keieisha no Kakugo" [Capital Liberalization and Executives' Preparedness], Keidanren Geppo (June, 1967).

Iwatake, Shosan. "Boeki no Jiyuka ni tsuite" [On Liberalization of Trade], Anarisuto (October, 1955).

Izawa, Minoru. "Boeki Jiyuka no Rodo Men e no Eikyo" [Effects of Trade Liberalization on Labor], Zaisei Shoho (July, 1960).

Johnson, Harry G. "Trade Preferences and Developing Countries," Lloyds Bank Review (April, 1966).

Kaizuka, Keimei. "Shihon Shushi o meguru Rongi to Jiyuka" [Debates on Capital Balance and Liberalization], Keizai Hyoron (December, 1963).

Kaji, Moto-o. "Keizai Shakai Hatten Keikaku no Mondai Ten" [Problematical Aspects of the Economic and Social Development Plan], Keizai Hyoron (May, 1967).

Kamakura, Noboru and Kazuo Noda. "Kigyo Seicho no Mittsu no Joken" [Three Conditions for Growth of the Firm], Chuo Koron (May, 1966).

Kamakura, Noboru, et al. "Shihon Jiyuka Jidai no Nihon no Keiei" [Japanese Management in the Age of Capital Liberalization]," Chuo Koron, Management Series (Fall, 1967).

Kamino, Masao. "BIAC ni okeru Nihon no Shihon Jiyuka Rongi" [Controversy Concerning Japan's Capital Liberalization at BIAC], Boeki to Kanzei (February, 1967).

BIBLIOGRAPHY   293

_____. "Seifu no Jiyuka to Minkan no Jiyuka" [Liberalization:
Government versus Private Versions], Keizai Hyoron (November, 1965).

Kanamori, Hisao. "Keizai Kakudai to Gaikoku Boeki" [Economic Expansion and Foreign Trade], Keizai Hyoron (May, 1955).

Kanamori, Hisao and Kazuo Noda. "Nihon Keizai no Seicho Yoin wa
Nanika" [Factors in Japan's Economic Growth], Ekonomisuto
(October 20, 1968).

Kanazawa, Yoshio. "Jiyuka to Cartel" [Liberalization and Cartel],
Keizai Jin (May, 1960).

Kase, Seiichi. "Yen Kawase Ron" [On the Yen Exchange], Tsusho
Sangyo Kenkyu (December, 1958).

Kashu, Ekizo, "Jiyuka to Chusho Kigyo Mondai" [Liberalization and
Small-Business Problems], Keidanren Geppo (September, 1960).

Katayama, Kenji. "Boeki Jiyuka kara Shihon Jiyuka" [From Trade
Liberalization to Capital Liberalization], Boeki to Kanzei (January, 1967).

Kato, Shuichi, et al. "Nationalism no Nihon teki Kiban" [Japanese
Bases of Nationalism], Chuo Koron (January, 1965).

Kato, Teiji. "Boeki Jiyuka to Chusho Kigyo" [Trade Liberalization
and Small Businesses], Chusho Kigyo to Kumiai (June, 1960).

Kawabata, Hiroshi. "Chusho Kigyo to Boeki Jiyuka ni tsuite" [Small
Businesses and Trade Liberalization], Sen-i Keizai (March,
1960).

Kawahara, Hideyuki. "Wareware wa Ima Dokoni Ikani Aruka" [Where
and How Do We Stand Now?], Anarisuto (October, 1968).

Kawajiri, Takeshi. "Sengo Nihon no Gaikoku Boeki" [Foreign Trade
in Postwar Japan], Keizai Hyoron (October, 1965).

Kawanishi, Saburo. "Yunyu no Katsuyo to Bukka no Antei" [Uses of
Imports and Price Stability], Boeki to Kanzei (May, 1968).

Kawashima, Shoji. "Shihon Torihiki no Jiyuka ni tsuite" [On Liberalization of Capital Transactions], Kosha Sai Kaiho (March, 1960).

Keidanren. "Genko Gaikoku Kawase oyobi Boeki Kanri no Mondai Ten" [Problems of the Current System of Exchange and Trade Control], Keidanren Geppo (October, 1954).

————. "Kawase Boeki Kanri Ho no Kaisei ni kansuru Yobo Iken" [Opinion and Recommendations concerning the Reform of the Exchange and Trade Control Law], Keidanren Geppo (July, 1959).

Keizai Hyoron, a special issue on "Capital Liberalization and Japanese Economy" (June 1967).

Keizai Hyoron, a special issue on "Liberalization—a Turning Point for the Japanese Economy" (March, 1960).

Keizai Hyoron, a special issue on "Japanese Economy and Foreign Investments" (March 1962).

Keizai Hyoron, a special issue on "Final Phase of Trade and Capital Liberalization" (November, 1969).

Kikuchi, Toshio. "Boeki Jiyuka to Dokkin Seisaku" [Trade Liberalization and Anti-Monopoly Policy], Keiei Gijutsu (September, 1960).

Kimura, Kihachiro. "Nihon no Gaika Seisaku o dou Tenkan subeki ka" [How to Transform Japan's Foreign Exchange Policy], Keizai Hyoron (May, 1968).

Kitagawa, Kazuo. "Jiyuka no Nihon Teki Arikata" [Japanese Approach to Liberalization], Nagoya Shoko (February, 1960).

Kitamura, Masaji. "Boeki Jiyuka to sono Genkai" [Trade Liberalization and Its Limitations], Waseda Shogaku (July, 1960).

Kobayashi, Yoshio. "Jiyuka to Naigai Shihon" [Liberalization and Domestic versus Foreign Capital], Anarisuto (April, 1960).

Kojima, Kiyoshi. "Japan's Trade Policy," Economic Record (March, 1965).

Komiya, Ryutaro. "Taxation and Capital Formation in Postwar Japan," Journal of Economics (July, 1966).

Kotera, Takeshiro. "En Kawase to Hi Kyoju Sha Jiyuen Kanjo" [Yen Exchange and the Nonresident Free Yen Account], Kobe Ginko Chosa Geppo (August, 1960).

Kusuoka, T. "Nihon Keizai to Boeki no Kozo" [Japanese Economy and the Structure of Trade], Tsusho Sangyo Kenkyu (January, 1958).

Kuwahara, Hidetaka. "Boeki Jiyuka to Tekko Gyo" [Trade Liberalization and the Iron and Steel Industry], Tsusho Sangyo Kenkyu (March, 1960).

Kuwahara, K. "Sangyo Seisaku ni okeru Shin Jiyu Shugi" [New Liberalism in Industrial Policy], Keizai Hyoron (May, 1958).

Landes, James E. "A Note on Japan's Liberalization of International Investments," Aoyama Journal of Economics (June, 1967).

Machida, Minoru. "Shokuryo Yunyu to Bukka Taisaku" [The Import of Foods and Price Policy], Boeki to Kanzei (February, 1969).

Maekawa, Seiichi. "Shihon Torihiki Jiyuka to Shoken Ichiba" [Liberalization of Capital Transactions and the Securities Market], Gaikoku Kawase (April, 1960).

Makiguchi, Hiroshi. "Jiyuka to Kinyu Seijo Ka" [Liberalization and Normalization of Finance], Zai Kei Shoho (April, 1960).

Makino, Noboru. "Shihon no Jiyuka to Gijutsu Kaihatsu" [Capital Liberalization and Technological Development], Japan Economic Research Center Report (September 1, 1967).

Marushige, Akinori. "Nihon wa Shihon Yushutsu Koku ni Natta ka?" [Has Japan Become a Capital Exporting Country?], Keizai Hyoron (August, 1967).

Matsuoka, Ryo. "Boeki no Jiyuka to Nogyo" [Trade Liberalization and Agriculture], Norin Tokei Chosa (May, 1960).

Mishima, Kazuo. "Kokusai Ka Jidai no Chusho Kigyo" [Small Businesses in the Age of Internationalization], Boeki Seisaku (May, 1968).

Miwa, Yoshiro. "Shihon no Jiyuka to Sangyo Kai no Koko" [Capital Liberalization and Trends in Select Industries], Japan Economic Research Center Report (September 15, 1967).

Miyajima, Nobuo. "Kokusai Shihon Senso to Nihon Kigyo" [International Capital War and Japanese Enterprises], Keizai Hyoron (July, 1967).

Miyamoto, Shiro. "Dai Niji Shihon Jiyuka to Nihon Sangyo" [Second Round of Capital Liberalization and Japanese Industry], Japan Economic Research Center Report (March 15, 1969).

Miyata, Kiyozo. "Boeki Jiyuka to Nihon Keizai" [Trade Liberalization and Japanese Economy], Bankingu (October, 1960).

_____. "Boeki Jiyuka to Rodo Mondai" [Trade Liberalization and Labor Problems], Rodo Tokei Chosa Geppo (September, 1960).

Miyawaki, Nagasada. "Shihon Jiyuka no Nicro to Macro" [Micro- and Macro-Aspects of Capital Liberalization], Ekonomisuto (November 16, 1965).

Miyazaki, Yoshikazu. "Takokuseki Kigyo Ron" [Theory of Multi-National Business Enterprises], Japan Economic Research Center Report (June 15, 1967).

Miyazawa, Kiichi. "Shihon Jiyuka to Nihon no Taido" [Capital Liberalization and Japan's Attitude], Chuo Koron, Management Series (Spring, 1967).

Miyu, Hoshin. "Boeki Jiyuka to Chusho Kigyo" [Trade Liberalization and Small Businesses], Anarisuto (July, 1960).

Murai, Hichiro. "Kawase Kanri Seido" [Foreign Exchange Control System], Juristo, special edition (January, 1967).

Nagasawa, Yoshitada. "Waga Kuni no Nogyo to Boeki Seisaku" [Japanese Agriculture and Trade Policy], Boeki Seisaku (December, 1968).

Najima, Taro. "Jidosha Sangyo e no Gaishi Shinshutsu" [Advancement of Foreign Capital into the Automobile Industry], Keizai Seminar (May, 1965).

_____. "Sekiyu Kagaku Shihon no Undo" [Movements of Capital in the Petrochemical Industry], Keizai Seminar (June, 1965).

Nakamura, Takafusa. "Jiyuka to Nichibei Kankei" [Liberalization and U.S.-Japan Relationship], Sekai (June, 1960).

_____. "Seicho ka no Boeki to Kokusai Shushi" [Trade and Balance of Payments in the Process of Growth], Keizai Seminar (January, 1967).

Namba, Katsuji. "Boeki Kawase no Jiyuka to Kinyu Seisaku" [Trade and Exchange Liberalization and Monetary Policy], Keizai Keiei Ronshu (October, 1960).

Namiki, Yoshinobu. "Tsusho Sangyo Seisaku no Vision" [Vision of Trade and Industrial Policy], Boeki Seisaku (August, 1969).

Noda, Kazuo. "Watakushi no Nihon Keizai Ron" [My View on the Japanese Economy], Japan Economic Research Center Report (February 1, 1967).

Noguchi, Hiroshi. "Boeki Jiyuka no Rodosha ni Oyobosu Eikyo" [Effects of Trade Liberalization on Workers], Chingin to Shakai Hosho (May, 1960).

Noguchi, Yu. "Jiyuka, Choki Kigyo Seisaku, Chingin Seisaku" [Liberalization, Long-Term Enterprise Policy, Wage Policy], Anarisuto (April, 1962).

Nomiya, Soko. "Boeki Jiyuka no Doko to Boeki Kanri no Arikata" [Trend of Trade Liberalization and the Proper Trade Control], Tsusho Sangyo Kenkyu (May, 1959).

Nomizu, Kyumatsu. "Gaijin Toshi no Doko to Sono Kadai" [Foreign Investment: Trend and Problems], Japan Economic Research Center Report (March 1, 1970).

Nomura, Teruo. "Jiyuka to Bloc Ka no Haikei" [Liberalization and the Background of Rising Trade Blocs], Sekai Keizai Hyoron (April, 1960).

Nomura, Yuzo. "Boeki Jiyuka to Chusho Kigyo" [Trade Liberalization and Small Businesses], Shinyo Kinko (March, 1960).

Numaguchi, Gen. "Shihon Jiyuka no Saikento" [Reexamination of Capital Liberalization], Sekai Keizai Hyoron (June, 1969).

Ohba, Tomomitsu. "Hogo Boeki Shugi no Jittai" [Reality of Protectionism], Boeki to Kanzei (January, 1968).

_____. "Hogo Boeki Shugi to Jiyuka" [Protectionism and Liberalization], Boeki to Kanzei (January, 1969).

Ohishi, Toshiro. "Hikanzei Shogai no Yukue" [Future of Non-Tariff Barriers], Boeki Seisaku (December, 1969).

_____. "Nichi-Bei Keizai no Shin Jidai" [New Era of U.S.-Japan Economic Relations], Boeki Seisaku (September, 1969).

Ohjimi, Yoshihisa and Hiroshi Kurokawa. "Dai Niji Shihon Jiyuka o dou Susumeru ka" [How to Proceed with Second Round of Capital Liberalization], Japan Economic Research Center Report (Februray 1, 1969).

_____. "Shihon Jiyuka Ichinen to Korekara no Mondai" [One Year after Capital Liberalization and Future Problems], Japan Economic Research Center Report (August 1, 1968).

Ohkita, Saburo. "Shigen Yunyu Koku Nihon o Jikaku seyo" [The Importance of Understanding Japan's Import Dependence upon Resources], Chuo Koron (December, 1967).

Okada, Minoru. "Kawase Boeki no Jiyuka to Kaiun Kigyo" [Trade and Exchange Liberalization and the Marine Transport Firms], Gaikoku Kawase (April, 1960).

Okatani, Eiichi. "Hikanron Tsuyomaru Shihon Jiyuka" [Rising Pessimism about Capital Liberalization], Keizai Seminar (October, 1966).

Okumura, Hiroshi. "Amerika Shihon to Nihon no Shihon" [American Capital and Japanese Capital], Keizai Hyoron (July, 1967).

Okumura, Tsunao. "Kongo no Shihon Torihiki no Jiyuka wa Dou Arubekika" [How Should Capital Transactions be Liberalized from Now On], Gaikoku Kawase (October, 1960).

_____. "Shihon Jiyuka ni taisuru Kihonteki Taido" [Basic Attitude toward Capital Liberalization], Keidanren Geppo (May, 1962).

Ono, Ichiro. "Nihon ni okeru Gaishi no Keitai to Genjo" [Pattern and Condition of Foreign Investments in Japan], Ekonomisuto (May, 1960).

Ono, Ryoji. "Boeki Jiyuka no Koyomen ni Oyobosu Eikyo" [Effects of Trade Liberalization on Employment], Shokugyo Antei Koho (August, 1960).

Onoichi, Ichiro. "Nihon Boeki no Kakudai Katei to sono Haikei" [Process and Background of Japanese Trade Expansion], Keizai Hyoron (May, 1965).

Ozaki, Eiji. "Junen Kan no Kawase Boeki Kanri" [Ten Years of Exchange and Trade Control], Gaikoku Kawase (March, 1960).

Ryokaku, Yoshihiko. "Sangyo Kyocho Taisei Ron" [Theory of Industrial Cooperation], Tsusho Sangyo Kenkyu, No. 100 (1962).

Saito, Takeo. "Kenzen na Kokusai Shushi towa Nanika" [What is the Sound Balance of Payments], Keizai Orai (January, 1965).

Saito, Y. "Sangyo Hatten to Boeki Seisaku" [Industrial Expansion and Trade Policy], Sekai Keizai Hyoron (November, 1968).

Sakairi, Chotaro. "Jiyuka Rongi Hihan" [Critique of the Debate on Liberalization], Nihon Zaisei Kenkyu (April, 1960).

Sakamoto, Nobuaki. "Kawase Jiyuka to Kokunai Kinyu Ichiba" [Exchange Liberalization and Domestic Money Market], Ekonomisuto (March, 1960).

Sakane, Tetsuo. "Jiyuka no Shinten to Kosei Torihiki" [Progress of Liberalization and Fair Trading], Zai Kei Shoho (July, 1960).

Sakurai, Y. "Yunyu Seigen Shochi no Ruikei to Sono Kangaekata" [Kinds of Import Restrictions and Associated Ideas], Tsusho Sangyo Kenkyu (June, 1958).

Segawa, Minoru. "Kawase no Jiyuka to Rodo Mondai" [Exchange Liberalization and Labor Problems], Sen-i Keizai (May, 1960).

Sekai Keizai Hyoron, a special issue on "Trade Liberalization" (October, 1959).

Seki, Osamu. "Jiyuka Go no Yunyu Seisaku to Vision" [Post-Liberalization Import Policy and its Vision], Boeki Seisaku (November, 1969).

Shimada, Haruki. "Boeki Jiyuka to Sangyo Soshiki Mondai" [Trade Liberalization and Problems of Industrial Organization], Tsusho Sangyo Kenkyu (July, 1960).

Shimomura, Osamu. "Keizai Seicho to Jiyuka" [Economic Growth and Liberalization], Kinyu Zaisei Jijo (March, 1960).

Shinohara, Miyohei. "Jiyuka to 360 Yen Reito" [Liberalization and the 360 Yen Rate], Ekonomisuto (November, 1959).

_____. "Kawase no Jiyuka—Keizai Teki Kosatsu" [Economic Analysis of Exchange Liberalization], Seisan Sei (July, 1960).

Shishido, Toshio. "Boeki Jiyuka to Choki Keiei Keikaku" [Trade Liberalization and Long-Range Management Plans], Sangyo Keiri (August, 1960).

_____. "Jiyuka no Keizai Gaku" [Economics of Liberalization], Zai Kei Shoho (April, 1960).

Shirojima, Kunihiro. "Boeki Jiyuka Seisaku o Megru Sho Mondai" [Various Problems Surrounding Trade Liberalization Policy], Gaikoku Kawase (February, 1960).

Shoda, Akira. "Shihon no Jiyuka to Kokkin Hosei" [Capital Liberalization and the System of Anti-Monopoly Laws], Japan Economic Research Center Report (May 15, 1967).

Soba, Seiichi. "Shihon Jiyuka Jokyoku" [Prelude to Capital Liberalization], Keizai Seminar (September, 1966).

_____. "Shihon Jiyuka to Kokkin Seisaku" [Capital Liberalization and Anti-Monopoly Policy], Keizai Seminar (February, 1967).

Sugahara, Fujiya. "Jiyuka ni Chokumen suru Nihon Boeki" [Japanese Foreign Trade in Face of Liberalization], Gaikoku Kawase (April, 1960).

Sugimura, Masahiko. "Boeki Jiyuka to Sen-i Sangyo" [Trade Liberalization and the Textile Industry], Kasen Geppo (June, 1960).

Suma, Tsutomu. "Boeki Jiyuka to Sekiyu Sangyo" [Trade Liberalization and the Petroleum Industry], Sekiyu Kai (July, 1960).

Sumita, Shoji. "Boeki oyobi Kawase no Jiyuka to Kaiun" [Trade and Exchange Liberalization, and Marine Transportation], Kaiun (March, 1960).

Suzuki, T. "Joyosha Jiyuka o meguru Shiwaku" [Speculation about Liberalization of Passenger Cars], Ekonomisuto (May 4, 1965).

Suzuki, Takeo. "Jiyuka to Zaisei" [Liberalization and Public Finance], Anarisuto (September-October, 1960).

Suzuki, Yukio. "Tsusan Sho ni Miru San-Kan Fukugo Tai" [Government-Industrial Complex at MITI], Chuo Koron (September, 1969).

Tachi, Ryuichiro, et al. "Nihon Teki Policy Mix no Arikata" [What Should be the Policy Mix for the Japanese Economy?], Japan Economic Research Center Report (October 15, 1967).

Tada, Ichiro. "Jiyuka ni Sonaeru Mitsui Mitsubishi no Saihen" [Reorganization of Mitsui and Mitsubishi in Preparation for Liberalization], Chuo Koron (May, 1960).

Takagaki, Katsujiro. "Boeki Kawase Jiyuka to Kongo no Shosha Katsudo" [Trade and Exchange Liberalization and Future Activities of Trading Companies], Keidanren Geppo (April, 1960).

Takago, Torao. "Sangyo Shihon no Kosei Hendo to Shihon Ido no Jiyuka" [Structural Changes in Industrial Capital and Liberalization of Capital Movements], Keizai Keiei Ronshu (June, 1960).

Takahashi, Kiyoshi. "Boeki no Jiyuka to Kanzei" [Trade Liberalization and Tariff], Tokai Ginko Chosa Geppo (November, 1960).

Takahashi, Masao, et al. "Boeki Jiyuka to Rodo Undo" [Trade Liberalization and the Labor Movement], Sekai no Rodo (March, 1960).

Takahashi, Takao. "Joyosha Jiyuka no Kokusai teki Haikei" [International Background of Liberalization of Passenger Cars], Ekonomisuto (March 30, 1965).

Takahashi, Tatsuya. "Zodai suru Yunyu Jyuyo ni Taisho shite" [Coping with Expanding Import Demand], Boeki to Kanzei (September, 1967).

Takashima, Setsuo. "Shosha Gaika Hoyu Mondai ni tsuite" [Problem of Foreign Currencies Held by Trading Companies], Keidanren Geppo (May, 1955).

Takeyama, Yasuo. "Dai Niji Shihon Jiyuka no Naiyo to Kongo no Mondai" [Contents of the Second Round of Capital Liberalization tion and Future Problems], Japan Economic Research Center Report (March 1, 1969).

_____. "Dai Sanji Shihon Jiyuka" [Third Round of Capital Liberalization], Japan Economic Research Center Report (September 15, 1970).

Tamura, Mitsuo. "Kage o Hisometa Shiwaku Yunyu" [Receding Speculative Imports], Boeki to Kanzei (June, 1965).

Tanaka, Hirohide, et al. "Boeki Jiyuka to Rodo Mondai" [Trade Liberalization and Labor problems], Rodo Tokei Chosa Geppo (September, 1960).

Taniguchi, Katsuhiko. "Kokusai Kyoso Ryoku to Kigyo Kibo" [International Competitive Strength and the Firm Size], Tsusho Sangyo Kenkyu, No. 86 (1960).

Tatemoto, Masahiro. "Sengo Boeki no Nazo o Meguru Shokenkai" [Interpretations of Some Puzzling Aspects of Postwar Trade], Keizai Hyoron (August, 1957).

Tokai Bank Research Department. "Jiyuka to Kokusai Kyoso Ryoku" [Liberalization and International Competitive Strength], Toshi Geppo (June, 1960).

Tokunaga, Kiyoyuki. "Boeki no Jiyuka to Wagakuni no Tachiba" [Trade Liberalization and Japan's Position], Koshisha Shogaku (June, 1960).

Toyosaki, Minoru. "Nihon no Keizai Seisaku to Jiyuka" [Japanese Economic Policy and Liberalization], Keizai Seminar (February, 1960).

Tsuchiya, Rokuro. "Shihon Jiyuka Mondai no Subete" [All about Capital Liberalization Problems], Toyo Keizai Shimpo (February, 1960).

Tsuchiya, Rokuro. "Shihon Torihiki no Jiyuka o Meguru Sho Mondai" [Various Problems Surrounding Liberalization of Capital Transactions], Toshi Geppo (June, 1960).

Tsukamoto, Ishigoro. "Jiyuen Kanjo no Setchi to En Kawase no Donyu" [Establishment of the Free Yen Account and Introduction of Yen Exchange], Zai Kei Shoho (June, 1960).

Tsusho Sangyo Kenkyu, a special issue on "Progress of Liberalization and the Japanese Economy," No. 109 (1962).

Tsusho Sangyo Kenkyu, a special issue on "Trade Liberalization and Industrial Policy," No. 87 (1960).

Uchino, Akira. "Technological Innovation in Postwar Japan," Developing Economies (December, 1969).

Ueda, Ren-ichiro. "Kinri Suijun to Kokusai Kyoso Ryoku" [The Rate of Interest and International Competitive Strength], Keizai Hyoron (June, 1963).

Umezu, Kazuro. "Nihon no Kokusai Kyoso Ryoku to Shosha" [Japan's International Competitive Strength and Trading Companies], Keizai Seminar (August, 1966).

Utsumi, Kenzo. "Boeki no Jiyuka to Nihon Nogyo" [Trade Liberalization and Japanese Agriculture], Nogyo Sogo Kenkyu (October, 1960).

Wada, Kenzo. "Kawase Men no Jiyuka Keikaku" [Liberalization Plans with Respect to Foreign Exchange], Gaikoku Kawase (July, 1960).

Wagstsuma, Tosaku. "Boeki Jiyuka to Nihon Nogyo" [Trade Liberalization and Japanese Agriculture], Noson Kenkyu (July, 1960).

Watanabe, Fukutaro. "Keizai Seicho Seisaku to Yushutsu Kyoso Ryoku" [Economic Growth Policy and the Export Competitive Strength], Keizai Hyoron (January, 1966).

Watanabe, Ikuro. "Nihon teki Niju Kozo to Boeki Seisaku" [Japanese Dual Structure and Trade Policy], Sekai Keizai Hyoron (December, 1967).

Watanabe, Takeshi. "IMF to Kawase Boeki Jiyuka Mondai" [IMF and Problems of Trade and Exchange Liberalization], Keidanren Geppo (August, 1960).

Watanabe, Taro. "Nihon no Kokusai Shushi no Ugoki o Kimeru Mono" [Determinants of Japan's Balance of Payments], Keizai Hyoron (April, 1968).

Yajima, T. "Joyosha no Jiyuka to Hanbai Kinyu" [Liberalization of Passenger Cars and Sales Finance], Kin-yu Journal (June, 1965).

Yamada, Ryozo and Yoshiro Miwa. "Nihon Kigyo no Kokusai Teki Jitsuryoku" [International Competitive Strength of Japanese Enterprises], Chuo Koron (May, 1967).

Yamamoto, Shigenobu. "Boeki Seisaku no Koka to Cost" [Effects and Costs of Trade Policy], Sekai Keizai Hyoron (January, 1969).

_____. "Kanzei to Hogo no Riron" [Theory of Tariff and Protection], Japan Economic Research Center Report (June 1, 1968).

Yoshida, Yoshizo. "Kokusai Shushi to Jiyuka Mondai" [Balance of Payments and Liberalization Problems], Keizai Seminar (August, 1967).

Yoshimura, Hisao, et al. "Hada de Kanjita Shihon Jiyuka" [Eye-Witness Report on Capital Liberalization in Europe], Japan Economic Research Center Report (August 1, 1967).

Yoshino, Toshihiko. "Jiyuka wa Plus ka Minus ka" [Liberalization, Plus or Minus?], Chuo Koron (April, 1960).

Yuhi, Shinogu. "Shihon Jiyuka no Shin Kyokumen ni Sonaeru Sangyo Kai" [Industries in Preparation for a New Phase of Capital Liberalization], Toyo Keizai (November 21, 1968).

GOVERNMENT PUBLICATIONS, PAMPHLETS, OTHERS

Agency of Science and Technology, ed. Kagaku Gijutsu Hakusho [Science and Technology White Paper 1967]. Tokyo: Ministry of Finance Printing Office, 1967).

Bank of Japan. Economic Statistics of Japan. Tokyo, annual.

Bank of Japan, Waga Kuni Kawase Kanri Seido no Aramashi [Outline of the Exchange Control System in Japan]. Tokyo, September, 1950.

Boston Consulting Group. What Makes Japan Grow? Boston, 1968.

Committee for Economic Development. Japan in the Free World Economy. New York, 1963.

Economic Planning Agency. Juyo Shohin no Kokusai Kyoso Ryoku [International Competitive Strength of Important Commodities]. Tokyo: Shoko Shuppan, 1956.

Economic Planning Agency. Keizai Hakusho [Economic White Paper]. Tokyo, annual.

Economic Planning Agency. Keizai Kikaku Cho Nijunen Shoshi [A
    Short Twenty-Year History of the Economic Planning Agency].
    Tokyo, 1966.

Economic Planning Agency. Sengo Keizai Shi: Boeki Kokusai Shushi
    Hen [Postwar Economic History: Trade and Balance of Pay-
    ments]. Tokyo, 1962.

Economic Planning Agency. Sengo Keizai Shi: Keizai Seisaku Hen
    [Postwar Economic History: Economic Policy]. Tokyo, 1960.

Gaikoku Kawase Kenkyu Kyokai. Gaikoku Kawase Sho Roppo [Foreign
    Exchange Laws]. Tokyo, 1968.

Hashimoto, Riichi and Masao Mukaizaka, eds. Gijutsu Donyu no Jiyuka
    ni tsuite [On the Liberalization of Technology Imports]. Tokyo:
    Sogo Seisaku Kenkyu Kai, May, 1968.

Ikeuchi, Tokuji. Jiyuka to Ginko—sono Eikyo to Taisaku [Liberaliza-
    tion and Banks—Effects and Policy Measures]. Tokyo: Kin-yu
    Zaisei Jijo Kenkyu Kai, 1961.

International Monetary Fund. Annual Report on Exchange Restrictions.
    Washington, D.C., annual.

International Monetary Fund. Articles of Agreement. Washington,
    D.C., 1968.

Japan Economic Policy Research Association, ed. Gendai Nihon
    Keizai ni okeru Kokka no Yakuware [The Role of the State in
    Contemporary Japanese Economy]. Tokyo: Keiso Shobo, 1961.

_____. Sengo Junen no Nihon Keizai Seisaku no Hensen [Changes
    in Japan's Economic Policy during the First Postwar Decade].
    Tokyo: Keiso Shobo, March, 1956.

_____. Sengo Nijunen no Keizai Seisaku [Economic Policy during
    the Two Decades after the War]. Tokyo: Keiso Shobo, 1968.

_____. Shihon Jiyuka to Keizai Seisaku [Capital Liberalization and
    Economic Policy]. Tokyo: Keiso Shobo, 1969.

Japanese Chamber of Commerce and Industry. Boeki Jiyuka no Eikyo
    oyobi Taisaku ni kansuru Chosa [Survey Concerning the Effects

of and Adjustments for Trade Liberalization]. Tokyo, November, 1960.

Japan Marketing Association. Boeki Jiyuka to Nihon no Kigyo [Trade Liberalization and Japanese Firms]. Tokyo: Japan Productivity Center, May, 1960.

Japan Society of International Economics, ed. Nihon no Keizai to Boeki [Economy and Foreign Trade of Japan]. Tokyo: Nippon Hyoron Shinsha, 1957.

Japan Tariff Association, ed. Gaikoku Kawase Gaikoku Boeki Kanri Nyumon [Introduction to the Foreign Exchange and Foreign Trade Control System]. Tokyo, 1953.

_____. Nihon no Kanzei [Japanese Tariff]. Tokyo, 1959.

Kagaku Keizai Kenkyu Sho, ed. Boeki Jiyuka to Kagaku Kogyo [Trade Liberalization and the Chemical Industries]. Tokyo, July, 1960.

Keizai Doyu Kai. Boeki Kawase Jiyuka Taisaku [Policy toward Trade and Exchange Liberalization]. Tokyo, July, 1960.

Keizai Hatten Kyokai. Sengo Nihon no Sangyo Seisaku [Industrial Policy in Postwar Japan]. Tokyo, June, 1966.

Kin-yu Zaisei Jijo Kenkyu Kai. Jiyuka to Nihon Sangyo no Kadai [Liberalization and Problems of Japanese Industries]. Tokyo, June, 1960.

Kokusai Toshi Kenkyu Sho. Gaishi Donyu Kankei Hoki Shu [Laws and Regulations Concerning the Induction of Foreign Capital]. Tokyo, 1967.

Mabuchi, Naomi. Kokusai Keizai to Jiyuka narabi ni Kongo no Hoko ni tsuite [International Economy, Liberalization and Future Directions]. Tokyo: Kigyo Keiei Kyokai, 1960.

Ministry of Finance, Ministry of International Trade and Industry, and Agency of Science and Technology. Gaishi Jiyuka to Nihon no Kigyo [Capital Liberalization and Japanese Enterprises]. Tokyo: Tsusan Kigyo Kenkyu Kai, 1967.

Ministry of International Trade and Industry. Boeki Jiyuka to Sangyo Kozo [Trade Liberalization and the Industrial Structure]. Tokyo: Toyo Keizai Shimpo Sha, November, 1960.

_____. Jiyuka Taisaku Kaigi Shiryo [Liberalization Policy Conference Materials]. Tokyo: Kigyo Keiei Kyokai, 1960.

_____. Keizai Kyoryoku no Genjo to Mondai Ten [Present Conditions and Problems of Economic Cooperation]. Tokyo, 1967.

_____. Nihon Boeki no Tenkai [Expansion of Japanese Foreign Trade]. Tokyo: Shoko Shuppan, 1956.

_____. Sangyo Gorika Hakusho [White Paper on Industrial Rationalization]. Tokyo: Nikkan Kogyo Shimbun Sha, 1957.

_____. Tsusho Hakusho [Foreign Trade White Paper]. Tokyo, annual.

_____. Tsusho Sangyo Roppo [Laws Concerning Foreign Trade and Industry] . Tokyo: Foreign Trade and Industry Research Association, 1968.

_____. Tsusho Sangyo Sho Nempo [Ministry of International Trade and Industry Yearbook]. Tokyo, annual.

Mitsubishi Keizai Kenkyu Sho. Sekai Boeki: Jiyuka Mondai no Haikei [World Trade: Background of Liberalization Problems]. Tokyo: Sangyo Keizai Shimbun, May 1956.

Nihon Boeki Kenkyu Kai, ed. Sengo Nihon no Boeki Nijunen Shi [A History of Japanese Foreign Trade: Two Decades after the War]. Tokyo: Tsusho Sangyo Chosa Kai, 1967.

Nihon Keizai Chosa Kyogi Kai. Nihon o Chushin to shita Sengo no Kokusai Choki Shihon Ido [Postwar International Movements of Long-Term Capital around Japan]. Tokyo, August, 1963.

_____. Tanki Shihon Taisaku [Short-Term Capital Policy]. Tokyo, May, 1963.

_____. Waga Kuni no Boeki Gai Shushi [Nontrade Transactions Balance in Japan]. Tokyo, November, 1965.

Nukazawa, Kazuo. Japan's Foreign Economic Policy: Options for the Seventies. Washington, D.C.: United States-Japan Trade Council, May, 1970.

Okita, Saburo. Causes and Problems of Rapid Growth in Postwar Japan and Their Implications for Newly Developing Economies. Tokyo: Japan Economic Research Center, March, 1967.

Organization for Economic Cooperation and Development. Code of Liberalisation of Capital Movements. Paris, January, 1969.

Sangyo Seisaku Kenkyu Kai, ed. Watakushi no Sangyo Seisaku Ron [My Vision of Industrial Policy]. Tokyo: Keizai Hatten Kyokai, June, 1967.

Sanwa Bank. Boeki Kawase no Jiyuka ni tsuite [On Liberalization of Trade and Exchange]. Tokyo, January, 1960.

————. On The Induction of Foreign Capital. Tokyo, May, 1960.

Seisaku Jiho, ed. Tsusan Sho [Ministry of International Trade and Industry]. Tokyo: Seisaku Jiho Sha, 1968.

Shoko Kaikan. Gaishi Donyu Nenkan [Induction of Foreign Capital Yearbook]. Tokyo, annual.

Sogo Seisaku Kenkyu Kai. Nihon no Kokusai Shushi Taisaku [Japan's Balance of Payments Policy]. Tokyo: Diamond Sha, 1964.

Sumitomo Bank. Boeki Kawase no Jiyuka ni tsuite [On Liberalization of Trade and Exchange]. Tokyo, April 1960.

Tokyo Chamber of Commerce and Industry. Boeki Jiyuka no Eikyo ni kansuru Chosa [Survey Concerning the Effects of Trade Liberalization]. Tokyo, April, 1960.

Tsusho Sangyo Kozo Kenkyu Kai, ed. Boeki Jiyuka to Sangyo Kozo [Trade Liberalization and the Industry Structure]. Tokyo: Toyo Keizai, 1960.

U.S. Congress, Joint Economic Committee. Japan in United States Foreign Policy. 87th Congress, 1st Sess. Washington, D.C.: U.S. Government Printing Office, 1961.

————. Subsidies to Shipping by Eleven Countries. 88th Congress, 2nd Sess. Washington, D.C.: U.S. Government Printing Office, 1964.

————. Trade Restraints in the Western Community. 87th Congress, 1st Sess. Washington, D.C.: U.S. Government Printing Office, 1961.

United States-Japan Trade Council. The Growth of Japanese Technology. Washington, D.C., December, 1967.

_____. U.S.-Japan Economic Relationships in 1969. Washington, D.C., August, 1969.

United States Tariff Commission, Postwar Developments in Japan's Foreign Trade. Washington, D.C.: U.S. Government Printing Office, 1958.

ROBERT S. OZAKI is a Professor of Economics at California State College, Hayward. He received his B.A. from Ohio Wesleyan University, M.A. and Ph.D. in economics from Harvard University.

His published works include numerous articles and monographs on the Japanese economy, an English translation of a collection of scholarly papers on Japan's postwar economic growth, and a heuristic introduction to economics.

He is a member of Phi Beta Kappa and Omicron Chi Epsilon, and has served on the Advisory Editorial Board of the Journal of Asian Studies.